UNINTENDED CONSEQUENCES

Ray O'Hanlon takes an unflinching look at more than 100 years of American immigration policy broadly and how it affects the Irish specifically, particularly since the passage of the Immigration and Nationality Act of 1965. With clarity and context, he provides an essential chronology of the many battles waged to correct the 'consequences' of that legislation and its impact on Irish America. His assessment is as eye-opening as it is sobering, squarely assigning credit and blame for the results where they belong.

Linda Dowling Almeida, author of *Irish Immigrants in New York City: 1945–1995*, Glucksman Ireland House, New York University

Ray O'Hanlon remains the pre-eminent chronicler of the Irish American experience, in large part because for him it has never been purely an academic exercise, but a lived one, experienced first-hand as an Irish person who made his home and his life in America. His grasp of history informs a nuanced understanding of the modern, real-time Irish America.

Boston Globe columnist **Kevin Cullen**

Ray O'Hanlon plays the role of historian and fly-on-the-wall journalist in this well-researched narrative about immigration, politics and culture. It is an Irish story and an American story, told by one of Irish America's foremost observers.

Dr Terry Golway, journalist, author, historian, and editor of *Being New York, Being Irish*

Unintended Consequences provides an essential chronology on the history of U.S. immigration policy as it pertains to the Irish. Full of fascinating insights, O'Hanlon's journalistic style makes it an engaging read about an era that has been rather understudied to date.

Miriam Nyhan Grey PhD, Global Coordinator for Irish Studies, Glucksman Ireland House, New York University

Unintended Consequences is meticulously researched and beautifully written. The legislation that systematically closed the door to Irish immigrants is skilfully juxtaposed against multiple delightful vignettes that remind us of the humanity and diversity of the emigration experience over the last seven decades.

Professor Christine Kinealy, Director, Ireland's Great Hunger Institute, Quinnipiac University, Connecticut

For Phyllis, mother of an emigrant,
for Ann, descendant of immigrants.

Ray O'Hanlon is the editor of the New York City-published *Irish Echo* newspaper. A native of Dublin, O'Hanlon has reported from four continents in a newspaper career spanning forty-one years. In addition to his work as a reporter and editor, O'Hanlon has been a frequent contributor to US, Irish and British media outlets reporting on Ireland, Irish American affairs, and Anglo-Irish relations. His book, *The New Irish Americans* (1998) was the recipient of a Washington Irving Book Award, and *The South Lawn Plot*, his first fiction work, was published in 2011.

UNINTENDED
CONSEQUENCES

THE STORY OF IRISH IMMIGRATION TO THE U.S. AND
HOW AMERICA'S DOOR WAS CLOSED TO THE IRISH

RAY O'HANLON

MERRION
PRESS

First published in 2021 by
Merrion Press
10 George's Street
Newbridge
Co. Kildare
Ireland
www.merrionpress.ie

9781785373787 (Paper)
9781785373794 (Kindle)
9781785373800 (Epub)

A CIP catalogue record for this book is
available from the British Library.

Typeset in Sabon Lt Std 11/14 pt

Front cover image: President Lyndon B. Johnson signs the 1965
Immigration and Nationality Act into law on Ellis Island.
Photo courtesy of the Lyndon B. Johnson Library Collection/
Yoichi R. Okamoto.

Back cover image: The inspection room on Ellis Island,
New York, *c.*1910s.

Unless otherwise stated, images are taken from the
Irish Echo archive, courtesy of the author.

Merrion Press is a member of Publishing Ireland.

Contents

Preface

As the 1980s proceeded towards the middle of the decade, tens of thousands of mostly young Irish packed their bags and reached for a better life. Leaving behind dashed hopes and economic recession, they would travel to different lands. America would be the land with the greatest economic pull, the brightest of bright lights. Once immigration and customs were behind them, these 'new' Irish plunged into a life in a country that was far from home, yet familiar in so many ways. The American Dream is the property of people the world over, or so the world had been led to believe.

But America was changing, and in ways not necessarily seen or sensed by the arriving Irish. Their admission to the United States was only a first step. Taking the next steps towards a fully accepted and legal American life, they would hit a problem – indeed, multiple problems – stemming from acts of Congress that few of the newcomers were aware of to any significant degree, if at all. And yet a political battle on their behalf, one sourced in the first of those congressional measures, the 1965 Immigration and Nationality Act, had already opened. It would resume as a result of another act that came into being in 1986.

My American life was not forced upon me by overwhelmingly negative economic travails. But it has comprised more than half of my life thanks to my wife Lisa, who hails from America's heartland. That sets me apart from most of those 1980s Irish who made the journey across the Atlantic with hope, fears, sometimes desperation as their traveling companions. My journey has been an easy one compared to those who became undocumented in a land that has, nonetheless, benefited from their presence. This book is dedicated to the undocumented Irish who have stayed the course in the hope of relief from a sensible practice of politics.

I want to pay tribute to those politicians who have faced the immigration issue in a sensible and pragmatic manner. There have been quite a few of them, but never quite enough of them. Some are mentioned in the following pages, and there are others. They come from both parties and not all are Irish American.

Particular mention should be made of Judge John Collins and the American Irish National Immigration Committee (AINIC). Judge Collins has made available his personal account of AINIC's story, and for that I am but one who is deeply grateful. I am especially indebted to Conor Graham of Irish Academic Press/Merrion Press for taking just a few moments, during a conversation in New York University's Glucksman Ireland House, to give the green light for this project. And thanks, too, to those whose books, writings, thoughts and analyses are drawn upon throughout the chapters.

The years since the 1965 Immigration and Nationality Act, a legislative measure that so radically changed the course of the American Irish story and the broader American story, have been witness to the Herculean efforts of individuals who took up the cause of legal Irish access to the United States under the banner of AINIC, the Irish Immigration Reform Movement (IIRM), the Irish Lobby for Immigration Reform (ILIR) and others. Those named groups were ad hoc, formed to meet particular challenges at particular times. ILIR continues to battle on the front lines. Throughout all the years of battling, the work of the Ancient Order of Hibernians (AOH) has been a constant. The work of the more engaged Irish politicians and a constantly engaged Irish Diplomatic Corps deserves recognition.

Nobody wants to see forced mass emigration from Ireland ever again. No fair-minded person wants, or expects, special consideration for the Irish at the expense of other nationalities. But it's fair to argue that the great majority of Irish and Irish Americans are uncomfortable with a prevailing situation where an Irish person can dream of a life in America and yet be denied it simply because he or she is Irish.

Immigration is, for sure, a complicated and challenging political issue. No system can ever be perfect. But it can be better – for the Irish, for everyone. In today's political climate, even the idea of it being just a little better seems a remote prospect. Nevertheless, the fight for a better American immigration system will go on. It continues because of legislation more than five decades ago, which would result, years later, in all too many Irish living in the shadows. The undocumented or illegal life is not to be envied. That life is not confined to the Irish. An estimated eleven million people live in the United States outside its immigration laws. This is a number greater than the population of Sweden. The unintended consequences of the '65 act have had a broad effect.

I hope these pages capture, at least to some degree, the extraordinary relationship between Ireland and the United States of America, and in doing so make clearer why so many have given their life's energy to maintaining and enhancing, indeed saving, that relationship in the face of an immigration door that is almost entirely closed to the Irish. This is a special relationship of the purer kind, as Ireland's contribution to the transatlantic bond down the years, across the centuries, has purely been its people.

The observant reader will note the American spellings in these pages. This is appropriate, as the book has been written by an immigrant, though one aided by an emigrant's memory and sentiment. And never underestimate the power of sentiment! It powers much of what passes for relations between an island people and a continental one. It powers the continued campaign for a fairer future flow, in both directions, across the Atlantic.

There is more to this narrative than these pages are able to reveal. But I hope the reader comes away with an enhanced sense of a story that is compelling, important for the future of the United States and Ireland, and worthy of the telling.

And, of course, the story continues, now given new life and impetus by the election of Irish American Joe Biden to the presidency of the United States.

Ray O'Hanlon,
Ossining,
New York,

CHAPTER 1

Searching for a Savior

Why were they here?
Why were they cheering, clapping, whistling and bursting into chants of olé, olé olé? Why, behind the near physical sense of purpose and oneness, were they all so worried? Worried about their futures, their kids, their homes and businesses, their lives in America.

The American dream, like any dream, is harder to live than it is to imagine. But when it is hard even to imagine, you don't hesitate to reach out and grasp for something, for a feeling of hope, a prospect of a more certain tomorrow. And if that prospect is buoyed by the presence of one of the most influential politicians in the land, where else would you be on a night such as this, the first of the twelfth month in the year 2006.

So it was to this hall that they came, from the city and the suburbs, and beyond. They had names that could be traced back to every corner of Ireland. Their accents varied, but they were all talking about the same thing: a legal life in America. The hall, attached to a Catholic church, came with a name, St Barnabas, an early disciple, described in the Acts of the Apostles as a Cypriot Jew.

Few if any would have made the link. The man they had come to hear speak in this Christian place was a Jew. His name was Charles Schumer, often referred to as 'Chuck', and formally addressed as 'Senator'. On this night he was both.

To the organizers of the event he was very much the Capitol Hill powerhouse politician, a man of potentially boundless force and influence. To Schumer himself, when it came to speaking to his audience, there was more of the Chuck, the friendly neighborhood pol with so many Irish staff members that he might as well have been, well, Edward Kennedy.

But he wasn't – though there was talk of Edward, or 'Teddy', in the room – another politician who had in his power, or so it seemed, the ability to throw a lifeline to the increasingly desperate throng. The room was filled with descendants of so many before them who had landed in America so effortlessly by comparison, at least in terms of American law.

All in the room that night weren't too worried about the politician's name, or his party affiliation. The title of US Senator was more than good enough for the throng – mostly Irish, but one interspersed with hopeful new arrivals from Mexico, Central America, Poland and other far flung places.

The Irish were not the major force they once were in American politics. But they were far from a spent force. And those leading the Irish part of the national campaign for reform and relief for as many as eleven million undocumented were very much conscious of the need for operating in a bigger tent.

So it wasn't entirely a bad thing that it wasn't Ted Kennedy on this night, but rather a senator with family origins to the east of Kennedy's ancestral island off Europe's western edge. Schumer certainly didn't sound or look like he was out of place. He played to the crowd with a big grin on his face, at least at the start of the evening's business. But his countenance would soon darken, his words uttered in a more urgent tone. He would look down and over the top of his eyeglasses. Before too long it was serious Schumer in full flow.

Schumer was, and remains, one of the most consummate of politicians, a legislator famous for his Sunday morning press conferences, perfectly pitched to any and all media on the week's slowest news day. The quip about the most dangerous place in Washington being the space between Schumer and a camera is not that wide of the mark. Those in the hall who had heard this half-joke were hoping it was true. If you're going to rely on someone in Washington to be your champion, best that he, or she, is feared as much as loved.

Schumer's zeal for pulling journalists into his inner orbit had been evident for years. Long before he secured his Senate seat, when he was still a member of the House of Representatives, he would wear out shoe leather doing to reporters what they were often required to do themselves in the course of their work. That was door-stepping them – literally turning up at the door unannounced, wanting to sit down and talk about this, that, anything.

Tonight, however, Schumer was the invited guest and the talk was about something very specific: comprehensive immigration reform. Schumer, famously, makes sure to visit each of New York State's sixty-two counties at least once a year. On this first night of December he was covering two of them. The St Barnabas hall (really a school gym used as a meeting hall) was in Bronx County, but a few paces outside the door would have you in Yonkers in Westchester County.

Schumer, in not a few respects, is a political micromanager. No issue seems too small, and none too big. The issue on the agenda at St Barnabas was big, very big, but with countless individual parts to it, parts that were people and their unrequited American lives. And if the crowd in the hall could be counted in hundreds, they were representative of millions. This was a good place for Charles Schumer then – indeed, a perfect place. Cometh the hour, cometh the man.

That's what everyone was hoping – not least the organizers, the Irish Lobby for Immigration Reform (ILIR), a group that was a twenty-first century successor to the Irish Immigration Reform Movement (IIRM) of the 1980s and '90s. It was a slightly different name, but it was very much the same issue: Irish physically present in America but legally on the outside looking in.

ILIR had called the meeting in the aftermath of that year's midterm elections. It described the gathering as a kick-start for a renewed 'Countdown To Victory' campaign, one aimed at securing more Irish immigrant visas by means of a bipartisan reform bill that, all things going well, would take shape and win congressional approval in 2007.

'We're calling on all the undocumented to turn up and be counted. We can't win this without the support of the undocumented. If they don't turn out, people will think they have gone away', Kelly Fincham, the ILIR executive director, told reporters in the run-up to the meeting. ILIR was planning another rally in Boston for Wednesday, December 13, while additional meetings were in the works for Philadelphia, San Francisco and Florida.

The undocumented did turn up at St Barnabas. The hall was filled to standing room only, with some spilling out onto the street. And though it was just a few weeks shy of Christmas, many were wearing just T-shirts emblazoned with words calling for the legalization of the Irish.

December 1, 2006 is something of a standout in New York meteorological history. The record shows that temperatures in the New York area reached a spring-like high of seventy degrees that day. The warmth had lasted into the evening, and indeed by the meeting's scheduled starting time had started to spawn thunderstorms. With Schumer in full flow, thunderclaps erupted and lightning flashed outside. The rally had the air of some climactic scene from a Shakespeare play. But what act was it? First or final?

Regardless, it had quite an array of dramatis personae. US Representative Anthony Weiner, still in his political pomp, and former congressman Bruce Morrison (who had secured thousands of green cards for luckier Irish in the early 1990s) spoke, as did leaders of ILIR. Schumer, the main act, outlined a scenario that had the immigration reform saga within sight of a successful denouement, albeit assuming certain things happened, and certain things did not. All embraced the heady combination of optimism and caution, rallying cry and warning that Schumer outlined to his audience.

Schumer committed himself and his Democratic Party to the pursuit of a comprehensive immigration reform bill in 2007. Given Schumer's pivotal role in securing his party's congressional majorities in the recent midterm elections, this was no lightweight pledge. Schumer went so far as to proclaim '*tiocfaidh ar lá*', Irish for 'our day will come' and for years a proclamation of intent for Irish republicans and a pledge of working towards a positive and desired result.

The significance of Schumer's words, frequently interrupted by applause and cheering from the crowd, was compounded by the fact that New York's senior senator had emerged from the recent midterm elections as one of the most powerful figures in the Democratic

Party on Capitol Hill. And though his speech to what was a friendly home-state crowd sounded like just that, experienced observers in the room were in broad agreement that Schumer had sufficient clout to set in motion a debate geared towards producing the kind of comprehensive reform bill that would secure the signature of a seemingly sympathetic President George W. Bush.

A successful outcome to the reform debate, it was stated more than once to an assembly that included Irish diplomatic representatives, would depend on the bipartisan nature of a final bill. That reality, however, did not prevent Schumer from taking a few distinctly partisan swipes at those Republicans in the outgoing 109th Congress who had worked against reform and had campaigned against it in the months before the midterm elections.

'The last time I spoke to you,' said Schumer, 'the Republican leadership was playing cheap games with immigration reform. Now they are in the minority and Schumer and Weiner are in the majority.' The response from the audience was typical on an evening that witnessed a new surge of hope coursing through an ILIR campaign that had its high points and more pessimistic moments since the group was formally launched in a midtown Manhattan hotel exactly one year previously.

Schumer had been led into the hall by two pipers who had to duel it out with the crowd in the battle to best raise the rafters. It was heady stuff. And there were emotional moments amid the rhetoric. Two ILIR volunteers, introduced as Mary and Samantha, described what it was like to miss the funeral of a loved one, or spend another Christmas Day dominated by tearful transatlantic phone calls to family members in Ireland.

For the most part, the focus of the various speeches was on how immigration reform would be achieved. Little attention was paid to the question of why the meeting was taking place at all. It was no time for a history lesson. All eyes were looking ahead, though the energy coursing through the evening was fueled by years of frustration.

If the Immigration and Nationality Act of 1965 was mentioned at all, it barely caused a moment's pause on anyone's part. Most people in the audience hadn't even been born in 1965. But they were living in a time of consequence, right smack in the middle of a nine-year period (2002–11) in which Ireland would receive less than 15,400 Green Card visas out of ten million issued globally.

That, according to the ILIR's calculation, was about 0.15 per cent of the US visas issued to the wider world in that timeframe. So those gathered in the church hall, almost all of them shut out of the exclusive 0.15 per cent club, cheered and applauded, dreamed and imagined. Some even prayed.

CHAPTER 2

Mustering for Battle

In the waning days of January 1969, members of a group called the American Irish National Immigration Committee (AINIC) gathered at the Conrad Hilton Hotel in Chicago to plan a course of action aimed at securing more US immigration visas for the Irish. Similar scenes would be played out in other US cities twenty years later, and indeed thirty and forty years on.

But while the calls for greater Irish access to the American dream would draw media attention and inspire some congressional sympathy in 1989 and 2009, the Hilton gathering would take place at a moment in time when an Irish call for a wider American immigration door seemed at odds with an American landscape that looked, in certain areas, as Irish as any part of the island three thousand miles to the north-east of the Statue of Liberty.

The year 1969 would see out a decade when the Irish of America scaled seemingly impossible heights. At its opening, the first Irish Catholic president was elected. At its closing, two of the three crew members on board Apollo 11 could claim some degree of Irish ancestry.

So what had the AINIC members so riled up at a time of year when even damp Ireland seemed a warmer prospect than frigid Chicago? Simply put, a group of American Irish and their Irish-born cousins were feeling discriminated against, marginalized, shut out. It wasn't easy to get this message across. Not in the America of Vietnam and Watts; not in the America of Kent State, Bull Connor and Love Canal. There were a lot of problems, issues, anxieties. A lack of visas for the Irish didn't seem to rank at the top of them, not even close.

Why the American Irish National Immigration Committee? Why the meeting in a city that had so recently witnessed a party convention that had morphed into a metaphor for a country deeply divided? And if so divided, why the need for more Irish, more outsiders, more immigrants?

In the answers to these questions, there was to be found the very essence of the United States and its fabled dream. No matter how bad things were in America, there would be people in other lands who would leave everything behind for a chance to live in one of its fifty states. The Irish were no different. When they imagined America, they could draw on a version of the place that was itself Irish. Every new Irish immigrant had the luxury of experiencing both a push and pull effect.

But by 1969 it was becoming more difficult to observe this phenomenon. That's because it was hard to spot the Irish newcomers. There were hardly any of them about. The reason for this was a combination with a positive side and a negative one. By the end of the 1960s, economic activity on the divided island of Ireland was beginning to show the kind of vibrancy that had been elusive for centuries. This belated development would mean that fewer would have to emigrate. But fewer wasn't all. Many Irish were still being pushed and pulled and, as it was for countless of their ancestors, the 1960s Irish felt the strongest social and economic pull coming from the United States of America.

Then it happened. In the middle of the decade, in 1965, a boom came down, a golden door was slammed shut. What was a pull became a counter-push. The Irish beneficiaries, like other European nationalities with a favorable visa quota system, found themselves about to be locked out.

Admittedly, what had once been a flood of transatlantic Irish migration had been reduced, by the mid-1960s, to a relative trickle. This was not altogether unwelcome, as an awakening Ireland needed its people. But the 1965 Immigration Reform and Nationality Act would advance the process of flow reduction to the point that Irish immigration to America would almost completely dry up.

In fiscal 1965, the Irish secured 5,378 visas, a number actually well below their quota allowance. In the following year, the total fell to 3,071. It dropped further to 2,665 in 1967 and rose slightly to 3,619 in fiscal 1968. 1969, the year AINIC members huddled in Chicago, the bottom began to fall out. What was coming down the pike was clearly discernible as the year opened, and it was a verifiable statistic at its close. Between July and December of that year, the number of US visas obtained by Irish immigrants was precisely 60.

In later years, Senator Edward Kennedy, a primary architect of the 1965 reform act, would speak of the 'unintended consequences' that the act would have for the Irish. A total of 60 visas in six months matched Kennedy's assessment perfectly. It was such a low figure that many Irish and Irish Americans were certain that it had to be unintended – a mistake. Whether or not it was unintended, it was, beyond argument, a significant consequence for the Irish who failed to make the lucky threescore.

The 1960s was a tumultuous decade for many reasons. The end of meaningful Irish migration to America wasn't one of the bigger headlines from those ten years. Far from it. But for the Irish, the negative consequences of immigration reform at the decade's mid-point would reach far into the future. They would reach deep down into the collective Irish and Irish American psyche. And the headlines, over time, would indeed grow steadily bigger.

CHAPTER 3

1965: The Year of the New Divide

By the middle of the 1960s, the great divide that had once been the Atlantic Ocean had been bridged. Jet aircraft, more often than not American-made Boeings, had pulled Ireland and the United States closer than would have been imagined just a generation earlier. But while geographic distance as an impediment to travel was becoming less of an issue, a new geopolitical obstacle was looming in the form of a major departure from previous practice in US immigration law.

Still, with economic change becoming daily more evident in Ireland, and chilly relations between both the Republic of Ireland and Northern Ireland seemingly defrosting – this against the backdrop of meetings on both sides of the border between their respective prime ministers – the most significant change to US immigration law in decades did not stir up the kind of reaction in Ireland that such a development would have generated in 1955, a mere ten years previously. Things were on the up in Ireland. There were more jobs and promises of yet more. The sitting government in Dublin was returned to power in an April election. The government in Belfast created a new ministry in charge of development. There was reason for hope on the island. Even more than that: there was reason, finally, to expect.

There was reason to expect much in America too: civil rights for all to go with two cars in the garage. That was the general idea, anyway. America was an extraordinary place in the eyes of people in most other nations, a vast land of astonishing contrast and sometimes glaring contradiction. American astronauts were by now halfway along their decade-long mission to reach the moon. Back on the ground, cities burned. There were jobs aplenty in the world's largest economy, though soon enough a job might entail a uniform, a rifle and a flight to a country called Vietnam.

In April, as voters in Ireland signaled relative content with their political leaders and returned Seán Lemass as Taoiseach and leader of a majority Fianna Fáil government, President Lyndon Johnson asked a joint session of Congress to rid the United States of any and all remaining barriers to citizens who desired to vote. His appeal was broadcast on national television. That same month, the world's first commercial communications satellite was launched into space. Early Bird would make it easier for people in Ireland to phone friends and family in the United States. Phoning a friend in America was one thing. Joining that friend would soon be quite another.

If the world seemed to be shrinking in 1965 – if a satellite orbiting at 22,300 miles could bring a war on one side of the planet into the living rooms of the other side – surely it would be no great task to get up and move a few thousand miles, not least those miles between Europe and America? By the opening days of October, that question would be answered. A long-open entry door for European travelers with one-way tickets would begin a proposed five-year process of closing. And what was no longer considered a great distance by telephone line or airline would again become an unbridgeable chasm defined more by terrestrial man-made law than by mere water and sky.

Back in Ireland, the water and sky part was what was attracting the greatest attention. More and more people were flying the Atlantic to America in passenger jets but, increasingly, it was not as emigrants.

In the first three months of 1965, 1,036 visas had been allocated to Irish applicants by the US Embassy in Dublin. Irish migration to the US was tailing off and was a mere trickle compared to the 1950s, a decade when Irish America paid host to one of the most concentrated periods of migration from Ireland in the history of that storied east-to-west passage.

More than a few of the new arrivals from Ireland had little or no inkling of the profound changes being pieced together in Washington. Indeed, as the debate reached its climax in Congress, those back in Ireland who were inclined to think of a future American life were a good deal less informed than they should have been in an age when television presented an array of shows to audiences in Mayo that would have been entirely familiar to viewers in Minnesota. That's because most people in Ireland living outside the east coast area, or Northern Ireland – particularly those living in the western parts of the country, traditional springboards for large scale emigration – had access to only one television channel, the national broadcaster RTÉ.

For hard news from America and around the world there was still a heavy reliance on nationally distributed newspapers. And as the clock ticked down to the biggest change in US immigration law in living memory, there were no newspapers to be had. From July 2 to September 12, a printing strike closed down Ireland's national dailies and an array of printing houses. There was, in those crucial months, a near total news blackout throughout the twenty-six counties of the Republic. British titles were available for sale, but unlike later years, there were no Irish editions of the main British titles. Irish visas for America didn't quite make the grade for editors in 'swinging' Britain, so the coming sea change went largely unreported in Ireland during the printers' work stoppage.

In Irish America, however, it was another story. The emergence in Congress of two bills, S.500 in the US Senate and HR 2580 in the House of Representatives, was raising an alarm among community members who advocated for a continuing clear passage to America for any and all Irish who wanted to make the Atlantic crossing. And there was an irony lurking in the background. The idea that the old ways of doing business were in the past, that the future of immigration was to be found in all corners of the globe and not just western and northern Europe, had for years been taking shape in one especially important Irish American grouping: the Brothers Kennedy.

Kilcullen, Maureen

43012

Saturday, November 27, 2021

31183202990898   The attic on Queen Street

CHAPTER 4

The Fading Drumbeat

In his memory, that sound of the drums beating slow time for the dead president is still carrying across the Potomac and up into the sloping meadows of Arlington National Cemetery. Each year, on the anniversary of the assassination of President John F. Kennedy, many recall, or try to remember, where they were when they first heard of the president's death. Michael McGrath thinks more of where he was when JFK was lowered into the ground. He was standing right beside the president's grave, standing stock-still, his eyes fixed on the scene, drawing every detail into a young mind that had yet to reach 20 years of age.

Many don't know, and many have forgotten, that twenty-four Irish soldiers comprised the front-line honor guard at the hallowed spot where the young president was laid to rest on November 25, 1963, three days after his death in Dallas. McGrath was one of those soldiers, a member of the Irish army cadet school's guard of honor and rifle drill team.

In later years, McGrath would perform numerous duties and missions, both for the Irish army's air corps and for the United Nations' peacekeeping forces in the Middle East. But there never would be a mission quite like this first one, not for him and not for his comrades who, on that November day, represented a bond between Ireland and America that transcended national borders.

The journey to Washington for McGrath and his comrades started with a journey to Ireland for President Kennedy, the immigrant homecoming to beat all homecomings. A few months before his last day of life, Kennedy had made his never-to-be-forgotten visit to the land of his ancestors. One of the ceremonies attended by the American president was a wreath-laying ceremony at the 1916 memorial at Arbour Hill, in Dublin, during which the cadet school's drill team went through its paces.

According to McGrath, Kennedy was so impressed that he requested a film of the drill, 'He wanted to use our drill with his own honor guard.' McGrath would rise to the rank of commandant (major) in the Irish Army Air Corps and would, after his retirement from military service, take up the post of first manager of Knock (later Ireland West) international airport.

Kennedy was sent a film of the Irish drill. His enthusiasm for it was apparently conveyed to Jackie Kennedy. 'She made a request just a short while after the assassination for us to be at the funeral,' McGrath said. 'It came out of the blue and was conveyed through the Irish embassy in Washington. She felt that her husband would have wanted it.' He continues, 'It was highly unusual. The president's own armed forces were moved aside to a certain extent to accommodate her wish. And she got her wish.'

Kennedy was assassinated on Friday, November 22. The following evening, Michael McGrath and the other members of the rifle drill team were still contemplating a night's sleep in their barracks at the Curragh.

It was at about 11 p.m. that McGrath and the rest of his unit were unexpectedly ordered to report to the Curragh military college's Pearse lecture hall. 'We were all shocked by the president's death but this was something that really left us astonished. So while we were saddened by what had happened, we also immediately realized that Ireland was about to be accorded the greatest of honors and that we would be representing our country,' McGrath explained.

The surprise of the moment was soon replaced by the urgent need to work out the logistics of the operation. First and foremost were the rifles used in the drill. They were Lee Enfields. But these older rifles had just been replaced by new and shorter FN models. 'All the old rifles were stored away and packed in grease,' McGrath recalls. 'We had to quickly take them out of storage, clean them up and bring them back to the required operational state. And all this in the middle of the night.' The rifles were put in order and the cadets managed to snatch a couple of hours of sleep.

Sunday morning had barely dawned when they were up again for Mass, a quick breakfast, some rapid rifle drilling and a bus trip to Dublin airport, where an Aer Lingus Boeing 707 was ready to fly President Éamon de Valera and the rest of the official Irish delegation to the funeral in Washington. 'None of us had passports, but we all had rifles and bullets,' McGrath said. At the airport, the cadets formed a guard of honor for de Valera as he went on board the jet. De Valera shook McGrath's hand during the presentation. Once the Irish president was on board, the cadets, led by their officers, piled on after him. So far as McGrath can recall, none of them had ever even flown before.

McGrath fell into a seat beside his close friend and fellow cadet Martin Coughlin. He remembers the emotions of the moment. 'We were sad, anxious and elated,' he said. 'We were representing out country, flying across the ocean with our president in order to mourn and salute America's president.'

The plane landed at Idlewild in New York, the airport that would soon be renamed after JFK. The Irish party didn't need passports. They were met on the tarmac by US Secretary of State Dean Rusk. The plane refueled and flew to Dulles airport outside Washington. The Irish cadets were driven to Fort Myer in Virginia, a few minutes' drive from Arlington National Cemetery. It was now Sunday afternoon.

The young Irish soldiers bedded down as best they could for the night. They were tired and jetlagged, but sleep was to prove elusive. First thing Monday morning, the cadets were roused for a full dress rehearsal at the graveside. 'I remember they were still digging the president's grave,' McGrath said. 'There was a gravedigger in the hole. I could see the top of his shovel coming out of the grave as he dug. We were ordered into our positions by an American general, at least three-star. We realized then that our position was to be right in front of the grave.'

After going through their drill, McGrath and his fellow cadets were bussed back to Fort Myer for breakfast. They were back at Arlington and in position by half past one that afternoon. 'The press were there and the cameras were rolling so we all had to be in position,' McGrath said. 'Because of that we couldn't stand at ease. We stood like statues for almost three hours.'

McGrath was tall, a shade over six foot, three inches. As a result, he was placed at one end of the line, in the second row. He was only a few feet from President Kennedy's final resting place. As the afternoon – which he remembers as being cold and largely windless – wore on, McGrath became conscious of the sound of drums leading the caisson carrying the dead president. 'The drums were coming closer and closer and later I could hear the horses' hooves,' he said. The arrival of the procession at the grave was the moment for the cadets to commence their drill. McGrath describes the scene:

> I remember thinking, here we go, we're on. How we performed the drill was of immense importance to us, here more than ever before. It was an old traditional funeral drill, the Queen Ann Drill, and it can't be done with modern rifles. It is very precise, snappy and visually precise, both in sight and sound. You hear the clash of the hand hitting the rifle sling.
>
> There was a moment when we all turned our heads left. I was looking straight into the eyes of Jackie Kennedy. It was heart wrenching. The drill then reached the point where we reversed arms and lowered our heads. It was the most solemn part, the salute to the dead.

The drill had passed off perfectly. All the orders had been given in Irish by Lieutenant Frank Colclough. At this point, the cadets raised their rifles in the air and fired three volleys over President Kennedy's grave.

The role of the Irish cadets at the graveside is not obvious in many of the films showing the graveside ceremonies. McGrath himself is seen in a photograph taken by the Associated Press and included in a commemorative book entitled *The Torch Is Passed*. The cadet seen in front of McGrath is Leo Quinlan. McGrath says:

> Waiting by the grave and listening to the drums seemed like an eternity at the time.

I can still hear those drums now. For me, and I think for the rest of us, they epitomized the overwhelming sadness of that day.

We were all emotionally charged up, but we had to keep it all in. We had to be at one hundred per cent because we owed it to the president, and our country.

We were deeply honored. It was the most significant event of our lives and the one thing we all go back to whenever we meet. I will never forget that day, every minute of it. I am immensely proud to have been there.

Over the years, McGrath kept newspaper clippings, copies of photographs and a memorial card for President Kennedy presented to the Irish cadets. But more than all these paraphernalia, Michael McGrath was in possession of extraordinary memories of a sad but standout moment in twentieth century history. It was witnessed by millions on television, but only a chosen few were at the place where the world said goodbye to John F. Kennedy. It was also a high moment in the relationship between two countries, one that had reached a rare altitude with the election of Kennedy to the presidency and a new depth of sadness when he was assassinated.

The presence of the Irish cadets at Arlington was also a salute to all the Irish of America, living and dead. But it would soon appear to be something of a false summit. Within a couple of years the idea of a passport-free flight across the Atlantic and a greeting at its end from the US Secretary of State would be replaced by a new barrier to travel for even those Irish with a passport. President Kennedy himself had a hand in this change of affairs. Over time, so would his brothers Edward and Robert.

CHAPTER 5

Teddy

It had always been Teddy. He was the beginning, the middle and the end of the story, the *primus inter pares*, the *sine qua non*, the main man. Teddy had taken away, but he could also give back. And he wanted to give back. Oh, how he wanted.

Senator Edward Kennedy has gone down in history, and lore, as one of the greatest legislators to ever walk the corridors and tunnels of Capitol Hill. For the Irish, be they Irish or American-born, Teddy was 'The Man', like the Edward G. Robinson character in 'The Cincinnati Kid'. When it came to legislative gambits in Washington you would be a fool to bet against Teddy, at least most of the time.

This was later in his political career, of course, when he was performing solo without the support of his brothers John and Robert. But even when his brothers were alive, and he looked to some like the Kennedy family political afterthought, Teddy was giving consideration to immigration: how it had been, how it was, how it might be in the future.

And why not? Immigration was central to his family's story – indeed, the very reason that he and his brothers had come into this world. Teddy – all the Kennedy brothers – could become sentimental when the family's own experience of immigration was the subject for discussion. But sentimentality could only go so far. It could not get in the way of reworking the American immigrant story. So the Kennedys, led at first by John, set about the retooling of a system that had never been an open door, despite popular mythology.

America had always been selective as to who was allowed inside its expanding borders, starting with out-of-luck foreign princes and potentates who, arguably, did not deserve much consideration.

This selectivity extended to all manner of people for a variety of reasons, most of them not especially noble or altruistic. The Alien and Sedition Acts, passed by President John Adams in 1798, were largely designed to keep out the Irish, specifically members of the (ironically) rebellious United Irishmen, who would be defeated by a man not unknown to Adams, General Charles Cornwallis.

John Kennedy, a son of Massachusetts like Adams, was little more than a toddler when the United States first went into sustained reverse gear on immigration. It was 1921, and the huddled masses yearning to be free were sent a first signal that their yearning might not be quite enough. There had been some restrictive laws enacted before that year. 'Lunatics, idiots, convicts and those like to become a public charge' had been barred under the first federally enacted immigration law in 1882. That same year, the Chinese Exclusion Act was introduced to stem the flow of Chinese labor.

But it was the 1921 Immigration Act, signed into law by President Warren Harding, that could be construed as being the first mostly rational piece of restrictive immigration legislation, in both conception and practical effect. It would not please everyone, of course. Immigration law invariably pulls people in opposite directions. But the act carried in its pages the idea of lowering the overall number of new arrivals, a view which has prevailed down the years. The 1921 act established a quota system based on the national origins of the US population in 1910. The act was revised in 1924 with a new point of reference being the 1920 census. Both pieces of legislation placed a ceiling on the number of immigrants permitted to enter the United States in any one year. But given the standout proportion of Irish in the now 'native' US population in both 1910 and 1920, Ireland would continue to do as well under the quota plan – confirmed again in 1929 legislation – at least as long as people in Ireland saw America as their way out, the most compelling alternative to their own economically backward native land.

By the mid-1960s there was another way out, and it was much closer to home. It was home. For the first time in living memory – and before it – Ireland was offering possibility to those who stayed on the island. The quota system was still in operation across the ocean, and Irish were still migrating westward across it, but the great

1950s surge had sharply tailed off. The annual emigrant number totals were now consistently falling short of Ireland's yearly quota, and those unused quota visas were not transferable.

Meanwhile, other countries – Poland, Italy and Greece to name but three – had far smaller quotas than Ireland. Huge numbers of people who had applied for US residence were being held back in waiting lines that would take years to process.

The pressure for changes in US law had built up noticeably during the late 1950s. But the reformers were battling deeply entrenched views. The 1952 Immigration and Nationality Act had added new cement to the quota system wall – so much so that President Truman was unsuccessful is his attempt to kill it with a veto. Truman's reaction was clear, 'The idea behind this discriminatory policy was, to put it boldly, that Americans with English or Irish names were better people and better citizens than Americans with Italian or Greek or Polish names.' Such a concept, Truman added ruefully, was 'utterly unworthy of our traditions and our ideals'.

The soon-to-be greatest living hero of the Irish everywhere, John F. Kennedy, agreed with Truman. Kennedy's pre-White House congressional activities included a 1957 amendment that allowed for family reunification without reference to national origin. Jack was laying the groundwork for Ted.

By the decade's end, the quota system was seen by JFK and others to be entirely inadequate when it came to dealing with divided families, survivors of natural disasters and, perhaps most importantly in the context of the day, refugees fleeing political oppression – not least that imposed by Washington's *bête noire*: communism.

Unlike some groups, the Irish had avoided the communist yoke and their country was blessedly free of large-scale, death-dealing natural disasters. The game was almost up. To Kennedy, it seemed only logical and fair. The times had absolutely changed and Cold War America had to base its intake of newcomers on entirely new criteria.

On July 23, 1963, four months before his death, JFK submitted to the 88th Congress proposals for 'revising and modernizing our immigration law'. This entailed the elimination of the national quota system after a five-year phase-out period. President Johnson, during his State of the Union address on January 8, 1964, took up where his late predecessor had already been. 'In establishing preferences,' said Johnson, 'a nation that was built by immigrants of all lands can ask those who now seek admission: "What can you do for your country?" But we should not be asking: "In what country were you born?"'

Irish Americans were prominent in the subsequent congressional debate. At first glance, the idea of family reunification seemed to pose no threat to Irish immigration so long as the Irish kept coming in numbers. The chief advocate for the emerging bill in the Senate was Senator Philip Hart. The chairman of the House Judiciary Committee was Congressman Michael Feighan. Feighan had problems with some aspects of the new bill but was not opposed to the elimination of the national quota system. And when the dead president's legislative legacy was first submitted for congressional debate, the acting chairman of the Senate Judiciary Committee was in favor of just about every last word. The acting chairman was Senator Edward Kennedy.

It would fall heavily on the youngest brother to ensure that JFK's views, as expressed in his 1958 book *A Nation of Immigrants*, found meaning in new laws. By virtue of his growing skills as a weaver of bipartisan deals, the brother would not fail in this task. As the bill was being debated in 1965, Ted Kennedy, as Senate floor leader with responsibility for presiding over the bill's amendments, gave advance notice of his talents as a broker of compromise.

As with all legislation, the bill that finally emerged was indeed a compromise arrangement, or an arrangement of compromises depending on one's point of view. The bill not only did away with national quotas but also introduced a controversial ceiling on migration from the Western Hemisphere. Against such broad-ranging change, Ireland looked like a dot in the ocean.

Ted Kennedy summed up the outcome as follows:

> There is little doubt that of key importance was the unusual parliamentary situation in Congress, where the large Democratic majority was generally responsive to the spirit, if not the letter, of the administration's proposal.

Republican leaders were also ready to act on the issue. Moreover, in the Judiciary Committees of both Houses, the balance of power lay with those who long worked for reform, or who readily recognized the need for changes in policy governing the admission of immigrants. And in the executive branch, for the first time in more than a decade, the White House, under both President Kennedy and President Johnson, was deeply committed to basic reform and actively mobilized its forces to see it through.

'The legislative history of the bill,' said Kennedy, 'especially the drawing of a consensus which, in effect, neutralized any significant opposition both within and without the Congress, generated an atmosphere receptive to reform which was consonant with changing attitudes among our citizens on questions of race and national origin.' He added, 'And not to be forgotten in any list of reasons is the tremendous effort put forth by the several private organizations, whose many years of work throughout the country were helping to bring the hope of reform into reality.'

Back in Ireland, very few had the slightest notion about what this new 'reality' would very soon mean.

CHAPTER 6

The Fighting Irish in Retreat

The Irish bled for America. And bled. And they are not shy about reminding themselves, and anyone else who cares to listen, that they bled profusely. So it is not surprising that a closing American door would cause unease, indeed anger. The Irish built America. They are not shy when it comes to making that claim either.

Of course, people from all over the world bled for America and forged a continent into a nation state. Every ethnic and racial group has its own story, its own version of the facts, its own mythology. But it being America, those who shout loudest tend to be heard the most. And with between thirty and forty million Americans claiming some degree of connection to Ireland, the Irish have no problem being heard. It's being listened to that can be a problem.

Nevertheless, the Irish of America have maintained a healthy chorus that proclaims their role in the nation's building. The idea of the 'Fighting Irish' can be found far and wide, and well beyond the campus of just one university. The first fighting Irishman on what would one day be American soil was most likely Edward Nugent.

Nugent turned up on Roanoke Island in the 1580s after being deposited in the ill-fated colony by a fellow Irishman, Richard Butler, who had served Walter Raleigh. The story of Edward Nugent is short, and not very sweet. It was recorded that Nugent was given the task of killing the Indian chief Pemisapan, deemed responsible by colonists for leading a series of raids. Nugent turned out to be an efficient killer, returning to the colonist camp with the slain chief's head.

This early clash between Irish and Indian would be followed by many others in succeeding centuries. And all this strife was tinged with more than a whiff of irony: a displaced people battling displaced peoples. But if the Irish were up for a fight it would have to be every fight. So it was inevitable that when America itself set out to fight for its independence, the Irish would be in the middle of the action, behind George Washington, and even sometimes in front of him in British army red.

The Irish role in the Revolutionary War was not insignificant. Many of the Irish in the ranks of the Continental Army saw the struggle not just in terms of winning American independence but also Ireland's. For these hopefuls, the battle three thousand miles and more from their home island amounted to a proxy war against the British Crown. Not surprising then that the many Irish, and their even more numerous Scots-Irish cousins, earned a reputation for toughness in what would be a drawn out, dour contest in which harsh winters and lack of supplies would prove to be every bit as hard to beat as the British.

Such was the case at George Washington's 1779–80 winter camp in Morristown, New Jersey, where perhaps as many as one in four soldiers were either of Irish birth or ancestry; generals born in Ireland, or who had Irish parents, commanded seven of the eleven brigades in the camp.

The conditions at Morristown were especially brutal, the record-breaking winter weather seemingly endless. So bad were the conditions that some who endured the long months of cold and damp longed for the comparative comforts of Valley Forge, now two winters gone. But Washington would deliver a denouement of sorts by declaring a holiday. And that day off would be March 17, 1780 – St Patrick's Day.

The declaration went beyond the bare detail of a routine general order. It linked the American Revolution to events in Ireland. In his order, written on March 16, Washington stated:

> The general congratulates the army on the very interesting proceedings of the parliament of Ireland and the inhabitants of that country which have been lately communicated; not only as they appear calculated to remove those heavy and tyrannical oppressions on their trade but to restore to a brave

and generous people their ancient rights and freedom and by their operations to promote the cause of America.

Desirous of impressing upon the minds of the army, transactions so important in their nature, the general directs that all fatigue and working parties cease for tomorrow the seventeenth, a day held in particular regard by the people of the nation.

Of course, this was no signal for rambunctious revelry. Washington was prickly when it came to form and personal behavior. He made it clear that the 'celebration of the day will not be attended with the least rioting or disorder'; that the officers were to stay in their own quarters, with troops remaining within their encampments.

Still, for those Irish who still felt unsure about their place in the new emerging nation, this nod from the great George Washington was no small thing. It was, in its own way, an official welcome to the new land from its uncrowned king. But it was not a welcome destined to last indefinitely. The affairs of Ireland were of undoubted interest to Washington and others among the Founding Fathers. But of far greater interest were the affairs of France.

With independence for the colonies ultimately secured, and Washington in place as the new republic's first president, it might have been an opportune time for the more politically motivated in what was also a nascent Irish America to steer eyes and interest towards an Ireland where leading political figures, Protestant and Catholic, were sounding very much like their bewigged American cousins. Ah, but France.

Washington took the presidential oath less than three months before the storming of the Bastille. That event, and what followed, would cast a long shadow, not just across France itself, but well beyond its borders. The French Revolution would cast a shadow over Ireland, and it would grip the imaginations and stoke the fears of many among the recent revolutionaries in America. And fear would, in time, lead to a wall, albeit a legislative one: the Alien and Sedition Acts of June and July 1798.

The French Revolution had all but run its course by then, its fervor steadily giving way to a new order under Napoleon

Bonaparte. Still, fear of Jacobin contagion yet prevailed within the ranks of President John Adams's Federalist Party, and to add to the concerns of America's young government were events in Ireland that appeared, from across the ocean, to bear a strong resemblance to Jacobin thinking.

The rebellion of the United Irishmen in 1798 did indeed draw inspiration from the French Revolution, but also from its American equivalent. The Irish rising spanned the months of May to September that year and included a battle, Vinegar Hill in County Wexford, which would have brought back memories of Bunker Hill to American minds. In that same county, Irish of a French Jacobin mind even went so far as to proclaim a revolutionary French Republic. No surprise then that French military support for the United Irishmen forged, in Federalist minds at least, an image of an expanding Jacobinism reaching across the Atlantic. It was the domino theory of its day. And it was enough for Adams and his administration to throw up the first significant obstacle to Irish migration to the United States.

As Ron Chernow notes in *Alexander Hamilton*, his biography of the first US Secretary of the Treasury and a man who shuddered at the spectacle of revolutionary France, the Federalist-controlled Congress would maneuver for partisan advantage and betray an unbecoming nativist streak.

Chernow writes:

> Federalists wanted to curb an influx of Irish immigrants who were usually pro-French and thus natural adherents to the Republican cause. Congressman Harrison Gray Otis of Boston set a strident tone when he declared that America should no longer 'wish to invite hordes of wild Irishmen, not the turbulent and disorderly parts of the world, to come here with a view to disturb our tranquility after having succeeded in the overthrow of their own governments'.

David McCullough, in his biography of John Adams, also highlights the widespread impression of the Irish as being somehow bestial and beyond the bounds of civilized society. 'In addition to the French,' he notes, 'there were the "wild Irish," refugees from the Irish Rebellion of 1798 who were thought to include dangerous radicals and in any case, because of their anti-British sentiment, gladly joined ranks with the Republicans'.

McCullough highlights a New York newspaper warning its readers that a Thomas Jefferson victory in the election of 1800 would mean civil war. The paper reported that hordes of Frenchmen and Irishmen, 'the refuse of Europe', would flood the United States and threaten the life of 'all who love order, peace, virtue and religion'. This broadside was primarily aimed at Jefferson himself, the 'refuse of Europe' – an unintended nod to the future Statue of Liberty as it would turn out – merely acting as props for the agitprop.

Jefferson and his fellow Republicans took a different view of the French, and by extension the Irish. But they were not in power, and the Irish, despite all that they had contributed to America's fight for freedom, suddenly found themselves on the wrong side of American laws and much of what passed for popular sentiment. And the consequences of those laws, as embodied in the four component parts of the Alien and Sedition Acts, were very much intended.

And they were effective. A little over two hundred years after Edward Nugent had stepped ashore, the Irish foothold in America was secure, but the precise size and shape of its future was becoming less certain. The Irish – the Catholic ones in particular – had been defined and categorized. As the eighteenth century gave way to the nineteenth, these Irish faced very significant obstacles to their claim of a share of the new country in the new world.

The Alien and Sedition Acts, then, were an early-days 'no Irish need apply' sign, one so big that it overshadowed a continent. The century to follow would witness a mighty struggle to sweep that shadow away. And it would take more than acts written on parchment to deny the Irish an unfolding destiny an ocean away from their home island.

CHAPTER 7

The Irish Fight Back

In the sixteenth century it would be a toehold. In the seventeenth, a foothold. In the eighteenth, the foot would be in the door. In the nineteenth century, the Irish put the shoulder to the American door and nearly took it off its hinges.

They were facilitated in doing so by Thomas Jefferson and his Democratic-Republicans, a grouping that would not meet later definitions of a political party but which harbored a great many political ideas, likes and dislikes. Jefferson and his allies disliked the Alien and Sedition Acts, and after the Virginian wrested the presidency from John Adams of Massachusetts in 1800 – with 'overwhelming Irish-American support', according to Kerby Miller in his definitive book *Emigrants and Exiles* – he lost little time in erasing the bulk of the 1798 laws. This was done by allowing the Sedition Act and Alien Friends Act to expire. A part of the package, the Alien Enemies Act, remained on the books.

Jefferson was an astute politician. He might have viewed the French with a benevolent eye and the Irish with something less than a malevolent one. But he knew well enough that America would always attract enemies. Later presidents would deploy the codified Enemies Act against nationalities who fought wars against the United States, most notably the Germans.

The Irish of the nineteenth century did not enjoy the dubious privilege of waging war as a nation against anyone. That said, of course, the Irish would find themselves in quite a few wars, and under an array of flags – none more notable than the star-spangled banner. They would fight under British colors, for the army of the Pope, for the United States against Mexico, for Mexico against the

United States, for the Union against the Confederacy, and for the Confederacy against the Union.

By so fighting, and bleeding, the Irish would register in the consciousness of the wider world and its fast-emerging new power, America. If the twentieth century was indeed the American century, the nineteenth would be the Irish century in an American context. That said, glory on the battlefield would only be part of the story. Most Irish immigrants who set foot in the United States between 1800 and 1899 were destined to live lives far from any front lines. They would be born, live, work and die in relative anonymity, and, in the great majority of cases, in near total obscurity.

In the first third of the century, it would be a relatively benign anonymity. The Immigrant Irish, the growing number of Catholics as well as Protestants, benefited in the eyes of native-born Americans because they were perceived to be hostile to America's old adversary, England.

As Kerby Miller notes, 'from 1800 through the 1828 election of Andrew Jackson, son of emigrants from County Antrim, a common republicanism largely obscured old antagonisms between Americans and Irishmen, Protestants and Catholics. But this would not last, as the number of arriving Catholics began to rise'. Miller additionally highlights, 'Sadly, later Irish emigrants would discover that an increasingly Anglophilic, nativist and evangelical Protestant America no long considered self-proclaimed Irish exiles to be almost honorary Americans.'

By the 1830s the effects of this assertion were becoming increasingly evident; and nowhere more so than in a stretch of woodland about thirty miles from Philadelphia, which was to enter Irish American lore in the early twenty-first century.

'Duffy's Cut' fits the definition of microcosm. It's a small place, not much more than an acre, just outside Malvern, Pennsylvania. It would appear at first glance to be just woodland, though it does have a ruined man-made structure and a modern-day rail line running through it. More importantly, what's running through Duffy's Cut is a story – one of immigration, exploitation, ill-luck, persecution and death. Most Catholic Irish immigrants in the 1830s would have quickly recognized all, or part, of this combination.

Duffy's Cut first began making news in 2004, a couple of years after it was identified as a place worthy of forensic investigation by Dr William Watson, of Immaculata University, and Rev. Frank Watson, William's twin brother. They identified it as such after setting eyes on what a *Smithsonian Magazine* report described as 'a long-secret railroad company document'.

The work at Duffy's Cut would make national headlines, spawn a book, and put names and faces on at least fifty-seven Irish immigrant rail workers and literal camp followers who died on the site in 1832. They died either from a condition known as cold cholera or, as the Watson team ultimately demonstrated, violent attacks by local nativists.

Though the dead of Duffy's Cut were condemned to anonymity locally, their Irish origins would not be so completely unknown. The existence of shipping records pointed backwards from the port of Philadelphia to Ireland's north-west, most especially counties Tyrone, Donegal and Derry. These records, coupled with DNA science, would eventually return personal identities to some of the dead.

But as much as Duffy's Cut was an exercise in historical curiosity, fueled by grit, patience and determination, it was also a fitting symbol of the Irish American desire to legitimize the Irish presence on American soil – and under it. It was a reminder that America's Irish have always taken pride in their own, be they presidents or paupers.

Every labor, however humble, was a brick in the wall of national acceptance. This was no less the case than at Duffy's Cut, named after a Philip Duffy, who was the recipient of contracts for work on the Philadelphia and Columbia railroad line. The 'Cut' in the name of the site is derived from the fact that a hill had to be cut away in order to create flat ground for the rail line.

Philip Duffy was himself an immigrant Irishman, more prosperous than most of his fellows. An 1829 newspaper account described him employing 'a sturdy looking band of the sons of Erin'. Irish immigrants of the time could be seen in such a light. But that was on a rare good day. In the great project that was building the new nation from sea to shining sea, the arrivals from poverty-stricken Ireland were more often seen as being a people inferior to Americans of Anglo-Saxon or indeed German stock.

This was nonsense, of course, though the arriving Irish tended to start off with various disadvantages. But one distinct advantage, as it would turn out, would be sheer numbers. 'There are more of us coming off the ships each day. I heard 15,000 Irish a week.' These words are from a movie, *Gangs of New York*. But someone could well have uttered this, or something resembling it, in just about any year in the decade after Ireland's Great Hunger.

Taking just one year: 1855, roughly 86 per cent of New York City's laboring force was Irish, and 74 per cent of domestic servants, mostly women, were Irish born. By 1860, there were about 200,000 Irish in New York City (this is excluding Brooklyn, which was still its own city, and home to roughly 60,000 Irish). This accounted for about 25 per cent of the total population.

New York was the main port of arrival for the post-Famine Irish, but they were streaming off the boats in other cities too, not least Boston, Philadelphia, Baltimore, Savannah and New Orleans. New Orleans would become as Irish as it was French due to ships laden with cotton for English ports that returned full of Irish who had made initial landings across the Irish Sea after quitting their home island.

That the Irish were laboring, loving and living, and doing so with some success in the young United States, would make it inevitable that many of them would end up fighting for their adopted country. Martin Scorsese's *Gangs of New York* includes a scene in which young Irish immigrants step off a ship in New York Harbor and march right into the ranks of a Union Army that would fight toe to toe with the Confederacy between 1861 and '65. This might be an example of Hollywood license, but thousands didn't march all that far from the Manhattan docks before donning blue uniforms.

When the 'War Between the States' erupted, it would ensnare an Irish-born population that lived far beyond the boundaries of New York and Brooklyn. The better part of two million Irish immigrants, or roughly 6 per cent of the national population, found themselves on both sides of the Mason–Dixon Line. The newly born confederacy included more than 100,000 Irish-born 'rebels'. That 6 per cent of the total population translated into 40 per cent of the nation's immigrant population. In New York State, there were about half a million Irish-born on both sides – roughly 13 per cent of the Empire State's total population. Boston, now significantly smaller in size than burgeoning New York, was home to about 50,000 Irish.

During the four years of war, in excess of 150,000 Irish immigrants would fight in Union blue, and more than 30,000 fought in Confederate gray and butternut. They often fought each other, such as at the Battle of Fredericksburg, Virginia, in December 1862. At Fredericksburg, the Union Irish Brigade stormed Marye's Heights only to be bloodily repulsed by the Georgia Rifles, who were 'Irish too', as Civil War historian Shelby Foote put it in the classic Ken Burns PBS documentary on the war.

The admiration for raw Irish courage at Fredericksburg would not be confined to academic neutrals. Confederate Major General George Pickett wrote the following in a letter to his fiancée just after the battle, 'Your soldier's heart almost stood still as he watched those sons of Erin fearlessly rush to their deaths. The brilliant assault on Marye's Heights of their Irish brigade was beyond description. We forgot they were fighting us and cheer after cheer at their fearlessness went up all along our lines!' Perhaps he was inspired by his own words, because just a few months later he would lead a similarly doomed charge at Gettysburg against Union ranks that would again bristle with Irishmen, though this time on higher and more easily held ground.

If the Irish had staked a claim on America's future in America's war for freedom; if they had staked a claim by being at the fore of the nineteenth century immigrant tide; if they had staked a claim by pushing inwards, ever deeper, into an empty continent, they would absolutely nail down their claim to an Irish share of America in the war for America's very survival.

While there is an Irish story in just about every clash during the war's four years, there is, perhaps, no tale to match that which came out of the Battle of Antietam – or the Battle Sharpsburg, from the southern perspective. Yes, the North and South even disagreed over the naming of battles. The Confederate side would typically name a battle after the nearest town or settlement. The Union side would plump for moving water. So, from the northern perspective, the Battle of Sharpsburg is remembered as Antietam. It's a name that sends shivers through the spines of those who study the great conflict between the states.

It also speaks of a day when the American Irish earned their place in American military lore by virtue of the shedding of a whole lot of Irish immigrant blood. It was the day of the great nailing down. That day was September 17, 1862. Antietam stands out as the bloodiest day in American history. More than 26,000 soldiers were left dead, wounded or missing after the battle.

Hundreds of the Union dead were members of the regiments of the Irish Brigade, which traced its birth to August 1861. Originally composed of the heavily Irish 63rd, 69th and 88th New York regiments, it quickly earned a reputation for fearlessness and tenacity, especially at the battles of Seven Days, Fair Oaks, and Malvern Hill.

Its leader, Brigadier General Thomas Francis Meagher, was an Irish nationalist who had participated in the Young Ireland uprising of 1848 and was duly exiled to Tasmania. He later escaped and came to America in 1852, where he assumed a leading role in the Irish nationalist movement. Meagher hoped his brigade's performance would raise the low standing of the Irish in American eyes and provide experienced recruits for a future Fenian uprising in Ireland. His men would have an opportunity to fight back against that low standing by standing tall in a Maryland farm field.

The Battle of Antietam took place as a result of Confederate General Robert E. Lee's decision – in keeping with his belief that a smaller army needed to wage offensive war – to invade the North. In early September 1862, he marched his force, 50,000 strong, into Maryland. Lee's goal was to win a decisive victory on northern soil, a victory he and other Confederate leaders believed would win them foreign recognition and independence.

Opposing Lee was the ever-cautious Union commander General George B. McClellan. Even after he acquired a copy of the Confederate battle plan left at an abandoned campsite, McClellan waited four days before striking. The delay allowed Lee to change his plans and consolidate his army at the town of Sharpsburg, near Antietam Creek.

Union forces attacked early in the morning on September 17. The first thrust came against the northern end of Lee's line. The

Confederates buckled but managed to hold their position against the furious assault. At 10.30 a.m., a second Union assault began against the Confederate center. It was here that Meagher and the Irish Brigade cemented their reputation as one of the toughest formations in the Union Army.

Marching behind three green banners, the Irish Brigade crossed the creek. On the other side they paused a moment to receive a general absolution from Fr William Corby, the brigade's chaplain. After taking out a small force of Confederates who fired upon them from behind a thick fence, the brigade marched slowly up a slight hill, from the lower part of a field to its crest.

Reaching the crest, they were greeted with a murderous volley of Confederate musket fire. The brigade's men took what cover they could find and began returning fire. They were at a distinct disadvantage because the Confederates held a protected position along a sunken road. In this critical respect, Antietam, from an Irish Brigade standpoint, would be a bloody rehearsal for Fredericksburg.

After six volleys of return fire, Meagher ordered a fixed bayonet charge. It was a courageous but ultimately suicidal assault. Roughly half the brigade's men fell in the first charge. Four more frontal assaults were ordered over the next three hours, each bringing the same horrific result. On several occasions, men of the Irish Brigade reached the sunken road – known thereafter as 'Bloody Lane' – and fought hand to hand with the Confederates before being killed. One of the Irish struck down was Captain Patrick Clooney from County Waterford and of the 88th New York.

Eventually, the Union center, including the Irish Brigade, was forced to pull back to a defensive position. Now it was their turn to mow down Confederates, who emerged from the sunken road several times in an effort to breach the Union line. By nightfall, the fighting ceased.

McClellan had nearly driven Lee from the field, but the last-minute arrival of troops under Generals Stonewall Jackson and A.P. Hill helped save the day for the Confederates. The battle ended with no clear winner, but when Lee took his tattered army back into Virginia the next day, Antietam was hailed in the North as a Union victory. It might have been more of a victory had McClellan chosen to pursue Lee, but the risk-averse general opted to stay put. His failure to seize the initiative would soon lead Lincoln to dismiss him.

The human cost of the battle was staggering, no matter which side was the formal winner or loser. In just one day, more than 26,000 men (12,410 Union and 13,724 Confederate) were killed or wounded. No unit suffered more than the Irish Brigade, with 540 either killed or wounded.

Meagher's brigade was not the only Irish unit to suffer terrible losses that day. The Irish 6th Louisiana, one of many Irish regiments in the Confederate Army, was part of the force that held off the initial Union assault. Like its Union counterparts, it suffered fearful losses, including its commanding officer, Col. Henry B. Strong. (In one of those twists of history, the modern-day National Guard successors to the Louisiana Irish of Antietam would stand shoulder to shoulder with the New York 69th in the Iraq War.)

The Irish Brigade was soon reconstituted with the addition of the Irish 28th Massachusetts and 116th Pennsylvania. There would be future battles awaiting, not least Fredericksburg. By war's end, when the Irish Brigade marched in the Grand Review along the streets of Washington, DC, on May 22, 1865, it was one of the most famous brigades in the Union Army. The Irish name was surely nailed down now.

Well, almost. The Irish would continue to fight for the now-unified United States as the push westward gathered pace in the years after 1865. If Antietam and Fredericksburg are historical markers for the Irish east of the Mississippi, the banks of the Little Big Horn River in Montana would be a western match.

The battle of the Little Bighorn – or the Battle of the Greasy Grass, from the Lakota perspective – was in every sense a tribal affair. Native Americans from the Lakota Sioux, Cheyenne and Arapaho were on one side. European tribes led by a German American named Custer were on the other. The bulk of George Armstrong Custer's Seventh Cavalry on that hot June day in 1876 was made up of Irish and German immigrants.

The debacle at Little Bighorn shocked the nation on the eve of its centennial celebration. Shock turned to revulsion when the press reported that all but two of the bodies of the slain cavalrymen had been stripped and horribly mutilated. The two exceptions were Custer, whom the Indians both feared and admired, and an Irishman, Captain Myles W. Keogh.

Keogh was born in County Carlow on March 25, 1840. The Keoghs were wealthy Catholic landowners whose resources enabled them to survive the famine. Eager for adventure, Keogh, after graduating from St Patrick's College, went to Africa to find work as a mercenary soldier. But when he learned of Pope Pius X's call for volunteers to defend the Papal States against revolutionaries bent on creating a unified Italy, he headed for Rome.

Made a lieutenant in the St Patrick Battalion, Keogh distinguished himself in several battles. Despite the defeat of the papal army, the pope awarded Keogh the Medaglia di Pro Petri Sede (Medal for the See of St Peter). He wore it proudly for the rest of his life.

By now the American Civil War had begun, so Keogh joined the Union Army. His military experience, limited as it was, exceeded that of many officers in the Union forces and earned him a position as a staff officer in the Army of the Cumberland in Tennessee. Over the next four years, he saw action in scores of battles and earned a reputation as a fearless fighter. Keogh especially distinguished himself at Gettysburg, after which he was promoted to brevet major.

Like many Civil War veterans, Keogh remained in the military after the war by signing on for service on the western frontier. The army was now engaged in a major offensive to pacify Indian tribes that resisted efforts to remove them from ancestral lands and force them onto reservations. The westward migration of white settlers brought increased conflict with Native American tribes that believed they had a right to the lands where they had lived for generations. Native Americans lacked the firepower and unity to withstand the army, but they nonetheless put up fierce resistance.

Keogh was hardly the only Irishman on the western frontier. With hundreds of thousands of Irish-born and Irish Americans having served in the Union Army, it was only natural that many of the soldiers who headed west were of Irish lineage. In the Seventh Cavalry, for example, 21 per cent (128 of 600) of the men were Irish-born. Irish Americans likely comprised another 10 to 20 per cent.

Accounts vary as to Keogh's reputation as an officer. Several contemporaries recorded favorable impressions of him and said he enjoyed the respect of the men he commanded. Others, however, spoke of him as a harsh disciplinarian and a heavy drinker who, like Custer, had a weakness for flashy dress and women. All seem to agree that the Carlow man was a brave and capable officer in the field. Custer certainly thought so, and placed Keogh in charge of the Seventh's Company I.

The road to Little Bighorn began in 1874 when prospectors, acting illegally, discovered gold in the Black Hills of the Dakota Territory. Only six years earlier, the Fort Laramie Treaty (negotiated by an Irishman named Thomas Fitzpatrick) had granted this land to the Sioux and Cheyenne, and had prohibited white settlement. But news of gold brought thousands of fortune seekers into the territory and hostilities soon erupted. The US government reneged on its promise to prevent white incursion and demanded the tribes renegotiate the treaty to allow for the inflow.

When the tribes refused and continued to defend their lands, the government dispatched a force under General Alfred Terry. The force included the Seventh Cavalry. The army eventually closed in on a large band of warriors near the Little Bighorn River. The Seventh made first contact on the morning of June 25, 1876.

Custer, typically eager for glory, decided to attack before the rest of the army arrived. He believed there were only a few hundred warriors in the encampment, when in fact the number was as high as 4,000. He divided his force into thirds and ordered an attack. It quickly disintegrated in the face of superior numbers and several tactical blunders. Within an hour, more than 200 men of the Seventh lay dead. More would die the next day as remnants of the Seventh fought their way to safety.

The precise reason why Keogh was spared the mutilations that followed will forever remain a mystery. The Sioux apparently mutilated enemy fighters in the belief that it prevented the dead from entering heaven. Many believe the Sioux were awed by Keogh's large papal medal and decided to leave him be rather than risk angering his god. This theory is supported by the fact that the Sioux did not kill or take Keogh's prized horse, Comanche, who remained tethered to his rider's body.

Keogh would go down in the annals as yet another fighting Irish hero. He had left his native land to escape oppression only to end up as an oppressor in his adopted land. But irony, like truth, has a hard time of it in war.

Either way, Keogh was a standout in an ever-expanding Irish American narrative that seemed limited only by the numbers of Irish who would arrive in America – reinforcement for those in the front line of the great American Irish story.

They would continue to arrive in great numbers, and the story, by now turning into an epic, would spill over into a new century. The story would mostly be true but, of course, would also carry in its lines half-truth and outright myth. But honestly held belief was a fuel that would propel the Irish from the old century into the new. And that belief was not only in a destiny now made clearer but also in an American story set out in very stark terms.

The flight from poverty and starvation in Ireland had been followed by a fight in the new land to carve out not just space, but a place. And so the Irish, along with, though not always alongside, their Scots-Irish cousins, had fought for the new land and built it up from the hard ground. Or, as James Webb put it more delicately in his landmark book on the Scots-Irish, *Born Fighting*, they had 'shaped' America.

No matter the precise claim on behalf of the Irish, there was no denying their very distinct presence. And they had a mind that there was no denying them anything much at all in the new twentieth century. Others, however, would be of a different mind.

CHAPTER 8

Revulsion, Rejection, Retreat

The Irish were never unconditionally welcomed in America. There were, however, some periods that were better than others. A young Irishman landing in a northeastern seaport in the spring of 1861 was more welcome than his counterpart ten years earlier – this, if for no other reason than that he might be persuaded to don a blue uniform and fire a musket for the Union.

Towards the end of the nineteenth century, there would be a less conditional welcome mat of sorts, often thrown out by other Irish with their eye on recruiting new voters of a particular bent. In the last years of that century, it was less about welcomes and more to do with consolidation. The Irish were now de facto if not entirely de jure in the eyes of their more reluctant hosts. And some of those reluctant hosts had not given up the battle to stem the green tide from the east. And a tide it was.

As Terry Golway notes in *Irish Rebel*, his biography of Fenian John Devoy, the Irish would absorb just about everything thrown at them by hostile nativists by dint of sheer numbers. In 1871, when Devoy landed in New York, Golway points out that the population of the city was approaching a million. And of this total, 20 per cent had been born in Ireland while 37 per cent could lay claim to at least one Irish-born parent. By contrast, based on a tally from the previous year, the city was home to a mere 2,800 Italian immigrants and 80,000 Jews. The city's future political culture based on the Ireland–Italy–Israel triumvirate, 'The Three I's', was still a long way off.

Golway writes, 'So Gaelic was this Anglo-Dutch city that one of its leading newspapers referred to the metropolis as 'New Cork' after Ireland's second largest city. And so Catholic was the mass of immigrants that an editorial in the *New York Times* wondered, 'How Long Will protestants Endure?' It was a fair question: in 1840, New York was 64 per cent native-born and predominantly Protestant; by the time of Devoy's arrival, it was 47 per cent foreign-born and, stunningly, 50 per cent Catholic.

Such numbers, according to Golway, 'repulsed the city's middle classes, who believed they were losing their city to feckless foreigners who brought with them alien customs, terrible diseases and a despised religion'. Those middle-class northeasterners were indeed repulsed, and to the point of placing, or attempting to place, legal barriers in the way of the teeming masses of Irish spilling off ships.

Dr Hidetaka Hirota, a teacher of American immigration history at the City College of New York and the author of *Expelling the Poor: Atlantic Seaboard States and the Nineteenth-Century Origins of American Immigration Policy*, writes in the *Irish Echo* that, in American history, 'there has been a myth that immigration to the United States was free from regulation until the introduction in the late nineteenth century of federal laws to restrict Chinese immigration'. He argues otherwise, writing, 'In fact, eastern states, especially Massachusetts and New York, developed extensive systems of state-level immigration control in response to Irish famine immigration. Long before the federal government launched Chinese exclusion, these states refused admission to the destitute Irish and deported them to Europe as government policy.' The Irish, Hirota contends, 'were indeed the first targets of institutionalized immigration control in the United States'.

Hirota points to the legal origins of American immigration control as dating back to the colonial period. Writing in the *Irish Echo* in March 2017, he states that, based on the model of the English poor law, which allowed each parish to banish transient beggars, English colonists developed similar practices to regulate the movement of the poor:

> When the famine Irish arrived in the United States during the 1840s, nativists in Massachusetts and New York built upon the colonial poor laws to develop laws for restricting the landing

of destitute foreigners and deporting immigrant paupers back to Europe. Throughout the era of state-level immigration control between the 1840s and 1880s, the Irish remained principal targets for these measures. Strong antagonism toward the poverty and dependency of the Irish lay at the core of immigration control in Massachusetts and New York.

Just like nativists today, Hirota writes, 'those in the nineteenth century framed immigration control as a matter of national security'. He continues:

> While they believed that the Catholic Irish attempted to overturn American Protestant and democratic society with despotic 'papism,' they viewed the poverty of the famine Irish as an equally dangerous economic and public health threat. In 1855, nativists called Irish immigrants receiving public relief 'leeches upon our tax payers.' The anti-Irish newspaper, *Boston Daily Bee*, asserted that 'most of the danger' to public health 'springs from the foul and disgusting habits of the Irish population.'

'The strict construction of deportability', according to Hirota, characterized state immigration law. Nineteenth-century Massachusetts law, for example, defined deportability on the basis of legal settlement, a symbol of membership in the state. 'One could acquire legal settlement by residing in the state for a certain period of time, and the law made deportable anybody seeking public relief without settlement in Massachusetts.'

What was striking about this law, Hirota contended, was that only American citizens could acquire legal settlement:

> In other words, however long they might have resided in the state and whatever contributions they might have made to the community, non-naturalized immigrants were permanently ineligible for settlement. And without it, they could instantly become deportable upon entering a public almshouse. Under this arrangement, some Irish immigrants were deported to

Ireland after having spent four decades in the United States. In the eyes of nativist officers, destitute Irish Americans were foreign and belonged to Ireland, rather than the United States. Irish Americans criticized citizen deportation as 'vile tyranny,' but nativists justified it as a necessary and sound measure to reduce the burden of 'the lazy, ungrateful, lying and thieving population of old Ireland.'

Hirota draws a lesson for contemporary times:

> Given the fact that the Irish not only survived this nativist backlash, but indeed ultimately thrived, it would be easy enough to dismiss efforts to block immigration from any national, racial or ethnic quarter to be doomed from the outset.
>
> But somehow that apparent lesson never seems to fully discourage those who see America through a very narrow and at times specifically tinted lens.

Neil Swidey, in *The Boston Globe Magazine*, has drawn a connection between sentiments uttered by Donald Trump, as presidential candidate, and words written and uttered over a century previously. Familiar themes of bans, borders and walls, and especially about how the radical and dangerous new immigrants don't measure up to the 'quality' ones we used to get, weren't crafted by Trump. Instead, Swidey writes, they 'were part of an immigration Ur-text painstakingly assembled, brick by nativist brick, in Boston, by three Brahmin intellectuals, beginning in 1894'.

The Brahmin trio – the word Brahmin being a commonly used reference to Boston's social and political elite – had founded the Immigration Restriction League, 'the equivalent of a modern-day think tank, just five years after all three had graduated from Harvard'. Swidey indicates that leading the group was Prescott Farnsworth Hall, a lawyer and Brookline 'homebody', who was largely unknown, even in his day. He writes:

> At the close of the 19th century, Hall and his colleagues began warning the nation about the consequences of unchecked

immigration. Their chief ally in Washington was Senator Henry Cabot Lodge, owner of two of the most storied surnames in Massachusetts history. For all their connections and zeal, though, these men had little to show for their anti-immigration efforts after 20 years.

But they would have something to show in February 1917, when 'restriction advocates scored their first big win with the passage of the federal Immigration Act of 1917'. Getting this law approved required a congressional override of a presidential veto. Swidey writes, 'The sweeping law opened a new epoch in the nation's handling of immigration. While there had been earlier measures relatively limited in scope or specific to certain groups, the 1917 law asserted a federal framework for broadly restricting, rather than merely regulating, immigration.'

Hall and his fellow Brahmin restrictionists celebrated the passage of the 1917 law with a quiet dinner at the Union Club on Boston's Beacon Hill. Far from being content, according to Swidey, 'they were just getting started'. And their efforts would have a more lasting payoff in subsequent years, culminating with a draconian quota law signed by President Calvin Coolidge. A former governor of Massachusetts, Coolidge had lamented that the country was becoming a 'dumping ground' and pledged that 'America must remain American'.

Immigration had peaked in 1907 when 1.3 million immigrants were allowed into the country, the vast majority of them coming through Ellis Island. Ellis Island is holy ground to pro-immigration America. But to the nativist point of view it was always more akin to a human landfill.

As Swidey points out, even organized labor got into the nativist act, arguing, with some justification, that a large supply of cheap foreign labor was turning their bargaining power into so much weak tea:

> Workingmen's Party leader Denis Kearney blended this practical economic argument with some high-test racism to gain serious political power.

A native of Ireland, Kearney had been an immigrant laborer himself. But he embraced the close-the-door-behind-me mentality that immigrants have been adopting probably since Siberians first crossed the Bering Land Bridge to get to Alaska. Kearney wrapped up all his speeches with this drop-the-mike line: 'And whatever happens, the Chinese must go.'

So, from the streets, from the labor union ranks, and right up to the rarified air of New England Brahmin society, the immigration door came with hinges – big ones.

Senator Cabot Lodge, a mega Brahmin, had introduced a literacy test for new immigrants in the Senate in 1895. The test was drawn up by the Immigration Restriction League (IRL). In a letter to Hall the following year, Lodge wrote of the test, 'I consider it one of the most vitally important measures which has been before Congress in my time.'

Why was a distinguished senator from Massachusetts so solicitous of a young, largely unknown lawyer? Swidey writes:

> The IRL never came close to attracting a mass following, but Hall was extremely effective at using the organization, and its output, to influence the influencers. Some notables were members of his group, like publisher Henry Holt and the presidents of Harvard, Bowdoin, and Stanford. Many more were leading politicians, business leaders, and newspapermen, who were on the receiving end of Immigration Restriction League policy papers, stats-dense talking points, and survey results. The IRL also directly lobbied Congress andsupplied ghostwritten editorials to newspapers around the country.
>
> In January 1897, he wrote, both houses of Congress approved the literacy bill, which would bar all immigrants over the age of 16 who were unable to read a 25-word passage of the US Constitution that had been translated into their native language. Hall cheered the breakthrough.
>
> However, President Grover Cleveland vetoed the bill on his way out of the White House. He told nativists it wasn't long

ago that 'the same thing was said of immigrants who, with
their descendants, are now numbered among our best citizens.'

Lodge and Hall were not done, however, and the IRL's rhetoric
'grew only nastier'. In 1913, Congress again passed the literacy test.
A few weeks before he left office, President William Taft announced
'with great reluctance' that he was vetoing it. Hall, Swidey writes,
couldn't contain his rage, writing, 'To hell with Jews, Jesuits, and
steamships!'

Hall, however, placed renewed hope in Woodrow Wilson.
After all, as Swidey notes, in the five-volume history of the United
States that Wilson had written when he was a Princeton professor,
the future president described eastern and southern European
immigrants pretty much the same way Hall had. They were 'of the
lowest class', having 'neither skill nor energy nor any initiative of
quick intelligence'. Swidey writes:

> Imagine Hall's shock in 1915 when, after the literacy test had
> once more passed Congress, Wilson struck it down with the
> stroke of his pen. The literacy requirement, Wilson explained,
> would serve as a test not of an alien's character but rather of
> his opportunity.
>
> Two years after the Wilson setback, Hall finally got his
> way. This time when Wilson vetoed the Immigration Act of
> 1917, Congress had the votes to override him. Twenty-three
> years after Hall began his crusade, the literacy test finally
> became law.

The reason for this U-turn was German U-boats. Swidey notes:

> In the one momentous week between Wilson's veto on
> January 29 and Congress's override on February 5, Germany
> announced its U-boats would be prepared to attack passenger
> ships in the Atlantic.
>
> When Germany sank the American liner Housatonic,
> Wilson broke off diplomatic relations.

Heading down the path to war, the nation erupted in jingoism. For decades, German-Americans had been perhaps the strongest political force blocking immigration restrictions. More than any other hyphenated group, they tended to remember their immigrant heritage and resist the 'close-the-door-behind-us' mentality. Now, on the cusp of America's entry into war, they found themselves under attack. That opened a wide lane for nativists.

Swidey indicates that 'In 1918, the first full year after the literacy test's passage, only 110,000 immigrants were let into the United States, the lowest number since the Civil War.' Nevertheless, according to Swidey, the literacy test wasn't as effective at keeping out 'undesirables' as Hall had hoped:

> For example, although there was a clear correlation between being poor and being illiterate, many European countries had improved basic education in the decades Hall was working to get the bill passed. And most Eastern European Jewish males, even impoverished ones, had no trouble passing the test because they had learned to read the Torah. The literacy test also entirely missed Mexicans, since the law didn't apply to immigrants from the Western Hemisphere.
>
> Still, the Immigration Act of 1917 opened a new age in how this nation – weary from a bloody, seemingly fruitless war in Europe – would treat foreigners. It reached a fever pitch in 1919 and 1920 with the Palmer Raids, the mass arrests and deportations of thousands of Eastern European immigrants. A key tool in those roundups had been the Espionage Act of 1917, which Hall's IRL cofounder Charles Warren had drafted during a stint in government.

Nativists, Swidey writes, continued to ride the anti-immigrant wave, and in 1924 Congress approved a tougher, permanent quota law:

> It cagily capped the number of immigrants allowed in each year from any particular nation to 2 per cent of the total number of foreign-born people of that nationality who'd been

here in 1890, before the big flood of immigrants from eastern and southern Europe.

Nativists were literally able to turn back the clock. Overnight, immigrants from northern and western Europe were effectively given free passes to come to the United States. Meanwhile, the total number of Syrians allowed into the country in 1925 was 100. That imbalance remained in place, more or less, for the next four decades.

Americans, Swidey contends, are more likely to look favorably on immigration if they sense there's a logical system guiding it. But absent of logical legislation, all manner of actors hostile to immigration are able to populate the vacuum.

Swidey concludes with reference to recent times:

> Session after session, Congress failed to pass comprehensive immigration reform, and illegal immigration continued to rise. Then Trump came along with his vows to turn back time, building a wall to keep out Mexicans and imposing a ban to keep out Muslims. He undoubtedly got more traction than he would have if there had not been a national consensus, among liberals and conservatives alike, that the current immigration system is broken.
>
> A close reading of history reminds us that there are no new ideas in immigration, just new people espousing them. Also, the pendulum always swings back – though sometimes it sure takes its time.

And it does indeed swing.

The story of the Irish in America from the opening of the nineteenth century to its closing was met with revulsion by many 'natives'. They experienced innumerable instances of rejection, and if it seemed at times that they were not only on the back foot, but in actual retreat in the face of seemingly insurmountable obstacles, the broader truth of the matter was that the retreat never amounted to much more than the tactical variety.

In the strategic sense, the Irish were on the march. They had arrived, and, critically, they had arrived in overwhelming numbers. The Great Hunger, while an end to an older Ireland, was the beginning of its bigger, bolder American version. That bigger, bolder version would flower in the twentieth century, or at least the first two-thirds of it.

CHAPTER 9

Restless, Ever Restless

Before Kennedy, there was Curley. For good or ill. If the nineteenth century was Irish America's version of D-Day, the twentieth would be the century of the big breakout (and big breakthroughs) from the landing zones.

James Michael Curley's assessment – that Irish Catholic families had seven or eight children while Brahmins had dogs – was a notable observation for the man in that it was largely in line with reality. The irascible Curley well understood the power of sheer numbers, and in the Boston of the early twentieth century – and in a few other major cities besides – the Irish had the numbers and then some.

Curley was born in 1874. In the decade of his birth – specifically between 1871 and 1880, a census year – 436,871 Irish immigrants would set foot in America. As had been the case in previous decades, the bulk of these new arrivals would congregate, at least initially, in large eastern cities such as Curley's Boston. And with large families following the large numbers of arrivals, the stage was being set for what some would see as a golden age for the Irish, or at least for those select few who were able to tap into the political opportunities presented by massed voter concentration.

In the year that John F. Kennedy was born, 1917, Curley was in the early days of his first term as Mayor of Boston. By the time he concluded his fourth and final term in 1950, JFK would be a member of the United States House of Representatives. He achieved this position after a congressional seat was vacated by a certain James Michael Curley, who, in turn, returned to his former job as Mayor of Boston.

In JFK's birth year, an initially reluctant United States went to war in Europe. And when it was all over, Johnny would be joined by Paddy in the great march home. If that year's immigration act sought to restrict entry to the United States, it was too late to hold back the Irish. The fox was not only inside the chicken coop, but it was running large swathes of it. And that very apparent fact of American political, economic and social life would make itself felt when federal legislators next got around to retooling the phenomenon that created America.

In keeping with the 'spirit' of the 1917 legislation, the Immigration Act of 1924, also referred to as the Johnson–Reed Act, was primarily an effort to suppress broad-based immigration and restrict arrivals in America to a group of favored nations and geographic areas. Senator David Reed, a Pennsylvanian, outlined his vision for America's future as a land of immigrants in the *New York Times*. He wrote, in the April 27, 1924 edition, 'Each year's immigration should so far as possible be a miniature America, resembling in national origins the persons who are already settled in our country.' Johnson–Reed became the law of the land one month later.

The 1924 act copper-fastened restrictions set down in 1921 under what was known as the 'National Origins Formula'. The favored countries – or relatively favored, it could be more accurately stated – were mostly to be found in Northwestern Europe, and their preeminence was codified in a companion piece of legislation to the overall act that was titled the 'National Origins Act'.

Out of favor, and distinctly so, were Arab, Asian and African countries and regions. This back of the American hand was highlighted by the inclusion in the legislation of the Asian Exclusion Act. Southern and eastern Europeans, especially Italians and Jews from Eastern Europe, where borders had long been fluid, were also singled out for restrictions.

Regardless of comparative advantage based on 1890 numbers, immigration from all corners of Europe took a hit – though Ireland, by virtue of its relative dominance in that year, faced much less of a cut than, for example, Italy. That country's immigration numbers fell over a cliff as a result of the 1924 act.

The act also introduced a series of preferences inserted into national quotas. So if a would-be immigrant was Irish, aged over

21, male, and had a background in agriculture, entry to the United States was far more assured than if the immigrant was a female physicist from Russia.

And if the act was hard on populations in Europe's east, it was downright brutal towards peoples of the Far East. Being Chinese, Japanese, or being any one of a number of designated Asian nationalities, was now virtually an automatic disqualifier.

For the first time, a system of visas allotted by the US State Department at its overseas diplomatic missions resulted in immigrants arriving on US shores only after going through a vetting process – and this was before going through a second one, courtesy of the Immigration and Naturalization Service (INS). This agency, prior to 1933, was actually two entities: the Bureau of Immigration, and the Bureau of Naturalization. To the hopeful immigrant, however, they were much the same thing.

It was not entirely the case in the first half of the 'Roaring Twenties' that America's door was closing. But, more than ever, there was now a firm hand on the door handle. And for many there was also a bolt. Still, the hand stayed itself somewhat when it came to the Irish, their next-door neighbors from Great Britain, and the Germans.

Dr Edward T. O'Donnell, Associate Professor of History at the College of the Holy Cross in Worcester, Massachusetts, penned, for some years, the Hibernian Chronicle column in the *Irish Echo*. In one of those contributions, O'Donnell set the scene for the significant changes in US immigration law and enforcement that came into play in both 1921 and 1924:

> The two years following the end of World War I were some of the most tumultuous in American history. The largest strike wave in the nation's history saw some four million workers walk off their jobs in 1919. Race riots broke out in Chicago, East St Louis, Tulsa and many other cities. A series of unexplained bombings hit targets from Wall Street to Los Angeles, leaving scores dead. Driven by these events, as well as news of the Russian Revolution, a wave of anti-radical hysteria (the so-called Red Scare) swept the nation. In all

these troubling developments Americans increasingly saw one
common thread: foreigners.

Nativists, according to O'Donnell, seized the moment and easily
pushed the Immigration Restriction Act through Congress; it
received President Warren Harding's signature on May 19, 1921.
According to O'Donnell:

> It sharply reduced the total number of immigrants admitted
> from some 800,000 in 1920 to an annual average of less than
> 300,000. More significant, however, was the quota system
> devised to allocate those 300,000 spots. Using an explicitly
> racist calculus designed to keep America's ethnic composition
> at roughly the levels revealed in the 1910 census, lawmakers
> assigned each country a quota. Preferred countries like England
> received large quotas, while nations like Russia, the principal
> source of Jewish immigration, received tiny quotas.
>
> Congress rewrote the law in 1924 making it even more
> restrictive. As a result, overall immigration dropped from
> 800,000 in 1920 to 165,000 in 1925. More importantly, many
> immigrant groups deemed 'undesirable' saw their numbers
> plummet sharply. Italians, for example, who had averaged
> 158,000 arrivals per year before restriction, were deemed
> undesirable and thus received an annual quota of just 5,802.
> Russia saw its number cut to 2,248. For Greeks the numbers
> were slashed from an average of 17,600 arrivals per year to a
> quota of just 307.

As for the Irish?

> In a word, their rising fortunes and improved reputation had
> gained for them the coveted status of 'preferred' immigrants.
> In the 1924 version of the law, the Irish Free State received
> an annual quota of 28,567 (later reduced in 1929, along with
> most other groups, to 17,853). Ireland received such a high
> quota despite the fact that it sent an average of just 22,000
> per year in the 1920s and a scant 1,300 per year in the 1930s.

The Irish, at least in the eyes of the quota makers, were finally welcome to apply.

Of course, O'Donnell added by way of a cautionary counterpoint, anti-Irish, and especially anti-Catholic, sentiment had not been banished entirely from the land, 'Al Smith's bitterly contested presidential campaign in 1928 revealed a shocking degree of bigotry across the heartland. Still, it was a far cry from the days of the Know Nothings and thirty-two years later John F. Kennedy would put the matter to rest once and for all.'

So 1917 was indeed a year that would resonate down the decades for the Irish of America. But this was not the case for the immediate years to follow, because immigration, and the policies surrounding it, were like the seas between America and all those countries where immigrant hopes were born. They were restless, ever restless. And never fully set.

Nevertheless, the years that witnessed a global catastrophe in the form of the First World War – years in which Ireland fought, voted, and fought again for what would turn out to be the securing of a significant measure of national independence – would also offer up something of a great settling.

The years 1916–21, according to Kerby Miller in *Emigrants and Exiles*, would serve up a 'last hurrah' for the image of the Irish emigrant as 'exile' in America. This was, according to Miller, because both the image and the activities it inspired evaporated almost entirely with Irish America's happy relief over the Anglo-Irish Treaty and with its subsequent confusion and embarrassment over the Irish Civil War.

'To be sure,' Miller writes, 'the disappointment over Al Smith's crushing defeat in 1928 and the traumatic setback of the Great Depression of the 1930s still lay ahead, but those were entirely American concerns. By 1923, except for the continuing trickle of embittered Catholic emigrants from Northern Ireland, the long, dark winter of Irish exile in America was over.'

A fact, of course, which would only make America an even bigger attraction when viewed from Ireland's now partially independent shore.

CHAPTER 10

Annie Moore and the Power of Sentiment

Immigration brings competing mythologies into stark relief. And the Irish know all about embracing mythologies. They are a source of strength and inspiration in dark times. They can also warp relations between emigrants and those they have left behind in the homeland. It does no good to place all the blame for this on those who have made the journey from land of birth to land of destiny.

There are official mythologies as well as popular ones. The Statue of Liberty is at once a symbol of reality and mythology. Whichever is precisely the case can vary from person to person, and from time to time. There are times when the lady with the lamp is seemingly triumphant. And there are times, most especially when politicians sign their names to what is regarded as anti-immigrant legislation, that she is left isolated, a prop, a mythological figure overwhelmed by dark politics. On most days, though, Lady Liberty is merely what the eye sees, an imposing neoclassical statue and work of art, an inspiration to the newcomer and native-born – at least most of them.

It would be impossible to calculate the collective emotive impact that the Statue of Liberty has had on the peoples of the world, most especially among those who, in the heyday of ocean-borne immigration, sailed into New York Harbor, their eyes fixed on a vision in greened copper, that stern but motherly face, the torch, the tablets, the broken chain around the feet, the whole blessed thing. No other country has anything to match this colossus. No other country would dare try to match it.

And no other country is a repository for so many stories of departure and arrival, longing and heartbreak, homesickness and the embracing of a new homeland – one like no other in history. It would be enough to make one weep, and it's probably the case that the volume of tears shed as a result of immigration to America could replicate the oceans bordering America. Which, of course, is a reminder of the essential humanity of the immigration story.

While politicians and bureaucrats obsessed over numbers, nationalities, ethnicities and diseases barely known to medical science, countless lives were being reborn and recast. This was no less the case for the Irish who streamed ashore – in huge numbers in the nineteenth century, somewhat lesser numbers in the twentieth, and in rapidly vanishing numbers in the twenty-first.

Who were they? The great majority would vividly remember leaving Ireland, voyaging across the Atlantic, and, in sometimes quirky detail, arriving in America. They would carry with them memories and mementoes, photographs and letters. And they would send back photographs and letters, millions of them. Words would express sorrow and homesickness, but they would also convey tales of new and magnificent sights, experiences and wonders, dangers avoided and difficulties overcome.

Immigration's deeply human core would generate its own inner and radiated strength. And it would act as something akin to gravity, pulling others across the ocean who would add their hopes and dreams, their labors and loves, to the grand collective story.

And the glue binding all these newborn American Irish? The unrelenting power of sentiment, often expressed in song, poetry or everyday conversation. Such sentiment would flow through the generations. It would join immigrant Ann in 1992 with immigrant Annie in 1892. And it would be entirely impervious to even the most hostile political forces.

The Annie of 1892 is Annie Moore, an Irish teenager who was the first immigrant to be admitted into the U.S. through Ellis Island and who, after fading into obscurity following a hardscrabble life, would emerge into the full light of Irish American consciousness in the waning years of the twentieth century and first few of the twenty-first. She would be eulogized, idealized, and newly recognized. Annie

Moore would be the Irish immigrant Joan of Arc, thrust into the front line of every argument favoring more Irish immigration – preferably, but not necessarily, legal.

Annie's life story began in obscurity; she was elevated into the public consciousness when she stepped ashore in America and was plunged into obscurity again as her life in New York City proceeded. So much so that after her death she would be confused in the public record with another Annie Moore whose life ended tragically in Texas.

At the end of it all, a hundred years after she stepped ashore on Ellis Island, Annie would be front and center in the public mind once more. And her elevation to the immigrant version of sainthood wouldn't stop there. With Annie Moore, the tide of sentiment would reach full flow on a day when the rain in her adopted city would have made Ireland proud.

That day was one of the waning ones in August 2006. It was indeed a soggy mess, but inside the meeting room of the New York Genealogical and Biographical Society all was warm and fuzzy. Most press conferences start late. This one didn't, as the organizers were just bursting to get the story out. The midtown Manhattan event went on for almost two hours and there were still people around at the end.

This, then, was that rare kind of press round up. All in the room were interested to the point of impatience for what was going to transpire beyond the usual professional courtesies. The start was at three, and just about right on that mark, Brian Andersson, New York City's Commissioner for Public Records – the keeper of the city's historical record – was up and running with the news that Annie Moore never left town, never went west, never got killed by a street car in Texas, and was now resting peacefully in an unmarked grave in a Queens cemetery. Annie's peace was about to be seriously disturbed.

A genealogist named Megan Smolenyak Smolenyak (in something of a genealogical coincidence she had married an unrelated man with whom she shared the same Carpatho-Russian surname) had led the charge for truth in the Annie Moore story and would steer the room through a historical detective story by way of slides.

One of the images was from an issue of the *New York Times* from the 1970s marking the hundredth anniversary of Annie

Moore's birth. The paper of record had been wondering if it was possible that Annie was still alive, and if so, what stories she would have to tell. Sadly, Annie was long gone by then. But her full story was yet untold.

By the end of the genealogical society gathering, the story had moved on with giant strides in a room where genealogy was king and Annie, for 120 minutes or so, was reigning queen. A dozen of Annie's descendants sat in the front as Smolenyak and Andersson unraveled an immigrant tale of Ireland, New York and America.

Annie had arrived in New York on the SS *Nevada*. The ship disgorged its first- and second-class passengers at a Manhattan pier. Annie and the steerage passengers were carried to Ellis Island on ferries. Get this, said Andersson, Annie had made the last short journey on a ferry called the, 'wait for it, J.E. Moore'.

Information kept pouring forth from the podium and the seats. Annie, someone said, had lived in King Street in Cork City before emigrating. Someone else had doubts about that. More work ahead for the Annie fan club. The extended family members, some meeting each other for the first time, traded stories and family lore. Photos, some of them borderline daguerreotypes, were produced to astonished gasps and pointed fingers.

Michael Shulman from Maryland, a great-grandnephew of Annie, said that all the first names in his family had tended to be Irish-sounding, a testimony to 'our Irish family'. Julia Devous, a great-granddaughter who had flown in with her sister from Phoenix, Arizona, could hardly contain her excitement. She was meeting a whole passel of new relatives, descendants of Annie's brother. Her father, who had passed away a decade previously, would have been so proud, she said. This was proof positive of his New York and Irish heritage.

It was that kind of gathering. Proof positive met affirmation, met pride. Annie Moore, you had to think, would have been wryly amused. She was famous, then obscure, and now famous again. And so it transpired, as the rain pelted down outside, that the long-believed story of Annie Moore moving west – variously to Indiana and New Mexico, and ultimately Texas – and getting married and dying in a Texas train accident in 1924 had nothing to do with the life of the teenage girl from County Cork who made immigration history on New Year's Day 1892.

Simply put, there were two Annie Moores. Their lives became entangled and intertwined in the historical record largely by accident and happenstance. The Annie Moore who died in Texas was not an immigrant from Cork. It appeared that she was the daughter of Irish immigrants and was born in Illinois. It had been Illinois Annie's descendants who had been linked, over the years, to the Annie Moore of Ellis Island fame.

The press and family who had gathered in attendance heard that Annie (actually Anna on her birth certificate) had reached New York after a twelve-day transatlantic voyage from Cobh (then Queenstown) along with her younger brothers Philip and Anthony.

The journey reunited the three Moore children with their parents, Matthew and Mary, who had made an earlier crossing to New York. The precise circumstances of Annie's landfall had become obscured a little with time. There was a story that several bearded Russian men were asked to stand aside and allow the young Irish teen to step ashore first; this was because there was a plan to strike a commemorative china plate in honor of the occasion. Another version of the story is that an Irishman named Mike Tierney called on a German man to step aside and allow Annie Moore first honors.

Either way, Moore led three shiploads of hopeful immigrants ashore that day and was duly presented with a $10 gold coin as a keepsake by officials, including Charles Hendley of the US Treasury Department. In being first, Annie Moore denied the second recorded immigrant, another young Irishwoman named Ellie King, a chance for undisputed immortality.

But while Annie's precise and recorded role in US immigration history was no longer disputed, it would have remained undisturbed but for the work of Megan Smolenyak. She could not join up the life of the Annie Moore who died in Texas with the young woman who had made history at Ellis Island. 'I really found out by accident,' she would recall. 'I was working on a documentary on immigration for public television and was planning on a segment on Annie Moore and her descendants.'

More in need of visual illustration than information on a life story that was generally accepted as fact, Smolenyak started down the paper trail in pursuit of Annie Moore. 'It was a bit like trying to find the needle in a haystack because it's not an uncommon name,' said Smolenyak, herself half Irish. 'But the documentation said that Annie Moore had been born in Illinois. I ignored this at first because documents are wrong all the time. But more and more documentation cropped up pointing to Illinois.' So began the search.

Curious and troubled by what she was finding, Smolenyak nevertheless had to set aside her investigation for several years because of other projects. When she returned to the Annie Moore trail, one of her first stops was the National Constitution Center in Philadelphia. It was holding an exhibit on immigration and included in the displays was a photograph of Annie Moore with one of her children.

This was Illinois Annie, and something about her facial features did not set well with Smolenyak. Still, the photo was not clear evidence pointing away from Illinois Annie because it was the only purported photo of Annie in existence. Nobody took Annie's picture at Ellis Island, or at least if they did it had remained unknown and hidden down the years.

Smolenyak, at this point, tried a novel approach. People are fascinated by family histories and the internet had made it easier for would-be genealogists to explore the darker corners of even the most widely accepted accounts. So she posted a reward of $1,000 on the internet for information that would solve the mystery. Regarding what happened next, Smolenyak said, 'So people went off on a chase and came up with results in just a few weeks. There was no intentional deception in the case of Annie Moore from Illinois. She was Annie Moore, and she was of Irish origin. But this was turning into a classic case of family stories getting mixed up.'

The case for Illinois Annie had been made a number of years previously by one of her surviving children, a daughter, who said that the young woman depicted on the Ellis Island china plate had been her mother. Smolenyak said, 'It was similar to the situation where anybody named Boone thinks they have to be related to Daniel Boone. This was a typical immigrant family story.'

And of course it was entirely plausible that Ellis Island Annie might have headed west to marry a man named O'Connell – who claimed his family was linked to Daniel O'Connell – and had ended up in Texas with a passel of kids only to die at 47 years of age after being struck by a train in Waco. Nothing was a stretch in the Annie story, except for the records that intriguingly pointed to a birth in a county in Illinois, not the Southern tip of Ireland, and a genealogist's hunch that the woman in the sole photograph attributed to Ellis Island Annie was someone else. Which she was.

It could be argued that, while the death of Annie Moore in Texas was testimony to the fact that Irish immigration to America was a transcontinental phenomenon, the death of Annie Moore in New York City, just a short distance from where she first made American landfall, was testimony to the extraordinary footprint that the Irish would leave in America's largest city.

Annie died in obscurity and was buried in an unmarked grave in Calvary Cemetery in Queens, just a few miles from Ellis Island. But the iconic status she was awarded decades after her passing was such that her resting place was never going to remain simply a plot of grass – though Annie herself might have appreciated her roof of green sward after a tough and all-too-short life on Manhattan's Lower East Side.

Annie had married a German immigrant named Joseph Schayer who worked at the Fulton Street Fish Market. The couple had eleven children, though not all survived birth and early infancy. Annie Moore Schayer, her husband and children moved address a number of times over their years together, as people did then, but never more than a few streets at any one time.

Megan Smolenyak's detective work was a gumshoe genealogical story spurred by nagging, unanswered questions, and a series of clues that began with a New York City death certificate for Annie's brother, Anthony Moore, dated 1902. He had died at just 24 years of age. The certificate listed a father named Matthew (the correct name) who had arrived in America at the right time: 1892. The certificate, however, named a Julia Moore as the mother, when for years it had been thought that Annie Moore's mother had been named Mary.

This, however, was due to an incorrect 1892 newspaper account. Annie's mother was indeed Julia Cronin Moore.

Undeterred by false trails, Smolenyak kept digging. It turned out that Matthew Moore, apparently a longshoreman, died in 1907. His son, who had been interred in a pauper's grave, was disinterred and buried with him. To back up these discoveries, record files uncovered by Commissioner Brian Andersson included a naturalization certificate for Annie's brother Philip. This was the so-called 'smoking gun' document that placed Philip alongside Annie and Anthony on the SS *Nevada* out of Queenstown.

With the investigation now focused on a family being naturalized, and living and dying in a crowded corner of Manhattan, it wasn't long before Annie was traced to a tenement in Monroe Street, where she first lived with her parents. From there she was traced to a number of other addresses, including one on Cherry Street, close by to the entrance to the Manhattan Bridge. A marriage certificate was unearthed by Andersson at nearby St James's Catholic Church.

It was the first chapter in a family life that would reach into succeeding generations and right across a continent. Five of Joseph and Annie's children survived to adulthood, but just three of them had children of their own. Annie herself died at 50 years of age in 1924, the year of the immigration reform act, from heart failure. Six of her children would share her grave.

By the fall of 2008, the Annie Moore story would receive its final marker – one of three. The voyage would be memorialized on both sides of the ocean with statues by Irish sculptor Jeanne Rynhart: one in Cobh, the other on Ellis Island. The Calvary gravestone would complete the troika.

The Cobh statue is of Annie and her brothers. The Ellis Island statue is of Annie alone and is located on the second floor of the island's immigration museum. It was unveiled by the Irish President at the time, Mary Robinson, at a dedication ceremony in 1993. The sculpture depicts Annie, one hand on her hat and the other holding a small suitcase.

The Calvary Cemetery headstone, inscribed with the name of Annie and the six children resting with her, would be the physical manifestation of New York and America's second official welcome to a young woman who was an iconic symbol – not just of Irish immigration but also of the arrival of people from all over the world. The unveiling ceremony, which included a rousing delivery of 'Isle of Hope, Isle of Tears' by tenor Ronan Tynan, was the culmination of a story more than a century old and of a much more recent chapter in which a new life of Annie Moore had been revealed to the public and nailed into the historical record.

Several hundred people gathered to witness the unveiling of the Irish blue limestone cross, which itself had crossed the Atlantic on a container ship a few days before the Calvary unveiling. On what was a warm October day – one in stark contrast to the January 1 of Annie Moore's arrival in New York Harbor – against the sheltering backdrop of the County Cork Association banner, descendants and invited dignitaries spoke of the life and legacy of a young woman who had lived a hardscrabble life on Manhattan's Lower East Side, had buried far too many of her children, and yet had a story that captured, and retained, the imagination of millions.

In one of a number of speeches at the grave site, the Celtic cross yet to be revealed, the Irish Consul General in New York, Ambassador Niall Burgess, spoke of Annie Moore being the human face of the story of Irish immigration; he spoke of how she stood for all the Irish who had crossed the Atlantic to America. Commissioner Andersson spoke of a young woman who had lived a typical life for her time, though 'more hardscrabble than most', and now rested close to the grave of both her parents and her German immigrant husband, Augustus Joseph Schayer.

The other member of the detective duet, genealogist Smolenyak, said that the full story of Annie Moore was being restored to history. 'In a sense we are getting Annie back,' she said. Smolenyak, who had been instrumental in uncovering the Irish ancestry of soon-to-be president Barack Obama, read out a letter of congratulations from the senator which stated that Annie Moore had been a symbol of immigration and, by proxy, the American dream.

Patricia Prior of the Arizona-based Irish Cultural and Learning Foundation said that Annie could be rightly described as the 'first lady' for the twelve million Ellis Island immigrants. The unveiling of the Celtic cross, which was given musical accompaniment by the pipers of the County Cork Pipe and Drum Band, was but a second-long culmination of a story stretching back, at that point in time, 116 years.

The gravestone carried the name of Anna 'Annie' Moore Schayer and simply stated that she was 'First Through Ellis Island' on January 1, 1892. It included a Gaelic blessing at its base and a cherry blossom motif at the end of each arm of the cross, depicting her home on Cherry Street. The ceremony was concluded with the release of doves and the playing of 'The Boys from County Cork' on the pipes in honor of a girl from County Cork whose spirit soared with the birds into a brilliant blue sky.

The Annie Moore story would never have been fully told if scrutiny of her passage across an ocean had merely settled for her being first in a line of passengers off a ship. Sentiment poured through the story and gave it a life that countless immigrants and descendants of immigrants, Irish and otherwise, could readily identify with. And it would be Annie's life, its enduring spirit, and the spirit of those countless others that would be the lifeblood for battles to secure legal landfall in America for future Irish, whether they arrived by ship or by plane.

Annie would be a Joan of Arc, all right – a de facto patron saint of Irish immigration. And the Irish place great store in their saints.

CHAPTER 11

Cold Prose Loudly Proclaimed

On a September day in 1990, Annie Moore was on the minds of many who had gathered on Ellis Island to mark the unveiling of a newly refurbished immigration museum. Not a few Irish at the time felt that that this was entirely appropriate, and that the story of Irish immigration belonged in a museum. Nevertheless, there was a significant Irish contingent at the gathering – and also one standout Irish guest. Annie Moore was a memory, but Johanna Flaherty was very much alive, her mind filled with memories of her arrival on Ellis Island in 1923, the year before Annie died.

Johanna was a sprightly 84-year-old with a sharp memory. One thing she remembered was the voyage across the Atlantic with her uncle Pat. The food on board her ship of passage had been dreadful. But things began to look up after she landed on Ellis Island. Her earliest memory of America, apart from the Statue of Liberty, was the brown-bag lunch that she and her fellow new arrivals had been given by American officials.

In that brown bag was a wonder, something Johanna had never clapped eyes on before: a banana. In Ireland in 1990, bananas were a popular and widely available fruit. What was not available was easy and legal passage to America. It seemed like a raw deal. A lot of young Irish would have traded access to bananas for access to green cards in a heartbeat.

Johanna had the jump on her future countrymen and women in more ways than one when presented with a new fruit and all the potential fruits of an American life on the same day.

The Ellis Island celebration had quite a guest list beyond Johanna.

Vice President Dan Quayle was there, as was broadcaster Barbra Walters, who spoke proudly of her Russian roots. The grand affair was presided over by then-Chrysler chief executive Lee Iacocca, who had been given the task some years earlier of turning a veritable ruin into a visitor hot spot.

From an Irish perspective, there was, of course, more than a whiff of irony in the harbor breeze. The elevation of Ellis Island to an even grander height in the American immigration story was taking place only four years after the 1986 Immigration Reform and Control Act, a measure that had made life more difficult still for those living beyond the bounds of legality.

The '86 act did contain an amnesty provision, but most of the Irish living illegally in the US had not qualified because they had arrived after the act's amnesty cut-off date. This had resulted in the birth of the Irish Immigration Reform Movement and a campaign for visas that was especially concentrated in New York City. The Ellis Island celebration, then, was an abstract matter to many Irish living and working just a few miles away across the choppy waters presided over by Lady Liberty.

The situation was a good deal less complicated on the day of Johanna Flaherty's first arrival on the island. The Irish immigrants of her generation, by virtue of the efforts and sacrifices of others who had come before them, were accorded sufficient status to start a new American life legally. Those who had come before them – most of them, at any rate – had been accorded a status in society that wasn't to be envied.

As Noel Ignatiev noted in *How The Irish Became White*, 'the Irish who emigrated to America in the eighteenth and nineteenth century were fleeing caste oppression and a system of landlordism that made the material conditions of the Irish peasant comparable to those of an American slave'.

They came to a society in which color was important in determining social position. It was not a pattern they were familiar with, and they bore no responsibility for it – 'nevertheless', according to Ignatiev, 'they adapted to it in short order'. That they did, though the concept of 'short order' might have eluded Irish immigrants in the thick of those years when they were viewed by some better-positioned Americans as being worth even less than slaves.

By the time the first quarter of the twentieth century was giving way to the second, the Irish had secured rough parity with the majority of their fellow Americans. They were ready and eager to seize their moment, and more besides. Just about anything in life was now possible. Or so it seemed.

The twentieth century has been hailed, in a global context, as the 'American Century'. In the narrower confines of the Irish story, it was a passage of years in which an independent Ireland would emerge on one side of the Atlantic, and a triumphant and self-sustaining Irish community would emerge on the other. Each would become dependent on the other, though not always in the same, or even similar, ways. And each would, at times, be suspicious of the other.

But as the 1920s proceeded, the bedding down of the Irish in America would be advanced sufficiently enough to allow them to spare additional time and energy for the land left behind. This would take its most personal form in the emigrant's remittance, a helping hand from those in the new country to those in the old.

But, in the broader political sense, the concerns of America's Irish would be directed at an island newly getting used to the idea of a partitioning border. Forces in America that had directed themselves towards attaining Irish independence would regroup and redirect their energies towards ridding Ireland of its new line in the sod.

Much of this energetic expenditure would be channeled through the pages of the Irish American press, an institution that had existed for the bulk of America's existence but was now found necessary to address a suddenly more complex political reality in an Ireland featuring a British-controlled northern region and a more or less free southern region.

By the time of Ireland's partition there had been a recognizable Irish American press going back more than a century. The *Hibernian Chronicle* had cranked into action in 1810. *The Emerald* came into view a few years later, as did the *Truth Teller*. The latter was actually a Catholic publication, but it was embraced by the Irish of New York because its voice projected to the surrounding world.

The *Boston Pilot*, which rolled off the presses for the first time in 1829, fulfilled a similar function, and as the nineteenth century rolled on it would become as much a cultural publication as it was a religious one while the Irish poured, in ever greater numbers, into the city.

The early Irish papers would vent about occupation, oppression and injustice in Ireland. And if the volume was high in the first half of the century, it would, fueled by the horrors of the Great Hunger, ultimately reach a crescendo in the second half. But not in the very first years of that second half.

In 1849, the *Irish-American* began rolling off the presses. It was a weekly published by Patrick Meehan, Patrick Lynch and Edward Cole, and it made its greatest impact during its first twenty years, a period of unprecedented Irish immigration.

Despite the hardest of hard times for the Irish, the *Irish-American* adopted a moderate tone on the situation back in Ireland; by doing so, it avoided the disapproval of the Church, which would have proved fatal for any publication purporting to serve the almost entirely Catholic Irish immigrant community. The *Irish-American* would cease publication in 1915, thus avoiding the challenge of reporting moderately on the 1916 Rising.

Patrick Ford's *Irish World and Industrial Liberator* cranked up its presses in 1870 and in the following years, became the dominant Irish newspaper in America, partly due to the fact that it paid close attention to matters of Irish American concern as much as issues in Ireland itself. The paper's main American focus was the cause of labor, which, as the century neared its close, would be heavily Irish, both in terms of rank and file and emerging leadership.

The *Irish Advocate* came into being in 1893 under the guidance of John C. O'Connor. It found its niche by largely avoiding politics and presenting its readers with general news from Ireland and social news deriving from immigrants off the boat.

Not avoiding politics was *The Irish Nation*, launched by Fenian John Devoy in 1881. It took part of the name of an earlier radical nationalist publication, *The Nation*, which lived and died within the confines of that rebellious year, 1848, just as another radical sheet, *The Citizen*, did in the twelve months of 1854.

Devoy's paper was devoted almost entirely to the situation in Ireland and went out of business after just four years. However, its agenda was revived by Devoy's *Gaelic American*, which was launched in 1903, survived Devoy's death in 1928, and was ultimately taken over by the *Irish World* after that paper shed the 'Industrial Liberator' part of its name from the masthead.

Devoy's mission did not mirror that of the earlier *Emerald*'s idea of creating a bridge between Irish and Americans. Devoy was more a man for blowing up bridges than building them – literally and metaphorically. His dedication to the loftier principles of journalism was never especially apparent.

Pandering, according to Devoy biographer Terry Golway, had been an established tradition in Irish American journalism by the time Devoy arrived on the scene. Granted, the pandering was often directed at sentiment that was born of legitimate grievance. But Devoy was a master when it came to whipping up sentiment and carrying it to previously unscaled heights. The man knew how to sell newspapers.

In the 1870s and 1880s, according to Golway, there were frequent crusades by Devoy against various evils, real and concocted. Devoy was never a man to do things by halves. The level of outrage often exceeded the offense, and he was guilty many times of going over the top with a story. Devoy did not believe in assimilation. He wanted an Irish America that was solely devoted to freeing Ireland. He would pander to anything that would keep Irish America separate, distinct, and in its own ghetto.

Devoy would live to see a free Ireland, or at least a partly free one. He would also be witness to America's Irish breaking out of their various ghettoes, an inevitability in a society as dynamic and fast-changing as the United States was in the first quarter of the twentieth century.

Devoy died in the closing days of September 1928. The island of his birth was by now divided into a Free State made of twenty-six counties and a still British-controlled province comprised of six of the nine counties of Ulster. The Irish were still arriving in America from all thirty-two, benefiting from the peculiar advantages now written into US immigration law. The border in Ireland was now a primary target for Irish republicans still smarting after defeat in Ireland's short but extremely bitter civil war, which had started in 1922 and concluded in 1923.

Perfidious Albion, of course, was not off the hook, but Ireland itself was presenting itself as a more complex story for those who labored in the gnarly field that was Irish American journalism. It might have been more complex still, but the solution was simple as a far as one new publisher was concerned.

Charles Connolly was a man for firsts. He was grand marshal of the New York St Patrick's Day Parade in 1918, the first parade that allowed women to march and the first to fly the green, white and orange Irish tricolor. Connolly was a printer and typesetter who stepped across the room to a publisher's desk – initially while the name atop the masthead of the weekly tabloid read *Sinn Féiner*, and ultimately as publisher of a weekly broadsheet, the *Irish Echo*.

An immigrant from County Monaghan, Connolly well understood the complexities of the new post-civil war Ireland. But he had a simple solution to Ireland's situation, one reflected in the sobriquet that would become linked to his birth name: 'smash the border'.

Connolly would set about his smashing with words on the printed page. And his readers were close at hand in New York City and its surrounding area, ready with nickels that would pay for a paper sold off the back of a horse and cart outside a church or dance hall.

Devoy was gone but his cause would be taken up by Connolly and his paper, supported by the sweat of the still-arriving immigrant Irish. It was the fall of 1928, the tail end of the Roaring Twenties. The roaring was soon to stop, but that would not curb Connolly. The man had much to say and now had the means of saying it.

CHAPTER 12

A New Divide

Irish immigrants in the years before the advent of everyday air travel had first-hand knowledge of the Atlantic Ocean's width. For most, the journey across the Atlantic would be the greatest adventure of their lives. For some immigrants in the days of sail, and especially during the years of the Great Hunger, it would be a final adventure. Most, of course, survived the voyage and gratefully stepped ashore into a new land.

But in addition to typically humble baggage, many would carry old habits and long-held beliefs, not least political ones. America would be a new home and an incubator for all manner of things from the old country. For those who spent their working days in America writing about the plight of the old country, the formula was fairly simple: England the persecutor, Ireland the victim. Countless words were written from this starting point, which also happened to be the ending point. With the creation of the Irish Free State, however, matters became more complicated.

There was now an Irish government as far as most people in Ireland were concerned. There was also a border on the island. Granted, Perfidious Albion was still in the picture, but not in the former absolute sense. This changed, Ireland required a change of tack in Irish American journalism, or at least in certain corners of it. And that, inevitably, would not be smooth-going. Just as there was a split in Irish ranks on the home front over the Treaty – a pact that granted a degree of independence while simultaneously creating the border – there would also be a divide in Irish American journalism. And that split would be most clearly evident between a man born in America but living in Ireland, Éamon de Valera, and a man born in Ireland and living in America, John Devoy.

Devoy's *Gaelic-American* was the most political of the Irish newspapers during the years leading up to the 1916 Rising and the turbulent years that followed.

John T. Ridge, in his chapter devoted to Irish county associations in New York during this period (from *Ireland's Allies, America and the 1916 Easter Rising*), points out that the variety of opinions on Irish nationalism were best reflected in the New York-published newspapers, *Irish World*, *Irish Advocate* and *Gaelic-American*.

Every issue of the *Advocate*, according to Ridge, had detailed reporting on the doings of a hundred or more Irish societies. The *Advocate*, he writes, 'had none of the pretensions of being a national newspaper for the American Irish like the *Irish World*, whose social coverage was briefer and much more sporadic'. The *Gaelic-American*, notes Ridge, was by far the poorest chronicler of the life of the Irish associations and societies, except for those with sentiments like those of Clan na Gael, or Cumann na Mban. Such differences in emphasis allowed the various papers to compete and coexist.

Devoy's *Gaelic-American*, with its near absolute emphasis on the Irish freedom struggle and the politics nurturing it, was, inevitably, on a collision course with the coming political divide in Ireland.

When the divide presented itself as a bloody rupture, Devoy would take the side of the newly born Irish Free State and was placed in opposition to a future leader of that entity, Éamon de Valera.

De Valera's fundraising tour of America in 1919 would be covered in detail by the *Gaelic-American*, but after the Treaty and partition, Devoy's paper – and it was Devoy's paper in every sense – turned on de Valera, 'challenging him week by week', as Terry Golway put it in *Irish Rebel*. Devoy also feuded with the *Irish World* and at one point sued it for libel. But de Valera would be the primary target.

Golway indicates that the *Gaelic-American* wrote 'with unseemly glee, and perhaps wishful thinking', featuring lurid reports about Devoy's rivals – reports that would be carried under breathless headlines such as 'Violence and Rioting Common at Meetings of the Organization Started by De Valera to Destroy the Friends of Irish Freedom and the Clan na Gael'. The de Valera-founded organization being referred to was the American Association for the Recognition of the Irish Republic.

For newly arriving Irish immigrants, many of whom doubtless hoped to put the chaos and confusion in Ireland behind them, America, the Irish version, presented itself as a veritable stew of argument and invective. And if they chose to jump into the stew, they could choose from a significant menu of organizations representing this and that point of view. And they could choose an Irish American newspaper that would support and underpin their views on events back across the ocean.

Devoy's preeminence, and that of his *Gaelic-American*, would be a boon to the pro-Treaty government emerging back in Ireland. De Valera, too, could rely on at least one newspaper – that being the one published by Joe McGarrity in Philadelphia, the *Irish Press*. The *Irish Press*, as Sean Cronin pointed out in *Washington's Irish Policy 1916–1986*, was initially favorable towards the Treaty but very quickly switched to the de Valera side and opposed it. De Valera, perhaps feeling grateful towards the County Tyrone-born McGarrity, would, some years later, found his own newspaper in Ireland and name it the *Irish Press*.

More than in any other country, the Irish immigrant population in the United States would be the target of a hearts and minds battle as the new Free State struggled to find its feet while the not-an-inch republicans stuck to the task of establishing a fully independent thirty-two-county Irish Republic. For most, concentrated as they were in the large east coast cities, the daily task of earning a living – often just scratching one – was enough to keep the mind focused on more near-at-hand priorities. But of course there was always their hearts, and Devoy and other community leaders with access to the mass media – the Irish version – were expert at pumping and priming the sentiments of those who had left Ireland in the physical sense but not always in the emotional one. All this stirring of sentiment was of grave concern to the new government in Dublin.

In May 1922, a few weeks before the outbreak of civil war, and seven months before the formal emergence of the Free State, Timothy 'T.A.' Smiddy, the de facto Irish ambassador in Washington – and later the first de jure ambassador for the Free State – wrote to George Gavan Duffy in Dublin on a variety of matters. Included in the lengthy correspondence, as recorded in *Documents on Irish*

Foreign Policy, Volume 1, 1919–1922, was a reference by Smiddy to a Mr McCullough, who had succeeded 'I think, in inducing the purely Irish Press ... and Mr J. Devoy, to abstain from personalities and bitterness. "The Irish Press" in its last two issues has shown a marked moderation in the pronouncements.' No small achievement given the habit of the time to go over the top in print on matters great, small, and even miniscule.

For Devoy, the dramatic change in the Irish political landscape presented more than enough challenge. He would have taken delight in the emergence of at least part of Ireland, the greater part, from under England's thumb. And if he was delighted, so was his newspaper. But as matters evolved to the east, Devoy was reminded of the fact that he was a primary opinion-maker against a backdrop of ever-widening opinion. This is always a challenge for a publisher or editor in the purely business sense.

So for Devoy's paper to initially describe the Treaty as a 'surrender' was certain to win agreement from many if not most readers. Later, on a return visit to the land of his birth, Devoy would embrace the Free State and be embraced by it in return. The readers of the *Gaelic-American* were simply required to go with the flow.

There was, of course, a new target for Irish American invective and that was the border. Invective, of course, sells newspapers. But by 1928, Devoy was less immersed in his newspaper than he was in his memoirs. And those memoirs threatened to be of biblical proportions.

Time, of course, waits for no man, even the greatest of the Fenians. On September 21, Devoy and his friend Harry Cunningham journeyed to Atlantic City. The sea air often reinvigorated Devoy, but this time he could not shake his assortment of ailments. By week's end he was in bed in his hotel room and a doctor was summoned. There was little the physician could do. 'At about 1 a.m. on September 29,' according to Golway, 'Devoy asked to be turned over on his side. He died minutes later.'

The voice of Irish America and its immigrant people was silent, but of course there would be other voices to follow. One of them did, and within a week of Devoy's passing.

CHAPTER 13

Read All About It!

On an April day in 1928, three men climbed aboard a boxy monoplane, a Bremen, at Baldonnell Aerodrome outside Dublin. Captain Hermann Köhl was the pilot, Irishman Captain James Fitzmaurice was the co-pilot, while Baron Ehrenfried Günther Freiherr von Hünefeld was, not surprisingly given his name, the plane's owner.

Their Hiberno-German venture had a tinge of irony to it as Fitzmaurice had fought in the British Army against Germany in the First World War. This, however, was in the fading past. What lay ahead of the intrepid threesome was a flight westwards across the Atlantic to North America – their destination being just about any part of the continent's eastern fringe where a safe landing might be made.

As it turned out, the flight of the Bremen would be a success and would enter the history books as the first successful east-west transatlantic flight. The Bremen would make a bumpy landing on Greenly Island in Labrador after a flight lasting more than thirty-six hours.

The plane wasn't carrying much in the way of cargo. But it had on board two copies of the *Irish Times*. This was the first time that any European newspaper had crossed the Atlantic in a plane. That it was an Irish publication was appropriate given the insatiable appetite of the North American immigrant Irish for news from 'home'.

The Bremen apart, Irish newspapers were being sent to America on ships in 1928. Copies were carried by new arrivals and the fact that the actual 'news' might be days or even weeks old mattered little. The Irish American newspapers carried reports from Ireland, but also voluminous coverage of events and argument on American soil. This was certainly true for John Devoy's *Gaelic-American* and was also the case with the weekly *Sinn Féiner* published by Charles F. Connolly.

The *Sinn Féiner* was a tabloid, but Connolly had dreams of something bigger, a broadsheet that would grab the attention of Irish immigrants in New York City and its immediate environs. Thus was born the *Irish Echo*. Planning a new newspaper takes time, so Connolly had little if any inkling that his new creation would be born just days after the death of Devoy. As it turned out, less than a week had passed since the death of the old Fenian when the first issue of the *Echo* ran off the printing presses in Harlem.

The *Irish Echo* would be the first major Irish American newspaper launched in the post-partition era. And partition would be its daily, or rather weekly, bread. As with its predecessor and contemporaries, the *Echo* would take its place in the broad American Irish world with its eye fixed on the far smaller Irish corner of that world.

The first issue of the paper – indeed, the first year of issues – has been lost to time but the oldest edition extant presents a clear image of what a newspaper aimed primarily at newly arrived immigrants saw as its focus. And that was where the immigrants had come from rather than the place to which they had arrived. So 'Severe Gales Sweep Over Co. Cork' was always going to be a headline topping, say, a blizzard in Connecticut.

As the first issue of the *Echo* was passed from hand to hand, its readers were significantly more attuned to the state of political play in faraway Ireland than in their new homeland. As such, many Irish-born inhabitants of New York City, New York State, and other cities and states where their fellow Irish had settled in numbers, would pay scant heed to Al Smith, the first Catholic nominated to head a party ticket in a presidential race. At the point of the *Echo*'s first appearance, Smith was just weeks away from an election drubbing at the hands of Herbert Hoover and not a little pre-vote skullduggery from the likes of the Ku Klux Klan.

Tom Deignan, in a 2007 issue of *Irish America* magazine, writes, 'The Smith debacle suggested that Irish Catholics had come far in America but had a long way to go.' 'And yet,' he continues, 'in the decade that followed, Irish Catholics would profoundly reshape America, and not just in politics. From books to radio, in front of Hollywood cameras and behind them, Irish Americans transformed America during the 1930s – for better or worse, it must be added.'

But first, the 1920s would draw to a close. It was the decade that had seen the birth of an Irish Free State and an 'occupied' six counties in the island's northern reaches. The Irish had mostly survived the effects of US immigration law changes that had dealt harshly with people from other lands. And many of the 1920s arrivals more closely considered the words of a Catholic political leader named de Valera than one named Smith.

On the *Irish Echo*'s picture-free, word-heavy front page on November 30, 1929 – among the various reports of wild and stormy weather in various counties and a right-side lead headline reading 'Ramsay MacDonald Is Denounced For Speech' – there was, in the very center of the page, a square block of print that read very much like a Western Union telegram. 'De Valera Arrives December 8th' was the heading. Below this was a line in quotation marks, 'De Valera will travel by Republic, arriving December eighth. Inform Promotion Committee. --- O'Connell.' This was the 1929 version of an email. It was hot news. And there would be plenty more of that in the decade that was to follow.

For decades, the precise date of the first issue of the *Irish Echo* was a mystery. The paper's year of birth was known: it was 1928. But what month of that year, what week of that month? The mystery would eventually be solved by the coming to light of an issue from late 1929 and an unusual numbering formula attached to it. Charles Connolly launched the *Echo* the same year that the Oscars came into being. But either no first edition survived, or, if it did, it had never come to light. For as long as anyone can remember, the sense among those working at the *Echo* was that the paper had first hit the streets of New York in the fall of that year.

This was really just a hunch. The fall was, and is, a time of year for many events in the Irish community, such as county association dinners, dances and socials. It would seem logical to plan the new paper in the earlier months of the year and launch it as the days grew shorter and people's minds became more focused after somnolent summer. That was the guess at any rate. As it turned out, the guess was spot on. And it was confirmed by the surfacing of an issue from 1929.

The 1929 issue was in the possession of John Feighery, brother of Frank, who for some years, had been the editor of the *Hibernian Digest*, the official publication for the Ancient Order of Hibernians. The issue is dated November 30, 1929. That was a Saturday. The *Echo* was published mid-week, as it would be in decades to follow, but for most of its twentieth century existence each issue would be dated for the following Saturday.

The front page of the 1929 paper, with an eye-catching ornate masthead – more of a work of art than a typical newspaper banner – carried the volume number, in this case two, denoting the second year of publication, and a separate number for the issue. Ordinarily, issues are numbered sequentially for the specific year denoted by the volume number. So this November 30 edition might have been number forty-eight or so for that year. Only it wasn't. It was actually listed as number sixty and what this revealed was that Connolly had continued the issue number sequence that had started in 1928 through the turning of the year and into 1929. Why he did this is a mystery. It might have been that he was trying to create the impression of the paper being around for longer than it was. The higher the number, the greater the appearance, and impression, of longevity and stability.

Regardless, going back sixty weeks from November 30 ended with Saturday, October 6, 1929. Go back an additional three days to the Wednesday publication day and the precise point of the calendar that the *Irish Echo* was born is reached: October 3, 1928.

This was less than a week after the death of the great Fenian John Devoy, a lead story for a first issue if ever there was one. But was it? The 1929 issue is in the care of the Archives of Irish America at New York University. The very first 1928 issue is in the lap of the newspaper gods.

CHAPTER 14

Saved Amid Depression

Irish immigrants and Irish Americans are separated by birthplace. They have traditionally been fused together when the descriptive term is 'Irish Catholic'. This is not to forget the Scots-Irish, a singular grouping that has received increased and deserved attention in recent years. But to the untutored eye, the descriptive word 'Irish' is often applied a little too quickly, too casually. There's Irish and there's Irish.

The most significant distinction to be applied to America's Irish is the difference between being 'off the boat' and being of a subsequent generation. The Irish were still disembarking from many boats as the 1920s roared their last. But strange days were ahead, difficult ones. America would always be a shining light over the western horizon, but it would lose some of its luster in Irish eyes over the course of the decade preceding the Second World War.

The Great Depression would be the agent of this. It would also have another effect on the great American Irish story. It would facilitate a settling in the American Irish community at a moment when that community was consolidating itself as a significant and increasingly influential part of the great American mosaic. Those Irish Catholics would, according to Tom Deignan writing in *Irish America* magazine, 'profoundly reshape America'. He continues:

> There were many great accomplishments by the Irish in the 1930s. There were the literary achievements of John O'Hara, James T. Farrell and, of course, Eugene O'Neill, who won the 1936 Nobel Prize for Literature. Power brokers such as Joseph P. Kennedy, meanwhile, slowly but surely made their way into the corridors of national political power.

But a figure such as Father Charles Coughlin suggests there was a dark side to this decade of Irish Catholic achievement and assimilation.

Wildly popular with both big-city Irish Catholics and rural Protestants, Coughlin was a radio commentator who evolved from a populist to an angry demagogue and anti-Semite. Both the Vatican and President Franklin D. Roosevelt worked diligently to silence the infamous 'radio priest.'

Father Coughlin's prominence in national and Irish American life during the decade might have been a new form of nativism delivered through a new medium. It was also a reminder that not all 'Irish Americans' were actually American, Coughlin being Canadian by birth.

Canada had long been a destination for the migrating Irish, not least since the Great Hunger years. The 1930s in Ireland would not replicate the 1840s, but they were nevertheless lean years for an Irish Free State struggling to find its economic footing – any kind of economic footing.

Matters were not helped when, at the end of June 1932, the Irish government, now headed by American-born Éamon de Valera, began withholding payment of land annuities still due to the British Treasury. The sum at issue was one and a half million pounds. It was a significant sum for the time, and its withholding would lead to the Anglo-Irish Trade War, also referred to as the 'Economic War'. This standoff between the Free State and Great Britain would amount to a blunderbuss-scale shot in the Irish foot. It would continue until April 1938 and ultimately cost the Free State economy a lot more than the original sum in dispute.

An ironic twist to the trade dispute was that many on the Irish side of the argument crossed the Irish Sea in search of work in England. This eastward movement, coupled with the effects of the Great Depression in the United States, would significantly reduce Irish westward migration across the Atlantic.

Nevertheless, those Irish who did cross the Atlantic – certainly, there were many – took the view that they were simply moving from a small depressed country to a much larger one. There was, then, merit enough in sheer geographic size.

As the Great Depression bit, the American political landscape began to shift and the American Irish – those born in the United States and their immigrant cousins – found plenty of time and reason to be involved. Also becoming more closely involved in the nation's politics were the Kennedys of Massachusetts. As Tom Deignan states, during the 1932 presidential campaign, the Kennedy family patriarch Joseph Kennedy worked tirelessly for Franklin Delano Roosevelt while directly contributing and soliciting significant sums of money for Roosevelt's ultimate election victory.

The Kennedys, of course, had once been off-the-boat immigrants, but the fourth decade of the twentieth century was, for them, a very different time than the final year of the 1840s when Patrick Kennedy, from County Wexford, stepped ashore in Boston. Patrick Kennedy carried hopes, dreams and fears, though he could at least count on there being many fellow Irishmen and women close by with similar baggage.

As Maureen Dezell notes in her book *Irish America, Coming Into Clover*, the Irish immigrant wave was swamping Boston at the point in time when Kennedy was taking his first American steps. James Michel Curley's biographer Jack Beatty puts numbers on the swamping, 'During the entire year of 1840, fewer than 4,000 Irish arrived in Boston, whereas on the single day April 10, 1847, more than 1,000 landed on its shores. By 1850, the number of Irish had risen to 35,000 in a total population of 136,900.' Those stepping ashore in Boston during the 1930s, named Kennedy or otherwise, would have more in common with the Patrick Kennedy of 1849 than his grandson Joseph. Leaving Ireland was one thing. Shedding it was quite another.

But these Irish people were ashore. And now ashore, they were reading reports from 'home' that would resonate due to the fact that the headline, especially if it was from the *Irish Echo*, would carry that irresistible hook: the name of a county. So 'Severe Storm Over Waterford' would provide a desired distraction from local headlines speaking of storm clouds over America's economy, or indeed literal ones in the Dust Bowl states.

It could be argued that the pullback effect of having a native country bedeviled by division was an impediment to the island Irish becoming more speedily assimilated in their new continent-sized home. That said, the Irish were not all that different from other immigrant groups in that, initially, they would huddle together in social re-creations of the land they had left behind.

Irish gatherings, however, would not always be merely social. Partition was an ever-present news leader, as the following banner headlines from *Echo* issues from the 1930s attest: 'Injustice of Partition Must Cease' (a line uttered by Éamon de Valera); 'Sailing to America: Forty Representatives of Irish Unity'; or (a classic page-topper from the July 2, 1938 issue) 'Britain Drives the Nail of Bigotry Into Ulster On the Cross of the North'. Even the Great Depression would have been hard put to distract Irish eyes from that one.

But the depression did have an easier time diverting the Irish from making the Atlantic crossing, as the numbers attest. Between 1921 and 1930, the number of Irish arrivals in the US was 211,234. Between 1931 and 1940, the total had plummeted to 10,973. The Great Depression was driving its own nails into Ireland. But it was everybody's depression; from an Irish perspective, that is what made it so very different to the state of affairs less than a century before. So while much had been written about the great exodus of the mid-nineteenth century, not a lot of ink was expended on departures during the 1930s – to America or anywhere else.

This is evident in newspapers such as the *Irish Echo*. Emigration from Ireland and immigration to America was hardly a story at all, and it was certainly not worth the time spent on crafting over-the-top headlines. Emigration or immigration was simply a fact of life, a non-story. Nevertheless, ironically, it was the very reason why Irish newspapers existed in America and they were able to report on bad weather in the counties and the evils derived from dividing twenty-six of them from the other six. Weather, of course, was a constant conversation piece.

But as the 1930s drew to a close, the possibility of war loomed. While the Great Depression had curtailed immigration from Ireland to America, often simply redirecting the Irish to England or at times Australia, the peaceful flow of people across the Atlantic had continued undisturbed. And at the tail end of the decade there was a hint of things to come.

On June 28, 1939 the Pan American World Airways flying boat *Yankee Clipper* landed at Foynes in the Shannon Estuary. Éamon de Valera was on hand to greet the eleven crew members and well-pampered passengers, all eighteen of them. The flight officially launched a regular service from Foynes to New York and was rightly seen as a miracle of the age.

But there was much going on at the time that could be described as far from miraculous. Within a few months, the Second World War would break out and the Foynes–New York service would be grounded. The Irish Free State would declare its neutrality. The Atlantic would be turned into a vast theater of battle and the idea of voyaging to America for work and a new life was consigned to the stuff of dreams.

CHAPTER 15

Cometh the Hour

It was a scant twenty years between the end of the Second World War and the end of relatively unencumbered Irish immigration to America. The vivid memory of the former made the latter much more than a mere slap in the face. The closing of America's door, by way of the 1965 Immigration and Nationality Act, was, for all intents and purposes, a declaration of war on a cherished legacy. Or, at the very least, a gratuitous insult – one to be long-remembered. And, of course, the Irish are said to have very long memories. Those long memories, in an American context, overflowed with stories of the Irish standing, fighting and dying in the cause of the republic.

'Being an Irish-American male has defined coming-of-age as service as an American soldier since the Revolutionary War.' So wrote Edward Hagan in his 2016 book, *To Vietnam in Vain*. Hagan, in later life a college English professor, was born and raised in Inwood, a neighborhood at the northernmost tip of Manhattan that sent many of its sons to Vietnam. Irish sons. Hagan was not long an adult when he was posted as an intelligence advisor with Military Assistance Command Vietnam, the 'MACV' made famous by Neil Sheehan in *A Bright Shining Lie*, his 1988 book account about the early days of American involvement in Southeast Asia as seen through the eyes of an intelligence officer, Lieutenant Colonel John Paul Vann.

At one point in his one-year-and-ten-day stint on the Mekong Delta, Hagan found himself in a helicopter that was shot down by the Viet Cong. The co-pilot was killed in the fusillade from a .50 caliber machine gun. The pilot survived. Hagan discovered that the pilot was also from Inwood, just a different street in a different part of the neighborhood. What were the odds?

Not all that long, in fact. The Irish, be they Irish-born or Irish American (Hagan's County Tyrone-born father had served in the US Army during the Second World War) bumped into each other all over the place and in every place that America fought. During the Civil War, they fought each other.

There is, of course, a degree of mythology to be considered whenever an ethnic group reflects upon itself in the context of war. The story of war carries multiple fogs. But certain things stand out about the Irish. One is that they wielded arms for America in great numbers, arguably disproportionate numbers.

One favored statistic for Irish American military boosters is the number of Congressional Medals of Honor won by Irish and Irish Americans. New Yorker John J. Concannon, who worked for many years as a journalist with Newsweek, Collier's, and as a frequent contributor to the *Irish Echo*, wrote in the mid-1990s about Gerard F. White, a military historian and one-time secretary of the Congressional Medal of Honor Society.

Writing on the *Wild Geese* history website, Concannon focused on White and White's associates, George Lang (a Medal of Honor recipient) and Raymond Collins, who had compiled 'the premier book' on the Medal of Honor, a two-volume 1,334-page history titled *Medal of Honor Recipients, 1863–1994*. The book listed the 3,401 men who, up until that point in time, had received the highest military award for gallantry.

Ireland, Concannon proudly noted, was the country with the largest number of medal-winners, 'by far', with 258 recipients. Germany/Prussia was second, with 128 recipients. 'We Irish can proudly note that five of the 19 fighting men who won a second Medal of Honor were born in Ireland.'

His evident pride was not isolated. It is common for Irish Americans to very quickly point to the Medal of Honor list as clear confirmation of the view that the Irish, and their Irish American cousins, have fought and died for America to a degree that is exceptional, indisputable and unassailable. And even with so many recipients, the Irish have long-campaigned for fallen heroes who came close to winning the Medal of Honor but, for various reasons that were at times dubious, failed to gain the highest possible recognition.

An example of this from the Korean War is to be found in the actions of Kerry native Corporal Patrick Sheahan. Following a long campaign by the late John Leahy, a fellow Kerryman, Sheahan was made a posthumous US citizen along with twenty-seven fellow Korean War Irish by virtue of an act of Congress in 2003.

Leahy, who had also served in Korea as a sergeant in the artillery, was of the view that Sheahan, who had won the Silver Star, should have been posthumously awarded the Congressional Medal of Honor. He battled for this up until his passing in November 2014. Sheahan's bravery (he was also a recipient of the Bronze Star) was never in doubt. But the Pentagon has a thing about paperwork. Think of the scene at the end of *Indiana Jones* where the crate is stored in a sea of crates in a warehouse the size of a small town. Something similar happened to Pat Sheahan.

Sheahan's heroism, which led to his death on October 4, 1951 on a Godforsaken patch of land in Korea dubbed Hill 281, is described in battlefield reports from the time. But the effort to secure Sheahan a higher award for valor was hampered down the years by the lack of subsequent paperwork – this, despite John Leahy's Trojan efforts.

Leahy argued that Sheahan would have been awarded at least the Distinguished Service Cross, the second highest military award for valor, or even the Medal of Honor itself, had he been an American citizen at the time of his death. Sheahan, like many of his post-war fellow Irish immigrants, wasn't long on American soil before being drafted. Citizenship wasn't required to put on a uniform and shoulder a rifle.

What didn't help Leahy's campaign – what, in a sense, stopped it in its tracks – was a fire that destroyed the army's records back in 1973 and a seemingly never-ending game of bureaucratic ping pong that saw the Sheahan case bounce back and forth in Washington, DC and elsewhere. And to add to this, the National Archives, which stores vast amounts of records on military personnel, lost track of Sheahan.

In a 2012 response to a letter from Leahy, the National Archives office in College Park, Maryland, said it could find no record of Sheahan in the casualty lists linked to the Irishman's final battle. 'We have examined casualty lists for Cpl. Sheahan's unit, the 7th Infantry Regiment, 3rd Infantry Division, but were unable to locate any listing for him', the National Archives response to Leahy stated. The archives office also said that it had examined command reports from the 7th Infantry Regiment for October 1951. 'We did not locate a mention of Sheahan', the letter stated, while adding that such records rarely cited individual names.

As it happened, the army's official battlefield report of Corporal Sheahan's final action had surfaced and was in the possession of the *Irish Echo*. And if the National Archives had copies of the paper from the early 1950s, it could have learned more about Sheahan and his fellow Irish immigrant Korean War fighting men. Their deaths were reported, as was a requiem Mass for Sheahan and some of his Irish comrades held at St Patrick's Cathedral in New York.

The Sheahan battlefield report states:

CORPORAL PATRICK SHEAHAN, US51064448, Infantry, Company 'A', 7th Infantry, 3rd Infantry Division, United States Army. On 4 October 1951, Company 'A', with the First Platoon serving as the assault unit, attacked Hill 281 near Chungseri, Korea.

Stiff enemy opposition prevailed and the sweeping fire of a hostile machine gun soon pinned down the platoon and halted the advance up the hill.

Corporal SHEAHAN, realizing the gravity of the situation and aware that the enemy weapon must be neutralized, courageously crawled forward under the lethal hail of fire and completely destroyed the emplacement with accurately thrown hand grenades.

Uncertain as to whether all the enemy soldiers had been killed by the explosions, he rose to his feet and, rushing forward, fired a long burst into the smashed entrenchment, eliminating all possible opposition.

It was while thus revealed to the enemy, as he carried out his singlehandedly brave action that corporal SHEAHAN fell, mortally wounded by the savage fire of an adjacent automatic weapon.

Corporal SHEAHAN'S aggressive gallantry and selfless devotion to duty were instrumental in the successful completion of his unit's mission and reflect the highest credit upon himself and the military service.

The 'highest credit' could, or should, equal the Medal of Honor. But it didn't. An effort by John Leahy to have the Distinguished Service Cross awarded posthumously to Sheahan also ended with Leahy's passing. But the story of Pat Sheahan did not pass or fade.

And it has reinforced the deeply held view that whether a medal is won or unjustly denied, it has always been from unassailable high ground that the American Irish have felt it well within their remit to take up arms for America, or, indeed, sometimes urge a retreat from war – and to do so without any questioning of patriotism or courage. This was the case at the outset of the Second World War, when prominent Irish Americans supported efforts to keep America out of faraway Europe's troubles and keep the Irish Free State out of those much closer troubles.

To that end, and as the so-called phony war was about to give way to the all-too-real version, a group called the American Friends of Irish Neutrality (AFIN) was formed in New York City in 1940. Its aim was to underpin Irish neutrality during whatever transpired in the still-nascent conflict. The records of the AFIN have been stored at St John's University in New York City since being donated by one of its leading members, the late Paul O'Dwyer, a lawyer, politician, and lifelong supporter of a united Ireland.

In the early months of the war, Britain was in need of using Irish ports and military bases in order to refuel ships and aircraft to better protect shipping in the North Atlantic.

Neutral Ireland would not allow Britain to use the bases, the so-called 'treaty ports' which had been returned by London to Dublin's control at the agreed conclusion of the Anglo-Irish Economic War in April 1938.

The United States believed that the Irish ports were vital to the British war effort and also to Anglo-American interests in the North Atlantic. Taoiseach Éamon de Valera viewed things differently. He would later state, by way of defending Irish neutrality and its control of the treaty ports, 'Our circumstances, our history, the incompleteness of our national freedom through the partition of our country, made any other policy impossible.'

De Valera sent an open telegram to John J. Reilly, president of the American Association for Recognition of the Irish Republic, and requested that the association put the Irish case, including partition, clearly before the American public. De Valera's request was aimed at diminishing the power of the 'propaganda' campaign initiated by Winston Churchill, who was trying to convince Americans that Dublin should give the port facilities to Britain.

Charlie Connolly, founding publisher and editor of the *Irish Echo*, responded to de Valera's appeal by calling on 'all people interested in assisting Ireland in preserving her neutrality' to meet at the Tuxedo Ballroom on 59th street and Madison Avenue on Sunday, November 24, 1940. About 2,500 responded to the call and, at the gathering, the American Friends of Irish Neutrality Association came into being.

Paul O'Dwyer, a St John's Law School graduate (class of 1929), was chairman, and James O'Brien, professor at Fordham University, was president. Another founding member was Sean P. Keating, a veteran of the Irish War of Independence who went on to become Deputy Mayor of New York City under Mayor Robert Wagner.

AFIN advocated American neutrality, but its main function was to keep Ireland out of the war by preventing the US from pressuring the Irish Free State into allowing British use of the ports. The ports in question were Berehaven in County Cork, the Cork Harbor facilities of Spike Island, Fort Camden and Fort Carlisle, and Lough Swilly in County Donegal. Churchill would bemoan the handovers when war broke out, but by then it was too late.

AFIN's brief existence was an active one. Meetings were called across the United States, prayer services were held, and there was a sustained and effective public relations effort carried out on behalf of the Irish Free State's freedom to exercise the neutrality option. The group organized a petition that gathered two million signatures advocating not just for US support for Irish neutrality but also for the supply of the Free State with military and non-military supplies from the United States. The treaty ports aside, it would be another anchorage that would ultimately decide the course of AFIN's story.

Less than a week after the attack on Pearl Harbor, the group disbanded. As was the case with the previous world war, the American Irish were being presented with a much bigger picture to consider. And this they would do, with characteristic energy and verve.

CHAPTER 16

The Hour Cometh

Emigration doesn't necessarily mean a total sundering. This is especially the case when large groups of people from a country congregate closely together in their newly adopted land.

The Irish in America congregated. They also dispersed. They also remained focused on their native land due to the very particular political realities there. That focus would only intensify as America became more powerful and globally influential. Rallying the American Irish to the cause of a free Ireland was a relatively simple task within the Irish community, but the outbreak of war would require a broader and more deftly-run campaign.

In the matter of the Irish Free State's neutrality in 1939, there was the complication of the effect this would have on America's closest ally, Great Britain. Still, Irish neutrality would have a relatively limited strategic effect. American neutrality was quite something else and that was an issue firing up varied opinion in every immigrant group – and across a broader American society where ties to old countries in Europe were not so recent or keenly felt.

The German American Bund campaigned for American neutrality from a position of supporting Nazi Germany. The success of such a campaign would clearly carry very significant strategic consequences. It wasn't successful. Joseph Kennedy, arguably the highest-profile and certainly the richest Irish American, wanted the United States to refrain from supporting the British war effort because he believed it to be in vain. He wasn't successful in pressing this viewpoint.

The arguments raging back and forth over just what America should do, or not do, in the face of the raging fires in Europe would become moot on December 7, 1941. At that point, Irish neutrality was accepted by Washington, if not exactly admired. And even the leaders of American Friends of Irish Neutrality realized that the picture had suddenly become much bigger and more dangerous.

America's Irish knew where their energies had to be directed, and those energies were employed from the very moment the first bombs began falling on Oahu. As it was, 2,403 Americans died in the attack on Pearl Harbor. More than a thousand others were wounded. Not a few of the dead were Irish Americans. Two Irish Americans would win the Congressional Medal of Honor that infamous day. They were John William Finn, who survived the attack, and Frank C. Flaherty, who did not.

Finn, a chief aviation ordnance man stationed at Naval Air Station Kaneohe Bay, earned his medal by manning a machine gun from an exposed position throughout the attack, despite being repeatedly wounded. Like just about everyone else on Oahu that day, Finn was rousted from the more somnolent duties of a Sunday. Finn didn't hesitate. He ran to a mounted gun and began firing at enemy aircraft. Two hours later he had twenty-one shrapnel wounds and a record of heroic action that would earn him the first Medal of Honor for the Second World War.

Born in 1909, Finn would live to be a hundred. He died in May 2010. He was born on July 24, 1909 in Los Angeles. His grandparents on his father's side were immigrants from County Galway. His father supported the family as a shipping clerk in a machinery firm and later as a plumber. Young John left school at 11 years of age to work. In 1926, at 17 years of age, he enlisted in the Navy.

He looked so young that his mother had to accompany him to the recruiting station to verify his age. Finn's lack of formal education didn't hold him back in the Navy, and by 1935 he had risen to the rank of chief petty officer. Six years later, in December 1941, he found himself stationed at Kaneohe Bay, Hawaii as Navy aviation chief ordnance officer.

The attack on Pearl Harbor and other military facilities on Oahu commenced a few minutes before 8 a.m. and caught American forces completely by surprise. The Pacific fleet was a sitting duck and the Japanese pilots took full advantage. Those Americans who could, eventually fought back. When John Finn reached his base, it was too late to launch any Navy pilots (their planes were in flames), so he ran to a mounted .50 caliber machine gun and began firing.

His position was completely exposed and soon came under fire. Despite numerous shrapnel wounds, Finn kept up the fight. 'I just kept shooting,' he later said in an interview, 'because I wasn't dead.' Witnesses later claimed that he shot down at least one Japanese plane. 'I'm not sure I shot a plane down, but I can take credit for shooting at every plane I could bear on.'

Two hours later, Finn was receiving medical treatment for his shrapnel wounds and learning the dreadful details of the attack. Eighteen ships, including all eight battleships of the Pacific fleet, were sunk or badly damaged. Over 350 aircraft, most while still on the ground, were destroyed.

Nine months later, Finn (now an ensign) received the Medal of Honor aboard the USS *Enterprise* from Admiral Chester Nimitz. The official citation bears reading in full:

> For extraordinary heroism distinguished service, and devotion above and beyond the call of duty. During the first attack by Japanese airplanes on the Naval Air Station, Kaneohe Bay, on December 7, 1941, Lt. Finn promptly secured and manned a .50-caliber machinegun mounted on an instruction stand in a completely exposed section of the parking ramp, which was under heavy enemy machine gun strafing fire. Although painfully wounded many times, he continued to man this gun and to return the enemy's fire vigorously and with telling effect throughout the enemy strafing and bombing attacks and with complete disregard for his own personal safety. It was only by specific orders that he was persuaded to leave his post to seek medical attention. Following first aid treatment, although obviously suffering much pain and moving with great difficulty, he returned to the squadron area and actively supervised the rearming of returning planes. His extraordinary heroism and conduct in this action were in keeping with the highest traditions of the US Naval Service.

Finn remained in the Navy for the duration of the war and stayed on after 1947, in the Navy reserves. He retired in 1956 (at 47 years of age) with the rank of lieutenant. He spent the next few decades running a repair shop in San Diego and then a ninety-two-acre ranch, seventy miles outside the city, that he and his wife, Alice, bought in the late 1950s.

Intensely patriotic, and proud of his Irish heritage, he attended Second World War memorial services and served for many years as a spokesman for causes such as the campaign to raise funds to secure and preserve the USS *Arizona* memorial.

While John Finn faced the enemy and survived that day, Frank Flaherty did not live to tell any tale. And his bravery was not displayed by hands on a machine gun, but, rather, a flashlight. There were many acts of extraordinary heroism at Pearl Harbor and they were performed in myriad ways. Flaherty, who was from Charlotte, Michigan, and an ensign at the time of the attack, was aboard the USS *Oklahoma*.

Flaherty's Medal of Honor reads in part, 'For extraordinary devotion to duty and extraordinary courage and complete disregard of his own life … when it was seen the USS *Oklahoma* was going to capsize and the order was given to abandon ship, Ensign Flaherty remained in the turret, holding a flashlight so the remainder of the turret crew could see to escape, thereby sacrificing his own life.'

There were 429 men entombed in the *Oklahoma* at Pearl Harbor, including Flaherty, after the great ship rolled over. The ship was raised for salvage in 1943, and the remains inside were eventually interred in mass graves marked 'Unknowns' at the National Memorial Cemetery of the Pacific in Honolulu.

In 1943, a destroyer bearing Flaherty's name was commissioned and it served for the duration of the war. The USS *John Finn*, an Arleigh Burke Class destroyer, was commissioned in July 2017. Flaherty and Finn opened the Irish American part of America's response in the opening minutes of the war. Their effort and sacrifice would be reinforced by countless Americans, men and women, with Irish blood coursing through their veins. And they were reinforced very quickly by one man.

As Ed O'Donnell would record, three days after the attack on Pearl Harbor, Captain Colin P. Kelly Jr took to the sky in his B-17 bomber. His mission was to bomb Japanese positions in Taiwan and was one of the first American responses to the attack on Hawaii. The mission cost Kelly his life, but in death he was celebrated by a grateful nation desperate for a hero.

Kelly was born in 1915 in Monticello, Florida, and graduated from the US Military Academy in 1937. He went on to become an aviator specializing in flying B-17s. His skills eventually earned him a job as a flight instructor. Soon after the Second World War broke out in Europe, Kelly was stationed in the Philippines. He knew, as did every soldier and sailor in the Pacific, that if war with Japan came, they would be among the first to know.

On December 8, Japanese planes attacked American bases in Manila, destroying hundreds of planes on the ground. Stationed nearby in Luzon, Kelly and the 14th Bomb Squadron, 19th Bomb Group to which he belonged, emerged unscathed.

Two days later, Kelly and his crew took off from Clark Field with orders to bomb Japanese positions in Taiwan. With so many planes destroyed, his bomber would go it alone without the customary escort of fighter planes. It would be a perilous 1,000-mile round trip.

Soon after takeoff, however, Kelly spotted a group of Japanese ships landing a large force at Luzon. Immediately, he radioed Clark Field. Did he have permission to bomb vessels? Left hanging without an answer as critical minutes ticked away, Kelly decided to attack. His target: the largest Japanese ship supporting the landing.

Kelly passed over the ship twice to give his bombardier a chance to home in on the target. On the third pass, they let fly three 600-pound bombs. One hit the ship dead on, while the other two exploded nearby, causing additional damage. Gazing at the huge billows of smoke below, Kelly and his crew were convinced they had sunk a Japanese battleship.

But there was no time to savor the moment, for Japanese fighters were on them in seconds. With no fighter support, the lumbering B-17 was a sitting duck. A fellow Irishman aboard Kelly's plane, Sergeant William Delahanty, was killed in the first strike. A second assault set the bomber ablaze. While Kelly struggled to control the plane, he ordered his crew to bail out. Moments after the last man climbed out of the escape hatch, the plane exploded and the wreckage hurtled to the earth.

One member of the Japanese fighter squadron later recalled Kelly's bravery in these final moments. 'Out of ammunition, I flew alongside the B-17 and saw the pilot trying to save the burning aircraft after allowing his crew to escape,' he remembered. 'I have tremendous respect for him.'

America, still reeling from the attack on Pearl Harbor, had its first hero of the declared war. From coast to coast, newspapers carried front-page stories of how Kelly had boldly sunk a Japanese battleship and selflessly gave his life so that his crew might live. Soon, word came that the commander of US forces in the Pacific had nominated Kelly for the Congressional Medal of Honor.

Over time, the details of Kelly's mission became clearer. An official report in 1942 determined that the Japanese ship Kelly hit was actually a light cruiser, not a battleship. And despite being nominated for the Medal of Honor, Kelly eventually received the Distinguished Service Cross. By then, of course, such details mattered little. Kelly's exploits, heroic by any standard, had provided a much-needed morale boost to his nation. His was an inspiring story that helped stiffen American resolve in the face of an uncertain future.

Finn, Flaherty, Kelly. Japan would have its work cut out, as would its Axis allies, as the Irish of America (Scots-Irish included) rallied to America's cause once again. Those American Irish would include the Sullivan Brothers, William 'Wild Bill' Donovan, James 'Jumpin' Jim' Gavin, Audie Murphy and of course John Fitzgerald Kennedy, whose *PT-109* included crew members with the obviously Irish names of Maguire and McMahon, and several others whose names indicated at least the possibility of partial Irish ancestry.

Of course, Americans of every ethnicity and race served America's cause between 1939 and 1945. But the movie, for reasons that might not ever be fully understood, was always going to be about saving a private named Ryan. And, fittingly, it would largely be filmed in Ireland.

At the end of it all, the American Irish were on the winning side and rightly felt proud of their contribution. Some also eyed a debt. The 1945 St Patrick's Day issue of the *Irish Echo* featured a front page with a range of stories that would give no clue whatsoever to a world war still raging. But the top-left lead carried a hint that all was not well with the world. Patrick Grimes, future publisher of the paper and newly installed president of the United Irish Counties Association, proclaimed that 200,000 Irish soldiers who had 'fought and bled' in the armies of the United Nations would not tolerate the continued 'dismemberment' of Ireland.

The world may have been turned upside down by what the *Echo* referred to as 'the present conflict', but some things absolutely remained the same. One of those things was partition in Ireland, while another was transatlantic immigration from Ireland. After the unsurprising shutdown during the war years, immigration was poised to restart as a result of America's traditional pull and the double-push exerted by a virtually inert economy in the neutral Irish Free State and the end to an unsustainable wartime economy in Northern Ireland where so many GIs had spent their dollars.

The hour had cometh. The Irish had answered its call. They had, as a result, heightened expectations.

CHAPTER 17

Back to Boston

The Irish crossed the sea in droves during the Second World War. The Irish Sea as opposed to the Atlantic Ocean. They did so to join up with the British armed forces and to work in British factories and munition plants. This suited the neutral Irish Free State for the simple reason that it amounted to jobs, a flow of income back to families in the state and, not least, a reduced potential for instability resulting from a lack of work in the Free State's twenty-six counties.

Some Irish did make the journey across the Atlantic, but this flow wasn't close to the numbers of former times. Still, the decade spanning 1941 to 1950 did see an increase in Irish immigration to America over the previous ten-year period. Most of the 19,789 Irish that made the westward journey in that span of time did so after the war had ended, in the second half of the decade.

In that second half, Britain – now rebuilding after the war and being led by a Labour Party government intent on considerable public works – was still the main draw for young Irish seeking a chance to make ends meet. But if the bigger part of the post-war Irish emigration story was the journey to Birmingham in England, a renewed part of it – and not an insignificant part – was back to Boston or a number of other big American cities. And in those cities, they would discover an Irish America that was well established, politically influential, and confident in its ability to take care of itself and, if the necessity arose, to extend a hand to the newly arrived cousins from Ireland.

From this was born a generation of new Irish who, combined with older immigrants and the American Irish, would witness the election in 1960 of the nation's first Catholic president. The '1950s Irish' have long been a recognized and distinct grouping.

Author Ed Hagan would refer to them, albeit a few years down the road, in 1972, and in the specific context of his own Inwood neighborhood in Manhattan. Inwood, he writes, was filled with members of the Transport Workers Union, the International Brotherhood of Electrical Workers, the Teamsters, Iron Workers Local 42, the Policemen's Benevolent Association, the Uniformed Firefighters Association, and 32B or 32J of the Service Employees Union International. 'They worked for Con Ed – the utility company – and for New York Telephone; they were construction workers, cops, truck drivers, letter carriers, firemen, bar tenders, doormen, subway train conductors, and bus drivers.'

Inwood, as John Thornton remembered it, was tight-knit and tightly controlled by the Democratic Party, a fact of life in most urban Irish immigrant communities in mid-twentieth century America. Thornton, known to many as 'Jack', edited the *Irish Echo* over three decades and died in 2004. His Inwood was a place where, as he put it, 'a turkey would arrive at the front door at Thanksgiving and a bag of coal would follow for Christmas'. Not quite gifts from the gods, but from the next nearest thing to permanence in the neighborhood: the party.

John Dunleavy, for many years the dominant figure in the running of the New York St Patrick's Day Parade, would describe his generation of Irish immigrants, the 50s Irish, as being people who had very little and did not enjoy the kind of educational opportunities in Ireland that would be available to later generations.

The 50s Irish, by his reckoning, had to scramble to reinvent themselves in their adopted homeland and would do so by availing of every available education opportunity, by serving in the military as he did, by reaching for any and every opportunity that came along, and by just working plain hard. Taking every opportunity often meant taking every opportunity that was offered, as opposed to an opportunity that could be defined as random.

Ireland might have enjoyed an immigration quota in the post-war years but that did not mean automatic entry to the United States for every Irish person who headed across the Atlantic. Patrick Joseph

O'Dea, 'PJ' to all who knew him, departed Kilrush in County Clare in 1957. He flew from Shannon to New York and from there to his intended destination, Toronto.

Canada, however, was not destined to enjoy O'Dea's talents for long. Those talents included county-level ability in both Gaelic football and hurling. As O'Dea tells it, John Kerry O'Donnell, the dominant figure in Gaelic games in New York, was aware of O'Dea's prowess on the field and was determined to secure the Clare man's services. O'Dea made several attempts to cross the border but was invariably asked to step out of the car and answer questions. 'I just couldn't tell a lie,' he said in a 2018 interview, at 92 years of age.

O'Dea was turned back at the border so many times that O'Donnell bought him a plane ticket and flew him to New York. Once he had landed on American soil, O'Dea began to play football and hurling for various teams. Given the times that were in it, a union membership with an attached job in a warehouse was procured. And the process of securing O'Dea permanent legal residence in the United States was initiated. This entailed a return to Canada and the nailing down of legality – this time, by the book.

Back in the US, and now with all the necessary papers, O'Dea headed for Los Angeles and San Francisco, still starring for Gaelic Athletic Association (GAA) teams, including one in San Francisco where he was teammates with a future mayor of the city, Frank Jordan. Following this, O'Dea would head east again to what would become his permanent American home: Chicago. It was in Chicago that he pursued a career in public relations and, ultimately, secured a position with the Cook County Sheriff's office.

Being able to play football and hurling, according to O'Dea, was 'a great asset'. Being simply Irish was no harm either now that the American Irish had reached the point of being those who often did the hiring, as opposed to being those who got hired.

The Irish who journeyed to America in the immediate years following the end of the war found themselves in a land that, unlike most of Europe, had not suffered the infrastructural ravages of war. The United States, of course, had suffered greatly in terms of the dead and injured in the campaigns to defeat fascism in Europe and Japanese militarism in Asia and the Pacific. But the America the Irish set foot in was, nevertheless, on the march into a stronger, bolder future. The Irish newcomers were only too happy to fall in lockstep.

This happiness would be on clear display on St Patrick's Day, 1946, when the first New York parade since the end of hostilities stepped off on Fifth Avenue. The 1946 parade would be loaded with a symbolism that combined American victory and Irish vindication. A century after the Great Hunger and a time when the Irish were vilified even as they suffered the ravages of poverty, disease and famine, they could rightly claim a central role in America's triumph and emergence as the greatest economic and military power on earth. This was certainly exemplified by the 1946 parade's most important spectator: the Mayor of New York, William O'Dwyer.

O'Dwyer was Irish-born and, as it had turned out, born to high American rank. His was a classic tale of being born into humble circumstances – in his case, County Mayo – traveling on a steerage ticket to America and landing on Ellis island. He seized the opportunities that his new homeland had to offer in terms of education, becoming a lawyer, a politician and, during the war years, a brigadier general in the United States Army.

In 1946, Johnny had come marching home. Paddy would be hard on his heels. And this grand march was to continue in the parade of 1947, which was led by a grand marshal, William Cavanaugh, who also held the rank of brigadier general. The 1948 parade would outrank the previous two years when it was reviewed by the commander-in-chief, President Harry S. Truman.

Of course, New York was only a fraction of the bigger story. The Irish still arrived mostly on ships making port on the east coast and found themselves on a continent that was being traversed by an ever-larger and more intricate transportation system – on the ground and now, increasingly, in the air. Back in Ireland, the Flying Boats that had taken off for North America from the Shannon estuary were giving way to planes that flew from land – specifically, Shannon Airport, which had announced itself as the first duty-free airport in the world. And the rising number of westbound air travelers would find, by the end of 1948, that they were no longer departing the Irish Free State but rather a free nation that was now describing itself as a republic.

A change of name, of course, was easier to accomplish than a change of economic circumstance. Ireland, in the years immediately after the war, was economically moribund and in a state of seemingly never-ending official 'emergency'. The push created by a lack of opportunity was only matched by the pull of opportunity elsewhere: in a rebuilding Great Britain and a rapidly expanding, bright-lights America. As the 1950s kicked in, those lights would shine ever more brightly; America, land of the free and home of the brave, turned into the land of the free-spending consumer.

In 1950, Washington and Dublin would sign a treaty of friendship, commerce and navigation – a de jure recognition of a de facto history. Two years later, the geographic divide between the two countries shrank markedly, at least in symbolic terms. In time for the New York St Patrick's Day Parade, Pan American Airways flew the first direct passenger flight from Shannon to New York. Flights, in former years, had mostly made initial North American landfall at Gander in Newfoundland. Now Gander seemed farther away from New York than Galway. That first Pan Am flight carried a large consignment of fresh shamrock in time for the big Irish day. It was now almost possible to smell Ireland on the streets of New York.

It was also yet possible to detect a whiff of xenophobia. Despite America's power and global dominance, many of the nation's leaders were still stricken with a siege mentality when it came to what kind of people could be allowed set foot in the United States. This state of mind, seemingly more nineteenth century than mid-twentieth, was exemplified by the Immigration and Nationality Act of 1952, more widely remembered as the McCarran–Walter Act.

The 1952 act, which came into being as American soldiers were fighting in Korea, further ratified the immigrant quota system, which disproportionately benefited northern Europe, Ireland included. It also opened America's door to Asian immigration, but at very low numbers. In response to McCarran–Walter, President Truman had wielded a veto, seeing in the act's provisions the 'dead hand of the past'. But Truman's effort to turn back the act was overridden by Congress.

Regardless of the debate in Washington, the Irish could still expect America to roll out the welcome mat. So they still came, more than

48,000 of them between 1951 and 1960. The vast majority would still arrive by ship, though a growing number would fly. And they would land or step ashore in a growing number of places. Few of them would pay attention to the closing of Ellis Island in November 1954. That was a place that spoke of another time.

It was perhaps fitting that the transition of the Irish Free State into the Republic of Ireland was confirmed in September 1948 by Taoiseach John A. Costello on New World soil – in this instance, Canada, in the still-British Dominion's capital, Ottawa. As Seán Cronin described it in his definitive *Washington's Irish Policy 1916–1986*, 'Asked at his press conference in the Canadian House of Commons ... if he intended to introduce legislation to repeal the External Relations Act, Costello replied "yes." He also said repeal meant secession from the Commonwealth. No Irish reporter was present. The first official notification that the Irish people received of their final break with the Crown and Commonwealth came via the wire services from Ottawa ... To say that the Republic was declared in Canada is hardly an exaggeration in these circumstances.'

CHAPTER 18

On Wings and Prayers

Countless things occurred in the America of 1958. But two occurrences, bookends in a sense, would have especially profound effects on the American Irish psyche, in the short term and in the longer.

The year would be the second last in a decade of unprecedented prosperity and economic expansion. The Russians might have been first into space but not too many citizens of the Soviet Union could boast a refrigerator big enough to accommodate Sputnik. Not too many of them could move to America either. In this regard, tiny Ireland had a distinct advantage over its vast neighbor to the east.

Throughout the decade – indeed, since the end of the Second World War – the psychology of migration had undergone a shift commensurate with technical and economic advances. An Irish man or woman fleeing hunger and destitution in 1848 was almost invariably leaving on a one-way ticket. This was not the case for the emigrant of 1958, though it could still be a hard task convincing those left behind that departure was no longer necessarily the end of the tale. If John Wayne's Sean Thornton could return to the land of his forebears in 1952, all the Seans who headed the other way in 1958 could also consider a future return, and a rather rapid one too.

It had been the case for some years that air services had accommodated some of the better-off Irish emigrants in their transatlantic foray. Those air services were typically American, Pan American and Trans World Airlines (TWA) being familiar names to the privileged few. Aircraft bearing the livery of airlines such as these tended to be associated with the westward journey. This would

change with the first landing in New York, on the second last day of
April 1958, of an airliner bearing an Irish name and livery.

The plane, named after St Patrick, took off from Dublin on a
Monday evening, landed in New York on Tuesday, and returned
to Ireland on Wednesday. All transatlantic airlines made the return
flight, but this airline, Aer Linte (Aerlínte Éireann, to give it its
full formal title) was a part of Ireland even before lifting off from
Idlewild.

It was thirty years to the month since the Bremen had landed
carrying copies of the *Irish Times*. The *St Patrick* carried the Irish of
their time. The inauguration of the new service was a big deal for
Ireland. It was also a pretty big deal for New York, home to so many
Irish. Mayor Robert Wagner had undertaken a visit to Ireland so as
to be on board the *St Patrick* for his return journey home.

The *Irish Echo* captured the spirit of the occasion, reporting on
its front page, 'There was a large crowd at Idlewild Airport when the
plane reached here on Tuesday morning. Many representatives of
Irish societies and city officials were on hand to greet the plane and
the Aer Linte guests. There was a cheer when the plane landed and
hearty congratulations extended to the Irish party.'

Even if they lacked the money for the fare, even if they couldn't
muster the time off for the journey, the Irish of New York, and some
distance beyond, could now imagine a winged Irish space just a few
miles away, not thousands of them. One-way emigration, the kind
with the truly final farewell to loved ones, had been fading into the
past. It was now well and truly in the past – in the mind's eye, at the
very least.

In the months that followed that first American landing, three
leased Lockheed L-1049 Super Constellations were used for a twice-
weekly service linking New York with Dublin. Times had indeed
moved on for the migrating Irish. The suffocating coffin ships in the
early days of their story had given way to 'Super Connies'.

Still, most Irish landing in America continued to do so from
ships, even as an (albeit growing) number of their kith and kin were
taking to the skies.

Dubliner John Timoney, who would rise to the heights of
law enforcement in New York, Philadelphia and Miami, sailed

majestically into New York Harbor in 1961. Well, at least the SS *Mauretania* did. The young Timoney was somewhat distracted from his first moments as a new American, distracted even from the majesty of the Statue of Liberty, by the agonizing discomfort of being trussed up in a wool communion suit on a hot summer's day.

Irish passenger airliners powered by propellers, and American ones powered by jet engines, clearly had the edge over ships when it came to the time taken to bridge the Atlantic. But new standards were quickly being applied and air journeys could sometimes be fraught.

Adrian Flannelly, who would become one of the most prescient observers of Irish immigrant life in America, made his transatlantic journey after leaving his native Mayo on October 18, 1959. Flannelly took off from Shannon Airport courtesy of Trans World Airlines. The anticipated travel time to New York was nine hours, with a refueling stop at Gander in Newfoundland included. The plane made it to Gander in good order, but a snowstorm kept Flannelly and his fellow passengers grounded for an additional seven hours. Flannelly, suffice it so say, would more than make up the lost time once New York was attained.

Not long after Flannelly's flight, on January 1, 1960, Aerlínte Éireann was renamed Aer Lingus – Irish International Airlines. Just before Christmas of that year, Aer Lingus significantly reduced the transatlantic travel time for Irish aircraft when it added three Boeing 720 jets to its fleet, for use on the New York service and a new route to Boston. Ships were not yet entirely redundant. Air travel would remain a luxury in those early years. But as a psychological salve, it belonged to everyone.

On board that first Aer Linte flight in April 1958 there was a man who well understood the importance of boosting a nation's psyche. Seán Lemass, the Irish government's Minister for Industry and Commerce and a future taoiseach, would become synonymous in the years ahead with the building-up of a viable Irish economy – one that would offer increasing numbers of Irish citizens an alternative to emigration.

In 1958, Lemass – destined to make the cover of *TIME* magazine – and his fellow government leaders had some way to go before that alternative would become meaningfully apparent. But 1958 was the year that Ireland unfurled its 'Programme for Economic Expansion', a document intended to 'redefine the objectives of national economic policy'.

In the Ireland of the late 1950s, the idea of economic expansion was novel. Then again, so was flying the Atlantic in a plane with a shamrock painted on its fuselage. Change was, in every sense, in the air. And this was also the case in American politics. By 1958, Dwight Eisenhower was in the second year of his second term, and at the beginning of the year, he was having to deal with an economic recession. He was also having to contend with criticism from his predecessor, Harry S. Truman, who was not spending all his time on his front porch back in Missouri.

Eisenhower could manage Truman, but there were other rising voices to be taken notice of in Washington and beyond. One of those voices belonged to John Fitzgerald Kennedy.

CHAPTER 19

A Favorite Son Rises

Given their history, the Irish can take irony. To a degree. The election of John Fitzgerald Kennedy to the presidency of the United States was Irish America's equivalent of scaling Mount Everest. Kennedy's presidential portrait would hang on walls and sit on mantlepieces from Wexford to Washington State. It would, more often than not, be displayed alongside a picture of the pope, John XXIII or Paul VI. Kennedy was the living symbol of triumph – political, social, religious and tribal. And though he loved his own tribe, he would be a prime instrument behind many of its members being shut out of an America that was home to the largest component of the global Irish nation.

On moral grounds it would be hard, if not impossible, to take issue with the 35th President of the United States on the matter of immigration to America and America's immigration policies. Morality, however, is not the key to a job, or food on the table. Kennedy, of course, did not live to see the signing of the 1965 Immigration and Nationality Act. But his spirit was about Liberty Island in New York Harbor as President Lyndon Johnson wielded his signing pen. His brothers, Robert and Edward, were but a few feet from the president as the ink flowed.

The spirit of JFK, his clear and cogently argued views on the nature and future course of immigration, had been evident for some years before that signing day, most obviously in the pages of his monograph *A Nation of Immigrants*, which was first published in that standout year of 1958. Fifty years later, in an introduction to a new 'revised and enlarged' edition, Senator Edward Kennedy wrote that his brother Jack's words rang true as clearly in 2008 as they had in 1958. He opined:

no one spoke more eloquently about our history and heritage as a nation of immigrants or fought harder on behalf of fair and rational immigration laws than President Kennedy.

One of his last acts as president was to propose a major series of immigration reforms to end the ugly-race based national origins quota system, which had defined our admissions policy in that era.

As he told Congress in 1963: 'the enactment of this legislation will not resolve all of our important problems in the field of immigration law. It will, however, provide a sound basis upon which we can build in developing an immigration law that serves the national interest and reflects in every detail the principles of equality and human dignity to which our nation subscribes.'

In 2008, it was plainly evident to many, not least Teddy Kennedy, that what had passed into the nation's immigration law in 1965 had indeed failed to resolve all those important problems.

Five years previously, Senator Kennedy had described the state of those laws as a 'national scandal' and had compared the plight of millions of undocumented immigrants to that of slaves.

As he wrote his introduction in 2008, Teddy was still smarting from a legislative battle on Capitol Hill that had seen the crafting of the bipartisan McCain–Kennedy reform bill, the Secure America and Orderly Immigration Act, in the United States Senate, and its ultimate failure to secure a floor vote in that august but oft-capricious body. The immigration issues in the first decade of the 21st century seemed, at first glance, to be significantly different to those in the sixth decade of the twentieth. But they also carried in them a perennial double-barreled question: Who gets in to America, and how many?

Back in 1958, as he put his thoughts down on paper, Senator John Fitzgerald Kennedy was primarily focused on the 'who'. But to properly address this part of the immigration conundrum he had to present evidence based on the 'how many'. With the benefit of hindsight, it is evident that JFK was contemplating a run for the presidency at the time. As such, *A Nation of Immigrants* is really two works: a homage to America's immigrant heritage and just about every immigrant group that had ever reached the nation's shores, and a stinging critique of immigration policy rooted, for the most part, in the 1920s. Kennedy concluded that, because of the composition of the nation's population in 1920, the system was heavily weighted in favor of immigration from northern Europe and severely limited immigration from southern and eastern Europe, and other parts of the world. So wrote the future president:

> To cite some recent examples: Great Britain has an annual quota of 65,361 immigration visas and used 28,291 of them. Germany has a quota of 25,814 and used 26,533 (of this number, about one third are wives of servicemen who could enter on a nonquota basis). Ireland's quota is 17,756 and only 6,054 availed themselves of it. On the other hand, Poland is permitted 6,488 and there is a backlog of 61,293 Poles wishing to enter the United States. Italy is permitted 5,666 and has a backlog of 132,435. Greece's quota is 308; her backlog is 96,538. Thus a Greek citizen desiring to emigrate to this country has little chance of coming here. And an American citizen with a Greek father or mother must wait at least eighteen months to bring his parents here to join him. A citizen whose married son or daughter, or married brother or sister, is Italian cannot obtain a quota number for them for two years or more. Meanwhile, many thousands of quota numbers are wasted because they are not wanted or needed by nationals of the countries to which they are assigned.
>
> In short, a qualified person born in England or Ireland who wants to emigrate to the United States can do so at any time. A person born in Italy, Hungary, Poland or the Baltic States may have to wait many years before his turn is reached. This system is based upon the assumption that there is some reason for keeping the origins of our population in exactly the same proportions as they existed in 1920. Such an idea is at complete variance with the American traditions and principles that the qualifications of an immigrant do not depend on his country of birth, and violates the spirit expressed in the Declaration of Independence that 'all men are created equal.'

Later in the text, Kennedy would argue that the national origins quota system had strong overtones of an indefensible racial preference. It was, he wrote, strongly weighted toward 'so-called Anglo Saxons, a phrase which one writer calls a "term of art" encompassing almost anyone from northern and western Europe'.

While many Irish would have winced at being lumped in with Anglo Saxons, there was no escaping the geographic location of their home island. For the Irish, the writing was on the wall, or at least the written page. Either way, the future form for Irish immigration to America was being suggested by a senator who would be president in the near future. And that form would be nothing like the past.

For Senator Kennedy, 1958 was an election year. In the fall he retained his seat in what was, for Massachusetts, a record-breaking margin of victory. On January 2, 1960 he announced his candidacy for the presidency. Not a few immigrant Irish would immediately fall in behind the man who had Irish ancestry and was also a Catholic. Not a few, but by no means all.

Adrian Flannelly remembers critical views of Kennedy and critical words directed at him and his family:

> Many Irish born and Irish Americans were wary of JFK. His liberal agenda did not sit well. Most were conservative-leaning and did not consider the Kennedys as Irish Catholics. Irish immigrants and Irish Americans were split. They (Irish Americans) were less vocal in their criticism of JFK. Democratic politicians were ecstatic and wooed the Irish vote. Many Catholic Church leaders detested the Kennedys and wove their opposition into sermons.

The opposition of some among the Catholic clergy was ironic, of course, given that so many voters were aware of Kennedy's Catholicism before just about anything else and considered it a potential barrier between the young senator and the White House. But in other areas, the clergy's doubts about Kennedy were not too difficult to understand. JFK's rejection of federal monies for parochial schools on constitutional grounds would cost him votes. And his assertion, to *Look* magazine, that 'religion is personal, politics are public and the twain need never meet and conflict' sounded downright Protestant to many Catholic ears, clergy and ordinary faithful alike. And, of course, many Protestants voted for Kennedy, as did many Catholics, people of other faiths and of no faith.

Some Catholics undoubtedly voted for Kennedy as a means of banishing the dark memories of the Al Smith debacle in 1928. Many voted for Kennedy because of his Irishness, forgetting, perhaps, that though Kennedy's roots could be traced back to County Wexford, Richard Nixon's were partly traceable to County Antrim. Kennedy's immigrant tale was, however, more upfront than Nixon's, and the Massachusetts man had penned a book that praised immigrants even as it proposed a fundamental change in how they would be received into American society.

Ed Hagan recounts:

> My father was really over the moon about it. It really meant that the Irish had made it in America.
>
> But the odd thing was that Nixon did surprisingly well with substantial numbers of Irish Americans.
>
> I'm rather certain that my sister was a Nixon supporter as were my cousins in Marble Hill. Apparently Nixon did well in Irish neighborhoods in Queens. I would find it easy to believe. I was a freshman at Fordham Prep in 1960. I remember that a student straw poll was won by Nixon. It was close, but Nixon won. I'd say that about sixty per cent of the students were Irish American, many of them first generation. The other forty per cent were mostly Italian.
>
> I don't recollect immigration being an issue at all in the election.

The new president's views on US immigration law were not mentioned in the *Irish Echo*'s front page report on the Kennedy victory. The two-line banner headline on page one of the November 12, 1960 edition proclaimed, 'Senator Kennedy Is Winner; First Catholic in White House'. The report went on to inform readers, or perhaps merely remind them, that 'the Boston-born Senator, whose ancestors came from Ireland, is the first Catholic to have been elected as head of the United States Government'. The remainder of the report focused on the numbers behind the Kennedy–Johnson win. Interestingly, it was not the only story on that issue's front page. The *Echo* ran with its typical cover format of multiple stories; what was a pinnacle moment in the story of the Irish in America – a triumph over centuries of struggle for acceptance – shared that front page with nine other stories. None of them touched on immigration policy or the views of the president-elect on immigration law reform.

There was, however, a brief report on plans to light bonfires along the Wexford coast in the event of a Kennedy victory. Kennedy, for sure, was a beacon of hope to the people of Ireland, an articulate affirmation of the island's emigrant legacy. But if Kennedy was to have his way, many more in Ireland, who might not have expected it, would have to consider the man and his presidency from the Irish side of an ocean. But such considerations were down the road. Now was a time to celebrate, to savor an Irish triumph in America like no other.

CHAPTER 20

A Favorite Son Falls

Some look at President Kennedy's thousand days and see a form of immortality. But that's a feeling rooted in the heart. More consequential than any visceral or emotional sense of immortality is the existence of a material continuity.

When the mind is focused on President Kennedy's legacy, it doesn't see an end in Dallas but rather an uninterrupted passage into the presidency of Lyndon Johnson. And when it came to changing the nation's immigration laws, Johnson would be the executor of Kennedy's will.

That Kennedy included immigration in that will might have been a surprise to many Americans. In the fall of 1960, and before the presidential election, Kennedy and Richard Nixon engaged in four debates. Immigration didn't figure in any of them. As such, it can be safely assumed that not many people voted for Kennedy because of his proposals, as laid down in *A Nation of Immigrants*, to fundamentally change the nation's immigration laws. And it can be safely assumed that not many voted against the Massachusetts senator on the same basis.

It's fair to say that the American Irish would ultimately be blindsided by the Kennedy-inspired reforms, in significant part because they were blinded by the overwhelming phenomenon that was the Kennedy family story and all its mystique. Both reached a peak during the waning days of June 1963, when President Kennedy, after laying down his marker for the Soviets in Berlin, traveled to the land of his ancestors for what would be a homecoming the likes of which the Irish, on their island, had never seen.

Those few days in Ireland meant a lot to Kennedy, the first serving president to visit Ireland. He would say so there, and he would say so again upon his return to Washington. They also meant a lot to the people of Ireland. Here, in the person of the American president, was living proof that the story of Irish emigration wasn't, in its entirety, some dark, tragic tale with no silver lining. Kennedy, silver-tongued and the most powerful political leader on the planet, was that lining, proof that the end of an old Ireland had actually given birth to a new and grander version in America.

This would only reinforce the profound feelings of shock and sadness that would wrap itself around Ireland like some malevolent cloud after Dallas. But for those four days in June there was magic in the air – hope, love even. And Kennedy was skilled enough, careful enough, to stick to a script that would enhance these feelings. He would not give the Irish much of an inkling of his plans for the future flow of various Kennedys and other Irish to America's shores. Not in his speeches, at any rate, and there would be half-a-dozen set piece speeches during the visit.

There were, of course, references to Irish migration and what the Irish had contributed to America. On June 28, Kennedy referred to this in his speech to the assembled Dáil (Assembly) and Seanad (Senate) in Leinster House:

> And so it is that our two nations, divided by distance, have been united by history. No people ever believed more deeply in the cause of Irish freedom than the people of the United States.
>
> And no country contributed more to building my own than your sons and daughters. They came to our shores in a mixture of hope and agony, and I would not underrate the difficulties of their course once they arrived in the United States.
>
> They left behind hearts, fields, and a nation yearning to be free. It is no wonder that James Joyce described the Atlantic as a bowl of bitter tears. And an earlier poet wrote, 'They are going, going, going, and we cannot bid them stay.'

But today this is no longer the country of hunger and famine that those emigrants left behind. It is not rich, and its progress is not yet complete; but it is, according to statistics, one of the best fed countries in the world. Nor is it any longer a country of persecution, political or religious. It is a free country, and that is why any American feels at home.

This address, according to journalist and historian Tim Pat Coogan, was one of the best of Kennedy's presidency, it being 'emotionally charged, pitch-perfect and replete with Irish references and Irish influences'. The Irish speeches to follow were also emotionally charged and perfectly attuned. In Cork, he said, 'Most countries send out oil, iron, steel or gold, some others crops, but Ireland has only one export and that is people.'

In Galway, he inquired:

> I wonder if you could perhaps let me know how many of you here have a relative in America, who you would admit to – if you would hold up your hand? I don't know what it is about you that causes me to think that nearly everybody in Boston comes from Galway. They are not shy about it, at all.
>
> I want to express – as we are about to leave here – to you of this country how much this visit has meant. It is strange that so many years could pass and so many generations pass and still some of us who came on this trip could come home and, here to Ireland, and feel ourselves at home and not feel ourselves in a strange country, but feel ourselves among neighbors, even though we are separated by generations, by time, and by thousands of miles.

In New Ross, the Kennedy family hometown, he stated:

> I am glad to be here. It took 115 years to make this trip, and 6,000 miles, and three generations. But I am proud to be here and I appreciate the warm welcome you have given to all of us. When my great grandfather left here to become a cooper

in East Boston, he carried nothing with him except two things: a strong religious faith and a strong desire for liberty. I am glad to say that all of his great grandchildren have valued that inheritance.

And in Wexford town, he had the following words:

I want to express my pleasure at being back from whence I came. There is an impression in Washington that there are no Kennedys left in Ireland, that they are all in Washington, so I wonder if there are any Kennedys in this audience. Could you hold up your hand so I can see?

Well, I am glad to see a few cousins who didn't catch the boat.

And I am proud to come here for another reason, because it makes me even prouder of my own country. My country welcomed so many sons and daughters of so many countries, Irish and Scandinavian, Germans, Italian, and all the rest, and gave them a fair chance and a fair opportunity. The Speaker of the House of Representatives is of Irish descent. The leader of the Senate is of Irish descent. And what is true of the Irish has been true of dozens of other people. In Ireland I think you see something of what is so great about the United States; and I must say that in the United States, through millions of your sons and daughters and cousins – 25 million, in fact – you see something of what is great about Ireland.

In Kennedy's hands, the story of Irish emigration or immigration was portrayed in a mostly positive sense – he being the embodiment of it. And this reflected the praise he had heaped upon the people of his ancestral land in *A Nation of Immigrants*.

For anyone who heard Kennedy speak, live at one of the public events, on radio, or by means of the still-young Irish national television service, RTÉ, there were hints and suggestions, invitations almost. Come to America, and if not you, your descendants.

A bare five months after Kennedy's triumphal homecoming, his life was ended in Dealey Plaza. The Irish of America, Ireland and the world over were in mourning. JFK was gone but his vision of an America that embraced immigrants from a wider array of nations, Ireland yet among them, would live on and be guided to legality by his brothers and his successor in the White House.

CHAPTER 21

The Torch is Passed

On just about every level, John Fitzgerald Kennedy and Lyndon Baines Johnson were as different as, well, Massachusetts and Texas. But it would be left to the latter to copper-fasten the legislative legacy of the former – or what JFK's legacy would have been had he lived to run for, and win, a second term.

On immigration, though, Johnson had to pay heed to living Kennedys, Robert and Teddy, the slain president's senator brothers and guardians of all that never was but, in their eyes, should have been. And when it came to immigration reform the brothers had a plan to draw upon.

Less than a month after his return from Ireland, and the delivery there of a promise to return in the springtime, JFK conveyed his proposals for the reform of the nation's immigration laws to a receptive Congress. On July 23, 1963 his message to the House and Senate stated by way of introduction:

> I am transmitting, for the consideration of the Congress, legislation revising and modernizing our immigration laws. More than a decade has elapsed since the last substantial amendment to these laws. I believe there exists a compelling need for the Congress to reexamine and make certain changes in these laws.
>
> The most urgent and fundamental reform I am recommending relates to the national origins system of selecting immigrants. Since 1924 it has been used to determine the number of quota immigrants permitted to enter the United States each year. Accordingly, although the legislation I am

transmitting deals with many problems which require remedial action, it concentrates attention primarily upon revision of our quota immigration system.

The enactment of this legislation will not resolve all of our important problems in the field of immigration law. It will, however, provide a sound basis upon which we can build in developing an immigration law that serves the national interest and reflects in every detail the principles of equality and human dignity to which our nation subscribes.

The president then outlined his proposal 'in detail', and in doing so drew on his analysis and assertions in *A Nation of Immigrants*. He concluded:

As I have already indicated, the measures I have outlined will not solve all the problems of immigration. Many of them will require additional legislation; some cannot be solved by any one country. But the legislation I am submitting will insure that progress will continue to be made towards our ideals and towards the realization of humanitarian objectives.

The measures I have recommended will help eliminate discrimination between peoples and nations on a basis that is unrelated to any contributions that immigrants can make and is inconsistent with our traditions of welcome. Our investment in new Citizens has always been a valuable source of our strength.

JFK portrayed his proposal as a wider opening of the American door that would make entry possible to people from a great number of countries.

To assuage fears that a country might find itself shut out, he proposed that existing quotas be reduced gradually and that natives of no one country receive over 10 per cent of the total quota numbers authorized in any one year. This was balm in the event of waters becoming troubled. The president's words and ideas latched on to a prevailing mood in Congress. As such, they didn't prompt much of anything in the way of argument, so there was little or no pushback from public opinion. And there was no pushback from the Irish, or the Irish government.

Four months after JFK charmed his ancestral nation, Taoiseach Seán Lemass made a reciprocal visit to the United States. Not surprisingly, Lemass was given the red carpet treatment, including a motorcade through the streets of Washington, DC. This was another high point in the relationship between two republics – one, the greatest power on earth; the other, a contributor to this greatness over the course of several centuries.

The contributor, however, was beginning to power up a bit, as exemplified by a profile of Lemass in *TIME* just days after JFK's triumphant Irish homecoming. Lemass adorned the cover of the July 12, 1963 issue of the famous news magazine along with, perhaps inevitably, an image of a leprechaun pulling back a shamrock-decorated curtain to reveal an industrial vista that was more Soviet in its muscularity than Irish. Nevertheless, the message was clear, and it was made clearer still by the headline: 'New Spirit in the Ould Sod'.

And indeed there was a new spirit. And there were aspirations, ambitions and plans, all of them needing people for fulfillment – people at home in Ireland and elsewhere, such as, well, JFK's Massachusetts. JFK was impressed and made that plain when writing to Lemass a few days after the *TIME* profile, 'Mrs. Kennedy and I look forward with great pleasure to your return visit here at your convenience, especially now that *TIME* has made you properly famous in this country.' Lemass would find October to be convenient. And he would be treated as a properly famous leader in Washington, Chicago, Philadelphia, New York and Boston.

Ryan Tubridy, in his book on Kennedy's Irish visit, *JFK in Ireland, Four days That Changed a President*, would sum the Lemass visit up as follows:

> As he was leaving the United States there was a sense that the Irish-American story was entering a new phase and that Ireland had cemented their own 'special relationship' with that powerful nation. As he sat in his plane on the runway at Washington airport, Lemass dictated a telegram to be sent

to the White House that read: 'I share your conviction that we do good work together and have demonstrated once more the close and enduring ties and real understanding that exists between our countries.'

Within thirty-two days, the President to whom he was writing would be dead.

Ireland, historically so used to premature death, and all too well practiced in the traditions of mourning, would treat the assassination of the American president as its very own national tragedy – the collective, profound sorrow heightened all the more by the still-vivid memories of the president's June visit. Tubridy writes:

> It was early evening when the first reports came through on the radio and television stations in Ireland. Other programmes were suspended as commentators talked endlessly about the president's recent visit, watched the tragic pictures of Jackie Kennedy, utterly shocked and still wearing her blood-stained suit, and covered the news that Lyndon B. Johnson had been sworn in as President on board Air Force One. According to the Irish Press, 'Cinemas, theatres and all places of entertainment rapidly emptied as the chilling facts of his death spread like wildfire among an unbelieving and bewildered populace. The rain-washed streets of Dublin were filled with hurrying people who made their way to the Pro-Cathedral and other churches to pray.'

President Éamon de Valera also spoke of Kennedy's recent visit, during which the Irish people 'came to regard the President as one of ourselves'. In a radio broadcast, he said:

> We were proud of him as being of our race and we were convinced that through his fearless leadership the United States would continue increasing its stature amongst the nations of the world and its power to maintain world peace. Our consolation is that he died in a noble cause, and we pray that God will give the United States another such leader.

Whatever about God, the US Constitution had given Lyndon Johnson, a man from Texas, a profound role in shaping the course of life for an unknown number of men and women from Tipperary, Tyrone and the rest of Ireland's counties. Johnson would do so by implementing the vision of his slain predecessor with regard to the rules of admittance to the land of the free and home of the brave. Adrian Flannelly recalls:

> After JFK visited Ireland in 1963, the word was about that de Valera had complained that the US was creating a brain-drain. Few believed that the impending change in immigration laws would affect the Irish. There were naive hopes that we were a superior breed with strong political connections and strong work ethic, and that these would garner an exception for us.

This would not turn out to be the case, but that impending change in immigration law would be delayed as a direct result of the passing of its main crafter and sponsor. Lyndon Johnson, suddenly and shockingly the president, had a lot of things on his immediate plate. In fact, as with only a minority of his predecessors, Johnson was having to deal with multiple plates. Immigration reform would have to wait a while.

CHAPTER 22

Paddy Goes Marching Away

Nobody would have begrudged Lyndon Johnson a few days to take stock. But of course that was not to be. In his first year of unexpected office, he would sign the Civil Rights Act and a range of measures under the heading of anti-poverty legislation; he would also be forced, more and more, to ponder Vietnam – a bequeathed quandary, if not quite yet a quagmire. And he would have to run for election. Which he did, and very successfully, with his vice presidential partner Hubert Humphrey. The November 3, 1964 election would give the Johnson ticket and the Democrats much to celebrate. Less than a year after JFK's assassination, the party had a lock on the White House and both houses of Congress.

From an Irish-American perspective, it didn't appear, based on the electoral outcomes, that there would be reason to expect any significant change in status or growth. After all, during his Wexford visit President Kennedy had made the point that the Speaker of the House of Representatives, John McCormack, was of Irish descent, while the leader of the Senate, Carl Hayden, was also Irish rooted. After the elections, both men remained *in situ*, and they were surrounded by House and Senate members, from both parties, with Irish roots – one of them being Senator Edward Kennedy, who had been elected for his first full six-year term in that November Democratic landslide.

The debate will forever linger with regard to JFK and Vietnam. If Lyndon Johnson was taking up where his predecessor had been stopped cold with regard to immigration, there is, perhaps, an argument that Johnson also carried forward Kennedy's standard with regard to the conflict in Southeast Asia. The argument can never be resolved conclusively, but what is beyond dispute is that the Irish of America, as was the case in all previous wars, took up America's cause in a prolonged conflict that would bring tragedy to the doors of all too many homes of every ethnic stripe and race, and on both sides of the Pacific.

The Irish were quickly in the fray. On December 5, 1964, President Johnson, himself the bearer of a Silver Star for gallantry, awarded the first Congressional Medal of Honor for a war in a place most Americans had yet barely heard of. The winner was an Irish American named Captain Roger Donlon, an upstate New Yorker and member of the US Army Special Forces. There would be other Irish American winners of the highest military award for gallantry; New Yorker Robert Emmett O'Malley was the first US Marine to be awarded the Medal of Honor, for his actions in the field in August 1965.

There would be many Irish and Irish American casualties too, despite the fact that the US forces that fought in Southeast Asia would be the most diverse in the nation's history. It is one of those numerical coincidences: in the Korean conflict, twenty-nine Irish-born members of the US armed forces gave their lives. In Vietnam, the number was only slightly lower at twenty-four, and that total included a woman, Second Lieutenant Dorothy Donovan of the US Army Nurse Corps. In his book, *Vietnam: The Irish Experience*, author James Durney additionally pays tribute to the Irish-born who served with Air America, USAID and the Australian contingent in Vietnam; he also writes of a sergeant in the Royal Canadian Army Service Crops, James Sylvester Byrne, whose plane was lost over Laos in October 1965. Added up, the number of Irish-born who gave their lives in Southeast Asia comes to twenty-nine, a precise match for Korea.

Against the backdrop of the appalling vista that was Vietnam, Cambodia and Laos, these numbers don't especially stand out. But they would be a subset of a bigger number: that of the Irish Americans who fought and lived, fought and died; that of the Irish who fought and lived throughout America's history, fought and died throughout it. The Irish are nothing if not sensitive when it comes to their contribution to the building and defense of the United States.

Putting numbers on the contribution settles arguments. Somewhere between two and three thousand Irish-born served in various capacities during the decade that the United States was most heavily involved in Vietnam. Mike Flood, from County Kildare, was one of them.

Flood had an early inkling of his future American life when he applied for a visa in the waning days of 1963. As part of his deal with America, he would have to sign on to the military draft. He set foot on American soil in January 1964 and, like so many before him, headed for the Bronx. As Flood recalls, at the time of his transatlantic journey, the immigration laws were not especially strict. The only requirements were that the would-be immigrant had to have a sponsor in the US, was required to go through an interview process, and, if male, had to register for the draft within six months. At the time, Flood's sister was already in the United States and acted as his sponsor. She also helped him prepare for his interview in Dublin. The questions that he was asked during the interview process were, in his view, very basic: reasons for going over, plans for work and so forth.

Once in the US, Flood registered for the draft by bringing his green card to the local post office. This was also how a male immigrant would renew his green card each year in January. All would change, however, and within a short period of time. When Flood's future wife Anne was attempting to join him in America, the requirements had become stricter. Flood remembers, 'You were required to have a job already secured before they would issue you a green card.' Coming up with a childcare job for Anne in the Bronx wasn't too high a fence to jump. The couple then returned to Ireland voluntarily in order to get married at their local parish. Flood recalls, 'The challenges that Anne went through attempting to get her green card made me aware that the laws were changing and becoming stricter.'

When he returned from Vietnam, those stricter immigration laws were becoming even more noticeable, 'This could especially be seen in regards to Gaelic games. It was becoming much harder to get footballers and hurlers out (from Ireland) to play. The older generation of Irish immigrants were dying out, or at least reaching those years beyond their playing days.'

Mike Flood came home to a changing America. But he came home. Patrick Gallagher did not. Like Flood, Gallagher was an immigrant from Ireland – in his case, County Mayo – and he found himself in Vietnam. Known as 'Bob', Gallagher was the second eldest of nine children born to Mary and Peter Gallagher. They lived at Derrintogher, three miles from Ballyhaunis in County Mayo.

When he was 18 years old, Patrick went to his aunt's on Long Island and began his new life in America. In 1966, he was drafted and joined the US Marines. In April of that year, Gallagher shipped out to Vietnam with Hotel Company, 2/4 Marines, 3rd Marine Division as an ammunition carrier. In July 1966, while other members of his unit slept, Gallagher's unit was attacked at Cam Lo, not far from the border with North Vietnam. The attackers threw grenades. Gallagher kicked a grenade away before it exploded and, as the citation for the Navy Cross he was later awarded read, 'another enemy grenade followed and landed in the position between two of his comrades. Without hesitation, in a valiant act of self-sacrifice, Corporal Gallagher threw himself upon the deadly grenade in order to absorb the explosion and save the lives of his comrades.'

As the three other marines ran to safety, two further grenades landed in the position and exploded, 'miraculously injuring nobody'. Another miracle was that the grenade under Gallagher had not exploded. His squad leader ordered him to throw the grenade into a nearby river. It blew up on hitting the water.

'It is a pleasure to pin this on your breast', said General William Westmoreland at the later presentation of the Navy Cross to the Mayo Marine. Gallagher's luck was to run out, however. He was shot dead while on Patrol in Da Nang on March 30, 1967. He was within a few days of shipping out of Vietnam and back to his adopted American home.

A look at the names of United States Navy ships down the years reveals many Irish names on hulls. Some of the names are those of Irish immigrants – most notably that of Commodore John Barry, the Wexford man recognized as the de facto father of the Navy (along with Rear Admiral John Paul Jones) and its first flag officer. Other fighting ships named after Irish immigrants include the USS *John*

King, named after another Mayo native who won two Congressional Medals of Honor after enlisting during the Spanish-American War.

The USS *Laffey* bore the name of another Irish immigrant Medal of Honor winner, Bartlett Laffey, from County Galway, who won his medal as a seaman in the United States Navy during the Civil War. There would be two ships named USS *Laffey*, the second being named after the first sank during the Second World War battle of Guadalcanal. The USS *Morrison* would be named after immigrant John Gordon Morrison, who won his Medal of Honor while serving aboard the gunboat USS *Carondelet* in July 1862.

That Patrick 'Bob' Gallagher would have a ship does not stand out as being unusual against the backdrop of so many US ships bearing the names of Irish Americans and their immigrant cousins. Not unusual, but a tad ironic. The future existence of the USS *Patrick Gallagher* was announced in the spring of 2018. In any of the four seasons of that year, a Patrick Gallagher from Mayo or any other Irish county would find it virtually impossible to legally land in America – never mind sign up for a branch of the US military as Patrick Gallagher did in November 1965, a mere month after that year's game-changing immigration act was signed into law on Ellis Island. There will be future navy ships named after Irish Americans. But will the USS *Patrick Gallagher* be the last named after an Irish immigrant? A fair question.

The Irish-born who died in the Vietnam conflict gave their lives between February 1966 and November 1970. Their names can be found on the panels of the Vietnam memorial in Washington, DC. In their time in Vietnam, they would have experienced an extraordinary array of sights and sounds, the full range of what only a full scale mid-twentieth century war could inflict upon the human senses.

What they did not hear was a sound from far away – one that would have profound implications for their fellow Irish and the story of Irish service in the armed forces of the United States. That was the sound of America's door being closed to their kith and kin.

CHAPTER 23

Aliens Ahoy!

A few days after Pat Nee, from South Boston (and before that Connemara), had splashed ashore with his Marine unit in South Vietnam, the *New York Times* reported under the headline 'Johnson Pushing For Aliens Law' that 'a new immigration law, stripped of the national origins quota system that liberals and foreign nationality groups have fought for a generation, appears now to have a reasonable prospect of being enacted during the current session of Congress'. The report stated that President Johnson had proposed the legislation the previous January. He had done so on January 13, 1965 with a message to Congress headlined: 'Correcting the Deficiencies'. In his message, Johnson might as well have been JFK. He stated:

> A change is needed in our laws dealing with immigration. Four Presidents have called attention to serious defects in this legislation. Action is long overdue.
>
> I am therefore submitting, at the outset of this Congress, a bill designed to correct the deficiencies. I urge that it be accorded priority consideration.
>
> The principal reform called for is the elimination of the national origins quota system.
>
> That system is incompatible with our basic American tradition.
>
> Over the years the ancestors of all of us – some 42 million human beings – have migrated to these shores. The fundamental, longtime American attitude has been to ask not where a person comes from but what are his personal qualities.

Violation of this tradition by the national origins quota system does incalculable harm. The procedures imply that men and women from some countries are, just because of where they come from, more desirable citizens than others.

The quota system has other grave defects. Too often it arbitrarily denies us immigrants who have outstanding and sorely needed talents and skills. I do not believe this is either good government or good sense.

Thousands of our citizens are needlessly separated from their parents or other close relatives.

To replace the quota system, the proposed bill relies on a technique of preferential admissions based upon the advantage to our nation of the skills of the immigrant, and the existence of a close family relationship between the immigrant and people who are already citizens or permanent residents of the United States.

Transition to the new system would be gradual, over a five-year period. Thus the possibility of abrupt changes in the pattern of immigration from any nation is eliminated. In addition, the bill would provide that as a general rule no country could be allocated more than ten per cent of the quota numbers available in any one year.

The total number of immigrants would not be substantially changed. Under this bill, authorized quota immigration, which now amounts to 158,361 per year, would be increased by less than 7,000.

I urge the Congress to return the United States to an immigration policy which both serves the national interest and continues our traditional ideals. No move could more effectively reaffirm our fundamental belief that a man is to be judged – and judged exclusively – on his worth as a human being.

Johnson had asked that the immigration measure be given high priority by Congress. Not high enough, the May 23 report in the *New York Times* was to indicate. More recently, within two weeks of the report, the *Times* reported how Johnson 'has turned the heat up another notch on his Congressional leaders. He has told them, according to reliable authority, that early enactment of such a bill would help to mitigate the unfavorable impression of this country in South Vietnam and in the Dominican Republic.'

The potentially negative headlines coming out of the Dominican Republic were made possible by a US military intervention to prevent a leftist government securing power after years of Rafael Trujillo and subsequent military dictatorships. Alarmed at the possibility of a Communist Dominican Republic on the lines of Cuba, President Johnson sent in the Marines and the 82nd Airborne Division, proclaiming that the US would not 'sit here in a rocking chair with our hands folded' while letting communists set up a government in the Western Hemisphere.

So all was not about immigration reform for its own sake. Vietnam and the Dominican Republic were spurs to action as far as the commander in chief was concerned. Reform would serve as much as a distraction from those conflicts as it would be a positive end in itself.

Johnson was a hard-nosed politician; one of the most, if not the most, capable of his generation. As such, he would view a piece of legislation not just for its own sake but also in the context of how it might help him in other legislative areas. So if success on immigration could draw attention away from potentially unpopular military action, so much the better.

Immigration reform, however, was far from being Johnson's top legislative action in 1965, as illustrated in a series of interviews with his primary biographer, Robert Caro. The interviews were conducted by the *New York Times*, *Paris Review* and *New York Review of Books* at a point when Caro had published four biographical works on Johnson and was working on his fifth and final volume. Immigration is mentioned in just one of the interviews. In the *New York Times* interview:

> Caro said he is now finishing a section of the book in which, in an 'incredible burst,' in 1965, Johnson oversaw passage of the Voting Rights Act, Medicare, Medicaid and more than a dozen separate education bills. Mr Caro called it a formative

moment of just a few months, during which Johnson 'rams through so much of what's made America what it is today.'

The *Paris Review* states:

> Since 1976, Robert Caro has devoted himself to *The Years of Lyndon Johnson*, a landmark study of the thirty-sixth president of the United States. The fifth and final volume, now underway, will presumably cover the 1964 election, the passage of the Voting Rights Act and the launch of the Great Society, the deepening of America's involvement in Vietnam, the unrest in the cities and on college campuses, Johnson's decision not to seek reelection, and his retirement and death.

In the *New York Review of Books*, Caro has the following words:

> Right. So I'm past the moment when Johnson has beaten Goldwater. Between January and July of 1965, he's passed the Voting Rights Act, Medicare, Medicaid, Head Start, twelve different education bills, a liberalized immigration law and much of the War on Poverty. What he's done is a great drama of legislative genius, almost without precedent ... And at the same time that he was passing this legislation, he was secretly planning to escalate the Vietnam War.
>
> It's fascinating. I don't know if I can write it well enough. But it's almost unbelievable. You can see these great ambitions, which Johnson is on the way to realizing, get swallowed up by Vietnam. You can follow it almost minute by minute.

Based on Caro's view, and his would be preeminent, it is arguable that the immigration act was going to be passed in 1965 or not at all. Historian Joshua Zeitz has written at length about the three-year debate in Congress leading up to the bill's passage. He has stated:

> During the long, three-year debate over the immigration act of 1965, members of Congress debated the wisdom and morality of removing 1920s-era quotas on immigration to the

United States. Not far from the center of this debate was the nettlesome issue of race.

'The people of Ethiopia have the same right to come to the United States under this bill as the people from England, the people of France, the people of Germany, [and] the people of Holland,' griped Senator Sam Ervin, a conservative Democrat from North Carolina. 'With all due respect to Ethiopia, I don't know of any contributions that Ethiopia has made to the making of America.'

Zeitz contends:

President Lyndon Johnson, hoping to tamp down concerns about the immigration act at a time when Congress was engaged in an even more ferocious debate over the voting rights act, sought to downplay the implications of the proposed immigration law: 'This bill that we will sign today is not a revolutionary bill,' he said upon signing it. The president, like many other of the law's supporters, sincerely believed that Europeans were most likely to take advantage of less stringent US immigration policy.

He was wrong.

Zeitz states that the Hart–Celler Act, 'so-called after its co-sponsors New York Congressman Emanuel Celler and Michigan Senator Philip Hart, opened the floodgates to new immigrants when it went into effect in 1968. But the vast majority of them didn't come from Europe; they came instead from Latin America, Africa and Asia.'

The Hart–Celler bill of 1965, he believes, turned out to be 'not only revolutionary, but perhaps also the most revolutionary act of the 1960s'. The new law favored newcomers with specialized skills and education, and those with existing family relationships with American citizens or residents; it also substituted the national origins standard with annual hemispheric limits: 170,000 immigrants from the Eastern hemisphere; 120,000 from the Western hemisphere. It was a breakdown that reflected lingering bias toward Europe. (This provision was later eliminated and replaced with a simple annual cap of 290,000 immigrants.) Critically, the bill exempted all immigrants with immediate family members in the United States from these caps.

Support and opposition to the bill fell along the same lines as civil rights legislation that Johnson signed into law in 1964: Southern Democrats and conservative Midwestern Republicans tended to oppose it strenuously; Northern Democrats and moderate Republicans embraced it. In signing the law, Johnson affirmed that the national origins standard violated 'the basic principle of American democracy – the principle that values and rewards each man on the basis of his merit as a man'.

Critically, states Zeitz, while the bill's champions, including Johnson and Celler, were committed to ethnic and racial pluralism, they anticipated that most of its beneficiaries would hail from Europe. He continues:

> But the story played out differently. As Europe's economy finally emerged from the ashes of World War II, fewer residents of Ireland, Italy or Germany moved to the United States, while those residing in the Soviet bloc found it all but impossible to try.
>
> Because of the family exemption, the 1965 act had vast, unintended consequences: Larger numbers of immigrants than expected established roots in the United States legally, and those who did so created a much more diverse population.

So, the 1965 Immigration and Nationality Act was a distraction from Vietnam and not a piece of legislation held up to the highest moral scrutiny, because, well, it wouldn't result in much change to the nature of immigration anyway. Perhaps it is no surprise that the act's unintended consequences were so totally unforeseen at the time. Certainly, in the months before congressional approval and presidential signing, it seemed to be a relatively unremarkable measure – so much so that it was never going to exert a gravitational pull on all those headlines away from something long-dreaded by America's leaders, JFK included: a major land war in Asia.

President Johnson found himself in something of a bind then: play the bill up to distract from Vietnam; play the bill down to secure its passage. But if there was an effort to play down perceived negatives in the immigration bill, there was also much support and positive force behind it. The *New York Times* report of May 23 pointed to proponents of immigration reform being encouraged by 'the persistent interest' of President Johnson and the 'wide spectrum' of bipartisan support that the proposal appeared to have garnered in both chambers of Congress. The report stated:

> The Senate bill, for example, introduced by Senator Phillip A. Hart, Democrat of Michigan, has 33 co-sponsors, including a number of Republicans.
>
> Another factor of significance, according to supporters, is the softening attitude of some groups that have steadfastly resisted changes in the existing laws. As an illustration, they point to the testimony of Daniel J. O'Connor, chairman of the American Legion, before the House Judiciary subcommittee last Wednesday.
>
> Mr O'Connor said that the Legion 'has re-examined its position with painstaking thoroughness.' While it is not ready to abandon certain basic principles in respect to immigration, it is prepared, he said, to consider alternative means to satisfy them.

O'Connor, the report stated, said that the American Legion was not unaware of the strength and direction of the current political winds, 'We have also had it dramatically demonstrated to us that over the past decade the national origins quota system has not worked in practice as in theory.'

The *Times* told its readers that the bill submitted to Congress by President Johnson would use a 'complicated formula' to abolish, over a five-year period, the forty-year-old system of allotting immigrant quotas annually on the basis of each country's representation in the population during the year 1920.

Critics, the report continued, had long argued that the system tended to favor the Western European countries at the expense of other regions, particularly the Far East:

Under the proposed legislation, quotas would be eliminated at the rate of 29 per cent a year for five years, the quota numbers going into a general pool. Ultimately, visas would be issued against this pool on a preferential basis involving, among other things, work and intellectual skills and the presence of family members already in the United States.

The bill would increase the total number of immigrants a year from approximately 300,000 to 350,000. It would retain, according to its sponsors, most of the present safeguards against the admission of undesirables, such as Communists and mental defectives.

The *Times* report noted that hearings before the Senate Judiciary Subcommittee had been suspended late the previous March to make way for the 'higher priority' voting rights bill. Hearings would be resumed June 2 and would run for possibly two weeks, primarily to give opponents of the measure a chance to be heard. 'The chairman of the subcommittee is Senator Edward M. Kennedy, Democrat of Massachusetts.'

CHAPTER 24

All Aboard!

As the summer of 1965 rolled into the fall, not everyone in Congress was singing off the same hymn sheet when it came to immigration reform. But reform backers were singing more loudly and their pitch was resonating with a public that was increasingly distracted by other matters, not least Vietnam.

From his seat in the Senate Judiciary Subcommittee, Ted Kennedy was proving to be an able choirmaster. He would later describe his early days on the committee in an interview in the Miller Institute at the University of Virginia:

> When I arrived in the Senate, I was appointed to the Judiciary Committee and the Labor Committee. We're all appointed to what they call two 'A committees.' The Judiciary Committee was chaired by Jim Eastland and he asked me, as the only new member on that Judiciary Committee, to think about what subcommittees I wanted. He said for me to come to see him the first part of the following week. So I thought long and hard and talked to different friends about the committees.
>
> The subcommittee I was very much interested in was the immigration subcommittee, which was a rather sleepy subcommittee, but it seemed to me that this offered an opportunity to be even more involved and engaged in the immigration issue. Its focus was immigration and refugees. It was the least desirable of the subcommittees because of both the subject matter generally and it had the smallest budget. I think it had a budget of $100,000 or so. You got only one staffer if you took that assignment. If you got one of the other

committees, like administrative practice or another one, if you got to be chairman of it, you got additional kinds of resources. We didn't have many staff people at that time, so there was always a lot of jockeying around to see who could try to get ahead in that field.

The subcommittee might have been sleepy but it was required to be wide awake while steering the president's immigration bill through the committee process and into the wider area of the full Senate chamber. This chamber could be hostile, but the bill had many backers who were ready to talk it up at various pre-vote congressional hearings. One of those backers was Ted Kennedy's brother, Senator Robert Kennedy of New York. Robert took the favored line that the bill was not going to change the nature of America in a fundamental way. He said:

> Out of deference to the critics, I want to comment on what the bill will not do. First, our cities will not be flooded with a million immigrants annually. Under the proposed bill, the present level of immigration remains substantially the same. Secondly, the ethnic mix of this country will not be upset. Contrary to the charges in some quarters, S.500 will not inundate America with immigrants from any one country or area, or the most populated and economically deprived nations of Africa and Asia.
>
> In the final analysis, the ethnic pattern of immigration under the proposed measure is not expected to change as sharply as the critics seem to think. Thirdly, the bill will not permit the entry of subversive persons, criminals, illiterates, or those with contagious disease or serious mental illness. As I noted a moment ago, no immigrant visa will be issued to a person who is likely to become a public charge. The charges I have mentioned are highly emotional, irrational, and with little foundation in fact. They are out of line with the obligations of responsible citizenship. They breed hate of our heritage.

Senator Philip Hart of Michigan, a Democrat like the Kennedys and a prime sponsor of the bill, took up a similar refrain:

In fact the distribution of limited quota immigration can have no significant effect on the ethnic balance of the United States. Total quota immigration is now 156,782; under the proposed bill, it would rise to 164,482. Even if all these immigrants came from Italy, for example, the net effect would be to increase the number of Italo-Americans by one-tenth of 1 per cent of our population this year, and less as our population increases. Americans of Italian extraction now constitute about 4 per cent of our population; at this rate, considering our own natural increase, it would take until the year 2000 to increase that proportion to 6 per cent.

Of course, S.500 would make no such radical change. Immigration from any single country would be limited to 10 per cent of the total – 16,500 – with the possible exception of the two countries now sending more than that number, Great Britain and Germany. But the extreme case should set to rest any fears that this bill will change the ethnic, political, or economic makeup of the United States. We bar immigration by those individuals who would compete for jobs for which the supply of labor is adequate for the demand. We bar immigration by individuals who have demonstrated that they do not hold such allegiance to our fundamental precepts of political freedom and democratic government. If it is true that those from northern Europe, as individuals, can make greater contributions to this country than can others, then this legislation will bring them here. If the legislation does not bring them here, then the assumptions on which defenders of the present system rely are wholly false. S.500 will facilitate the entry of skilled specialists. The level of immigration now proposed is far less than that thought 'assimilable' by the most restrictionist Congress (1924) in our history. As far as the quota system, it (S.500) increases it about 9,000 and as far as a practical matter, it increases it about 50,000. It is not a large number.

The support for the bill wasn't only to be found in the ranks of Democrats. Senator Hugh Scott, a Pennsylvania Republican, had the following to say:

the people who have built up America, Anglo-Saxons, and the northern peoples of Europe, are not discriminated against in this bill. The people from that part of the world (the Asia-Pacific Triangle) probably will never reach 1 per cent of the (US) population. Our cultural pattern will never be changed as far as America is concerned. It will become more cosmopolitan but still there is that fundamental adherence to European culture. We feel those people (from northern Europe) who have been preferred in former immigration bills would still be treated fairly. One of the reasons why the United States was attacked, on December 7, 1941, was because of these exclusionary laws (the 1924 Immigration Act) which had fomented so much bad feeling between the peoples of Japan and the United States.

Speaking of Pearl Harbor, Republican Senator Hiram Fong of Hawaii had the following take on S.500, 'the notion was created that somehow or another, 190 million (the population of the US in 1965) is going to be swallowed up. None of us would want that, this bill does not seek to do it and the bill could not do it.'

Senator Claiborne Pell, a Rhode Island Republican, thought that the reform was still a sufficient defense against what he would view as the wrong kind of immigrants:

With the exception of the provisions relating to epilepsy and certain mental conditions this legislation does not alter the qualitative standards for immigration which prevent the entry of those whom we can, in justice and in logic, exclude. It preserves our national security and our domestic welfare; it continues to exclude subversives; it retains the provisions of existing law which makes aliens who become public charges deportable.

His colleague in the Republican Party (GOP), Senator Thomas H. Kuchel from California, was also assured, or at least seeking to reassure himself, 'S.500 does not open the gates to all aliens applying for immigration. Any bar to true assimilation is ours, not theirs. It is how we welcome to our country, not how much they (immigrants) want to be welcomed.'

Over in the House of Representatives, there was a matching chorus. When President Kennedy made his pitch in July of 1963, Congressman Emmanuel Celler of New York, chairman of the House Judiciary Committee, opined, 'It is my considered opinion that the President's bill offers a broad and firm basis for a long overdue revision of our policies and practices in this most important area of domestic and foreign relations.' Representative William Ryan, a fellow Democrat and New Yorker, said he believed that President Kennedy's proposals represented 'a giant step forward in the creation of a sensible and humane immigration policy'.

Two years later, though under a new president, Representative Celler was the House sponsor of the reform push, an effort that was being backed by prominent members of President Johnson's cabinet such as Attorney General Nicholas Katzenbach:

> I do not think it (S.500) amounts to a serious increase in the number of persons admitted. I have read the statements of the Malthusian pessimists, and they may be right, of course, but I doubt if this bill will really be the cause of crowding the present Americans out of the 50 states. I do not believe an increase of 66,000 opens the door wide.

Secretary of State Dean Rusk had the following words on the subject of the bill:

> This bill is not designed to increase or accelerate the number of newcomers permitted to come to America. This bill would retain all the present security and health safeguards of the present law. The overall effect of this bill on employment would, first of all, be negligible, and second, that such effect as might be felt would not be harmful, but beneficial. The actual net increase in total immigration under this bill would be about 60,000. Those immigrants who seek employment are estimated at a maximum of 24,000. Our present labor force, however, is 77 million. Statistically or practically, we

are talking about an infinitesimal amount; 24,000 is about three one-hundredths of 1 per cent of 77 million a good part of even these 24,000 additional workers would not even be competitors for jobs held or needed by Americans. I would expect very little change in the immigration from the Western Hemisphere.

Legislators presented their views at various Senate and House committee hearings to which representatives of various ethnic groups also delivered their verdicts. Joseph A.L. Errigo, acting chairman of the Sons of Italy National Committee, told one Senate gathering, 'This bill emphasizes not primarily increased immigration but equality of opportunity for all people to reach this Promised Land.'

James B. Carey, President of the International Union of Electrical, Radio and Machine Workers of America, was not speaking for any Irish American organization, but his view would have been reassuring to Irish American ears:

S.500 will do little or nothing to add to unemployment. We estimate that by the fifth year of operation only about 24,000 quota immigrants will have joined the labor force each year. At that time, we will have a labor force of 86 million. The newcomers will constitute three-thousandths of 1 per cent of that group of workers. We can expect that a good number of these immigrants will bring badly needed skills to this country.

Secretary Rusk had this to say on the House version of the reform bill, HR 2580:

This bill itself draws some distinctions in favor of, gives preferences to certain types of people in terms of talent and training. It is not one which others have objected to. We haven't had any indication of disagreement on that from abroad, from any government, certainly we are dealing here with a level of immigration that is fully within our ability to absorb, and our needs as a Nation to receive. We do not get the impression that 3 billion people are all at the starting line, waiting to take off to come to this country, just as soon as the bill is passed.

Pennsylvania Republican Representative Richard S. Schweiker was another legislator who saw at least a degree of global equity in the proposed legislation, 'The administration bill favors nations of Latin America and North America. It favors nations of northern Europe.'

Representative Patsy T. Mink, a Democrat from Hawaii, was based a long way from Europe but he was certainly thinking of it, 'this bill is but a step in the right direction. It is estimated that in the total 5-year period 679,663 of the 828,805 persons entering the United States will come from Europe.'

All the reassuring words from legislators in both parties, almost all of them male and white, had a calming effect on America's Irish – or at least tamped down any loud protest. Nevertheless, there were those who were sounding the alarm; *Irish Echo* reporter Frank O'Connor was an especially prominent voice, and the largest Irish American organization, the Ancient Order of Hibernians, was certainly paying attention.

The mid-1960s, even taking into account the body blow that was JFK's assassination, was a time of prominence and plenty for Irish America. There were numerous Irish American legislators at local, state and federal level, and Irish neighborhoods in big cities were flush with immigrant arrivals, even if the Irish quota was no longer being completely taken up each and every year. There was confidence aplenty. But also complacency. Adrian Flannelly remembers, 'Grassroots attempts to address the immigration issue were not coordinated among the Irish societies and there was a view that it could all be left to politicians to deal with.'

CHAPTER 25

Finally!

The year of 1965 was one of remarkable highs and dubious lows for the United States of America. Gemini capsules soared into space and, back on earth, city neighborhoods went up in flames. Satellites circled the planet and, at lower altitude, B-52 bombers flew for the first time in the skies over Vietnam. There was certainly a middle level in the nation's affairs, and immigration reform hovered in that sphere, more or less.

President Johnson's push to have Congress rewrite immigration law had its passionate followers and entrenched detractors. Most legislators were seemingly happy to go with a flow partly generated by mostly supportive press coverage. President Kennedy's pitch to Congress in July 1963 had gotten the press ball rolling.

The *Chicago Tribune*, for one, had opined that the idea of 'shifting the basis of immigrants' admission from the arbitrary one of country of origin to the rational and humane ones of occupational skills and reuniting families deserves approval'. The *Washington Post* described the proposed change as 'the best immigration law within living memory to bear a White House endorsement'. The *New York Times* concluded that adoption of the president's 'wise recommendations would be an act of justice and wisdom, as well as evidence that we fully understand the true nature of the changed world – now grown so small – in which all humanity lives'.

Two years on, the world was that little bit smaller again and Kennedy's successor in the White House was doubtless happy enough to accept an inherited mantle of being just and wise. Johnson was savvy, and immigration reform, played correctly, was a distraction from other issues that the press viewed as being less deserving of praise for the White House occupant. Johnson's support for reform was solid enough, but he was dependent on a supportive Congress.

Ted Kennedy was certainly supportive, and he was determined to ensure that his dead brother's dream would become a living reality. In an interview with James Sterling Young as part of the Edward M. Kennedy Oral History Project at the University of Virginia's Miller Institute, Kennedy explained his own early-life observations that would merge with his lost brother's views as outlined in *A Nation of Immigrants*. The interview was conducted on Cape Cod on October 8, 2007, less than two years before the senator's own passing. Kennedy was relating early life lessons imparted by his grandfather John F. 'Honey Fitz' Fitzgerald:

> It was clear to me at the time that the laws in existence basically prohibited certain groups from coming into the United States and impeded the reunification of families, particularly the Southern Europeans. The Greeks couldn't reunify with their families. The Italians were probably the most notoriously prohibited, some Portuguese – those were the major groups. So this was a factor and something that was very much on his (Fitzgerald's) mind.
>
> I didn't know the details about reunification of family provisions, the order of priorities, the different sections of the immigration laws. But what was very clear to me was that some groups were excluded and other groups were permitted. What was also very evident was that there was real tension between the various groups in terms of getting jobs and getting homes. It reflected at the ballot. Italians voted for Italians and Irish voted for Irish, and it was reflected in those ethnic communities.

Ted Kennedy would reflect on the 1965 act as his 'first major piece of legislation, both in terms of shaping it and conducting the hearings on it, and getting it through the committee, and getting it to the floor, and effectively floor managing it'. Once on the congressional floor, the bill, as Ted Kennedy put it, faced a big stumbling block in the form of a group of 'southerner and westerner Senators' who wanted to get more control of immigration through a limitation of the Western Hemisphere flow:

> They delayed the bill for a few days, and for a short period of time it made its passage somewhat uncertain. Eventually we were able to get an agreement taking this amendment, which put a limitation of the Western Hemisphere flow. We'd have the support and eventually vote on the immigration bill, which in effect knocked out the national origins quota and the Asian Pacific triangle, which were the two most discriminatory aspects of the law, and the most egregious part of our immigration policies. We were able to get it passed by a vote that was very similar to the final votes on the civil rights bill, somewhere around 73 or 74 to 18. They had a signing ceremony at the Statue of Liberty, but for one reason or another, I missed that occasion.

By the time of the interview with Sterling Young, it is fair to say that Ted Kennedy had lived a very full life, one packed to the brim with meetings, rallies and signing ceremonies. Perhaps it's not entirely surprising that he might have forgotten that in fact he was on Ellis Island for the signing ceremony of a bill that he would describe to Sterling Young as his 'first major legislative undertaking and success'. Senator Kennedy was standing just a few feet behind and to the left of President Johnson at the moment of signing. His brother Robert was standing right beside him.

The signing followed congressional passage of the bill on June 30. Those Irish with an eye on the historical tea leaves would have noted that passage came on the fiftieth anniversary of the death in New York of the Fenian leader Jeremiah O'Donovan Rossa. Those with long memories would, years later, see more than the burial of one man figuring into the historical record for the last days of June.

Senator Kennedy argued on the Senate floor during the debate on what would also be known as the Hart–Celler Act; he argued that America's cities would not be flooded with a million immigrants each and every year, as some were predicting, and that the ethnic mix of the country would not be 'upset'. Given the time and Kennedy's own experience growing up in Boston, that 'ethnic mix' was a familiar lineup of mostly European national groups. And the same lineup dominated the Senate and House where the big change or non-change in immigration law was taking shape.

It was a delicate political dance, but when the votes came there was no doubt. The House voted 320 to 70; the Senate voted 52 to 14, with one abstention. A greater percentage of Republicans – 85 per cent – voted for passage, while 74 per cent of Democrats supported approval. The Senate had just 2 women members out of 100; the House had 14 women out of 435. Congress, then, did not reflect even the current immigration lines at the time of approval but few were taking notice of this seemingly minor detail.

And so it was on to Ellis Island and signing day, October 3, 1965. The bill that President Johnson signed came with its House designation, HR 2580. A few minutes after 3 p.m., the president delivered a speech which opened with a few lines of levity:

> We have called the Congress here this afternoon not only to mark a very historic occasion, but to settle a very old issue that is in dispute. That issue is, to what congressional district does Liberty Island really belong to – Congressman Farbstein or Congressman Gallagher? It will be settled by whoever of the two can walk first to the top of the Statue of Liberty.
>
> This bill that we will sign today is not a revolutionary bill. It does not affect the lives of millions. It will not reshape the structure of our daily lives, or really add importantly to either our wealth or our power.
>
> Yet it is still one of the most important acts of this Congress and of this administration.
>
> For it does repair a very deep and painful flaw in the fabric of American justice. It corrects a cruel and enduring wrong in the conduct of the American Nation.
>
> Speaker McCormack and Congressman Celler almost 40 years ago first pointed that out in their maiden speeches in the Congress. And this measure that we will sign today will really make us truer to ourselves both as a country and as a people. It will strengthen us in a hundred unseen ways.

I have come here to thank personally each Member of the Congress who labored so long and so valiantly to make this occasion come true today, and to make this bill a reality. I cannot mention all their names, for it would take much too long, but my gratitude – and that of this Nation – belongs to the 89th Congress.

We are indebted, too, to the vision of the late beloved President John Fitzgerald Kennedy, and to the support given to this measure by the then Attorney General and now Senator, Robert F. Kennedy.

In the final days of consideration, this bill had no more able champion than the present Attorney General, Nicholas Katzenbach, who, with New York's own 'Manny' Celler, and Senator Ted Kennedy of Massachusetts, and Congressman Feighan of Ohio, and Senator Mansfield and Senator Dirksen constituting the leadership of the Senate, and Senator Javits, helped to guide this bill to passage, along with the help of the Members sitting in front of me today.

This bill says simply that from this day forth those wishing to immigrate to America shall be admitted on the basis of their skills and their close relationship to those already here.

This is a simple test, and it is a fair test. Those who can contribute most to this country – to its growth, to its strength, to its spirit – will be the first that are admitted to this land.

The fairness of this standard is so self-evident that we may well wonder that it has not always been applied. Yet the fact is that for over four decades the immigration policy of the United States has been twisted and has been distorted by the harsh injustice of the national origins quota system. Under that system the ability of new immigrants to come to America depended upon the country of their birth. Only three countries were allowed to supply 70 per cent of all the immigrants.

Families were kept apart because a husband or a wife or a child had been born in the wrong place. Men of needed skill and talent were denied entrance because they came from southern or eastern Europe or from one of the developing continents.

This system violated the basic principle of American democracy – the principle that values and rewards each man on the basis of his merit as a man.

It has been un-American in the highest sense, because it has been untrue to the faith that brought thousands to these shores even before we were a country.

Today, with my signature, this system is abolished.

We can now believe that it will never again shadow the gate to the American Nation with the twin barriers of prejudice and privilege.

Our beautiful America was built by a nation of strangers. From a hundred different places or more they have poured forth into an empty land, joining and blending in one mighty and irresistible tide.

The land flourished because it was fed from so many sources – because it was nourished by so many cultures and traditions and peoples. And from this experience, almost unique in the history of nations, has come America's attitude toward the rest of the world. We, because of what we are, feel safer and stronger in a world as varied as the people who make it up – a world where no country rules another and all countries can deal with the basic problems of human dignity and deal with those problems in their own way.

Now, under the monument which has welcomed so many to our shores, the American Nation returns to the finest of its traditions today. The days of unlimited immigration are past.

But those who do come will come because of what they are, and not because of the land from which they sprung.

When the earliest settlers poured into a wild continent there was no one to ask them where they came from. The only question was: Were they sturdy enough to make the journey, were they strong enough to clear the land, were they enduring enough to make a home for freedom, and were they brave enough to die for liberty if it became necessary to do so?

And so it has been through all the great and testing moments of American history. Our history this year we see in

Viet-Nam. Men there are dying – men named Fernandez and Zajac and Zelinko and Mariano and McCormick.

Neither the enemy who killed them nor the people whose independence they have fought to save ever asked them where they or their parents came from. They were all Americans. It was for free men and for America that they gave their all, they gave their lives and selves. By eliminating that same question as a test for immigration the Congress proves ourselves worthy of those men and worthy of our own traditions as a Nation.

Never missing an opportunity to make extra political capital, Johnson went on to declare 'this afternoon to the people of Cuba that those who seek refuge here in America will find it. The dedication of America to our traditions as an asylum for the oppressed is going to be upheld.'

He told all assembled that he had 'directed the Departments of State and Justice and Health, Education, and Welfare to immediately make all the necessary arrangements to permit those in Cuba who seek freedom to make an orderly entry into the United States of America'.

With his words on Cuba certain to make a major headline, Johnson returned to the broader story:

> Over my shoulders here you can see Ellis Island, whose vacant corridors echo today the joyous sound of long-ago voices.
>
> And today we can all believe that the lamp of this grand old lady is brighter today – and the golden door that she guards gleams more brilliantly in the light of an increased liberty for the people from all the countries of the globe.

Johnson was as politically adroit as they came. On the one hand he was talking about a partial but significant closing of the golden door while on the other he was able to talk up a fully open door to Cuban refugees thanks to a decision just a few days previously by Fidel Castro to permit his countrymen and women with relatives in the United States to leave the island. As he spoke on Ellis Island,

Johnson might have been quietly thanking Castro for taking some of the edge out of what had actually just occurred.

The Irish weren't thanking Castro, and they weren't about to thank Johnson or Congress. Adrian Flannelly's main memory of the signing, and he was just a few miles away from it, was 'instant shock and horror'. He recalls, 'How could this happen to us? Didn't we build America? Has the US not realized how much she owed us? How could our Irish American politicians sell us down the river? It would take a few years to really feel the effects. Many Irish assumed that a special accommodation could be worked out.'

In fact, Ireland's special accommodation had just evaporated into the fall air that had settled over New York Harbor and its famous little island.

CHAPTER 26

An Explanation of the Problem

Some might take the view that a call to arms would be a natural and expected occurrence for the Irish. But no less than any other national group, the Irish can be reluctant fighters. It all really depends on the issue at hand. Having America's door slammed shut was an issue at hand. And it would require, in return, the playing of a strong hand. To do that the American Irish formed a committee.

This wasn't a literal fighting response. Words, however, were going to be the weapons, so a committee it was, and the American Irish National Immigration Committee (AINIC) would be its *nom de guerre*. AINIC had an aim: to turn back the negative effects imposed on the Irish by the 1965 Immigration and Nationality Act. It got to work as the ink on the legislation dried and its far-reaching consequences became clear. Steering its course was an attorney and son of immigrants, John P. Collins.

Collins was born in New York. His parents hailed from Limerick. His future wife, Ellen, was born in Galway. Collins, then, was predisposed to being sensitive towards immigration and immigrants. Such sensitivities can be ignored. Collins was not inclined to ignore. After graduating from law school, he served as an assistant district attorney and senior trial assistant in the office of Manhattan District Attorney Frank S. Hogan. Subsequently, Collins served as law secretary to New York State Supreme Court Justice Joseph Sarafite, and later as Chief of Consumer Protection in the office of Manhattan District Attorney Robert Morgenthau.

In 1978, Collins was appointed to a ten-year term as a judge of the New York City Criminal Court by Mayor Ed Koch, a politician who worked hard to forge ties with his city's Irish American and

Irish immigrant communities. Collins was reappointed by Mayors Rudolph Giuliani and Michael Bloomberg. In 1982, Judge Collins was appointed as an acting justice of the Supreme Court of the State of New York. For ten years he served as Administrative Judge of the Criminal Division of Supreme Court, Bronx County. In 2009, Governor David Patterson appointed him as a justice of the Supreme Court. After a thirty-two-year career on the bench, Collins retired in 2012.

Collins also had a link to that long-venerated Irish job description: military service. A veteran of New York's Seventh Regiment, he served in the New York Army National Guard for nine years.

He also had ties to his native city's Irish social life, serving two terms as president of the Limerick Association and a period of time as a member of the New York City St Patrick's Day Parade Committee. Collins was a feis competitor and winner. He served at various times as a feis adjudicator and vice-president of the United Irish Counties Association of New York. Collins was a regular visitor to Ireland.

For twenty years, he was a member of the faculty of Fordham College, teaching a course in American Criminal Justice. He would lecture at the Faculty of Law, University College Dublin, and at the University of Limerick.

Collins also had a family story that highlighted the difficulties the Irish could experience in trying to move legally to the United States, and this was well before the 1965 act brought the boom down. His father departed Ireland in 1923, but before settling in the United States, he would spend five years in Canada; after that, he gained legal entrance to America based on being a legal resident of Canada.

John Collins covered all the bases. He was a natural to lead a fight on behalf of the historical Irish claim on an American life. He would also, in later years, write about his years as chairman of the American Irish National Immigration Committee during the years of its existence – 1966 to 1973. By his side, as vice chairman, was a Carmelite priest, Fr Donal O'Callaghan. A judge who interpreted earthly law. A priest who interpreted the heavenly. Judge and priest would be a formidable combination – one with the ability to open doors.

Perhaps because of their history, the Irish have a keen sense of justice and a knack for sniffing out its opposite. Being a lawyer, John Collins would combine his Irish instinct for injustice and his formal jurist's training when it came to assessing the 1965 Immigration and Nationality Act. In his memoirs, and in an opening chapter entitled 'An Explanation of the Problem', he would describe the act as being 'neither fair nor just, but beggarly and miserly, to the Irish'. He might have been referring to centuries of English rule in Ireland, but here he was referring to American law.

But in casting a critical eye on that law, he would invoke England, albeit in the context of what had preceded the law's arrival. The national quota system, sourced in the 1920s (the decade of his father's arrival), and the 1947 McCarran–Walter or National Origins Act were, he would write, 'inequitable'. And Britain, with Germany and Ireland were drawing particular advantage from this inequity by virtue of pre-1965 annual visa allocations of 63,361, 25, 814 and 17,756 respectively. Collins would point out that southern Europe would not fare as well as northern Europe, and that some nationalities, 'particularly Asians', were excluded from the United States under the National Origins Act.

Separately, but critically, Britain, Germany or Ireland were not meeting their annual quotas in the lead up to 1965 while applicants from countries such as Italy and Greece were exceeding the annual limit placed upon them. Collins would take particular note of Italian efforts to change this state of affairs and of the supportive role of the Catholic Church. He would also pay close attention to President Kennedy's clearly stated intent to turn America away from the national quota system. He didn't need a law degree to realize that whenever any significant change came about in immigration law, there would be winners and losers in the numbers game.

'The ethnic Irish newspapers began to take note of the issue', he writes in the opening of his memoir. 'Columns were written descrying that the Irish might lose out. At meetings of the Irish American social, cultural and sports organizations in New York, murmurs about the issue could be heard.'

Those murmurings would filter through Irish organizations such as the United Irish Counties of New York, which had an immigration committee. It was not overly busy beyond supplying assistance 'for the odd immigrants who arrived with no relatives, contact or employment'. The committee would become aware of proposed law changes but, according to Collins:

> the general consensus was that it was unlikely that the Kennedy administration assistants or their successors would hurt the Irish.
>
> At least one member of the UICA [United Irish Counties Association], former New York City Deputy Mayor Sean Keating born in County Cork was serving in the Kennedy Administration as northeast regional postmaster general. Additionally, since the Irish never filled their quota anyway, there was sure to be enough numbers left. It was wishful thinking but these men can hardly be blamed for these rosy thoughts. At the time the US State Department was predicting to the Senate and the Congress that 5,113 Irishmen and women would be entering each year for the first three years under the legislation.

As time passed, the US-based Irish newspapers would present a clearer picture of the proposals. Frank O'Connor, lawyer, educator and *Irish Echo* columnist, would, according to Collins, write 'clearly and concisely on the issue'. And there was always more to be written, as would be the case, later in the 1980s, when the concerns of the Irish community would congregate in the ranks of a particular county society. In the late 1980s, it would be the Cork Association in New York; in the mid-1960s it would be the Limerickmen's Benevolent and Social Association of New York. Collins was a member. He had joined in 1963, but his first couple of years of membership were uneventful.

Collins, did, however, become more involved in the spring of 1965. He now had more time available as his military commitments had ended. Being a jurist with a military background, it was hardly surprising that Collins would take the lead as the Limerick Association focused on the new immigration law. Along with another attorney, he was appointed to a committee tasked with drafting a formal resolution, a document that would ultimately be approved by the association. He would later write:

> Little did I then realize that this document and its results were to become my avocation for a number of years. It was to cause me to meet and work with some wonderful people and dedicated individuals. It would mobilize the Irish community for some years to come. Although we in the Limerick Men's Association did not realize it at the time, there were at least two other societies that were producing similar resolutions, the Kerrymen's Association and the Sligo Men's Association. All ultimately were brought to the floor of a general meeting of the United Irish Counties Association.

The Limerick resolution, which was ultimately submitted to the United Irish Counties in June 1966, stated that members were 'deeply discouraged' by the effect of the immigration law of 1965: 'Recent statistics issued by the US government indicates that during the period December 1965 to March 1966, only 82 US immigration visas were issued in Ireland. One year earlier, prior to the enactment of the new law, from December to March 1965, 1036 US immigration visas were issued in Ireland.'

The resolution preamble continues:

> Some say that the fault lies within the provisions of the Immigration Act itself, some say it lies in the administration of the act's provisions and still others say it is a combination of both. However, we all can agree as we observe the plain facts, that there has been a drastic reduction is the issuance of immigration visas to Irishmen while the issuance of immigration visas to many other nationalities has increased.
>
> Our association feels that this matter should be of concern to all Irishmen, regardless of county and regardless of political affiliation. The death knell has been sounded for the county organizations and before long the bell will toll the death of Irish immigration to the US. Limerick opposed the initial enactment of the bill last year and publicly registered its

protest in a formal resolution sent to the President of the US and to Senators Javits and Kennedy.

The actual resolution states in part:

> Whereas, realizing that for decades past, Irishmen and Irishwomen have been freely allowed to enter the United States, and they came not as professionals for the most part, but with minds willing to learn and bodies willing to work and they served in the growth and building of the nation since its founding in war and peace, in the cities and on the farms, in the factories and in the offices, in the arts and in the sciences, in the professions and in the trades.

The resolution notes that one descendant out of all these Irish immigrants, John Fitzgerald Kennedy, had become President of the United States. It continues:

> Whereas, observing that the effect of the present immigration law and the administration of such law has been to drastically cut and strangle Irish immigration into this country, and whereas, seeking to penalize no nationality, but being specially interested in Ireland and desiring that what Ireland held she should continue to hold, therefore, Be It Resolved, that we delegates to the United Irish Counties Association protest the drastic reduction in the issuance of visas to Irish men and women desiring to immigrate to the US and call upon our elected and appointed government officials to remedy this situation by necessary amendments and administrative regulations, and Be It Further Resolved, that copies of this resolution be sent to the President of the United States, the Secretary of State, the Secretary of Labor, the United States Senators from New York and the judiciary Committees of the United States Senate and the United States House of Representatives.

Thus, the battle line was drawn: the United Irish Counties versus the United States. The former was not lacking in confidence, and was certainly invigorated by a strong sense of grievance. The latter wasn't even aware at the outset that it was in a fight. But that would change.

CHAPTER 27

Attention Ladies and Gentlemen

The meeting on the field of Irish America and America would involve quite a few individuals and groups. The United Irish Counties Association could depend on the support of an array of organizations in New York City and its surrounding metropolitan area. And additional groups in other cities and states could be relied upon to enter the fray. There was certainly sufficient body and volume available to bend political ears at a high level. But the very highest? Well, it would not be for the want of trying.

Judge John Collins would very quickly find a fellow jurist at his elbow. Judge James Comerford had fought in the IRA during Ireland's War of Independence. He landed in New York in 1927 and, in a classical immigrant tale, worked his way up from a job in a grocery store to a city judgeship.

Comerford was a larger than life figure. Calvin Trillin, writing in the *New Yorker* in 1988, states, 'Before there was democracy, there was Judge James J. Comerford'. Trillin was referring to Comerford's position atop, and near absolute dominance of, the committee running the New York St Patrick's Day Parade. Collins would later add another line about Comerford, 'It is often said that he sat on more daises, made more speeches, installed more officers and chaired more meetings than any Irishman in the history of New York.'

In the fall of 1966, Collins would receive word from Comerford that he wanted a meeting. The latter wanted the former to chair a revamped United Irish Counties Association immigration committee. Fr Donald O'Callaghan would be the vice chairman of what would become known as the American Irish National Immigration Committee.

Like Comerford, O'Callaghan was a ubiquitous figure in New York's Irish community. Unlike Comerford, a native of Kilkenny, O'Callaghan was a native New Yorker. With Comerford's blessing, Collins and O'Callaghan would become the de facto joint leaders of the effort to turn back aspects of the 1965 act deemed injurious to the Irish. Collins and O'Callaghan would also become close friends until the latter's death in 1973.

But in the closing weeks of 1966, the two were focused more on how best they could advance a new cause among so many long-established Irish causes. Judge Collins was focused primarily on action at the legislative level; Fr O'Callaghan was, not surprisingly, conscious of the effects of the new legislation at a community and individual level.

Collins describes those early days in his later account of the American Irish National Immigration Committee (AINIC).

> My thoughts concerning the immigration issue had always been along legislative lines. We should make the community aware of the situation and get Congress to act but I realized that this would be no easy task.

Father O'Callaghan argued that we must also be a service organization. We must set up an office and assist undocumented Irish in need of immigration help. It would be necessary to learn what the law required for entry, what papers were needed and how to fill out the applications. We knew none of this …

Even before we had an office – through word of mouth – we had a young illegal immigrant in need of help. Joseph Harte of County Galway. Father, through contacts, found a job for the lad in the kitchen of the Mission of the Immaculate Virgin, an orphanage on Staten Island. He picked up young Harte and took him by taxi to Staten Island. He obtained immigration forms for him and took Harte to the Immigration and Naturalization Service on West Broadway in Manhattan in order to file the papers. We had no treasury at that time and Harte had no money. Father O'Callaghan paid the expenses himself …

We began a practice then which we continued faithfully of never asking a prospective immigrant for a fee and personally refusing any money. If the immigrant's friends or relatives wished to make a contribution to the committee, we urged them to mail us a check made out in the name of the committee.

The committee needed space as well as friends:

Through the graciousness of Paul O'Dwyer and the Irish Institute, we were given a small room at 326 West 48th Street for our files and supplies as well as free use of a room for meetings and conferences. It was more than adequate for our needs. As our financial status improved, we installed a telephone, obtained a listing and added an answering machine.

Our general meetings were held once a month at the Irish Institute. The Irish-American newspapers advertised the time and place. The *Irish Echo*, under the supervision of John Thornton, Editor; the *Irish Advocate* operated by James, Elsie and Pearl O'Connor (whose nephew and son is the actor Carol O'Connor); and the Irish World and Gaelic American owned by the Ford family were always more than generous in printing items about our committee ...

Once each week, in the evening, we opened the office to be available for immigrant inquiries. Father O'Callaghan was available about three times a week, in the afternoons, at the Institute office. At our first general meeting, the opening of the office was approved. John 'Kerry' O'Donnell (a preeminent figure in New York's Gaelic Athletic Association) gave us a loan of five hundred dollars. Some years later, when we offered to repay the loan, he offered it as a contribution ...

One of the committee members correctly recognized that we needed some literature to properly explain our purpose. We prepared a card which informed the public that 'it is a committee of American Irish organizations and individuals who have banded together to protect the interests of those members of the Irish race who desire to immigrate to the US. We recognize that the former US immigration policy discriminated against some nationalities. Now, however, we find that the present law discriminates against the Irish.'

A few statistics were provided – the monthly average number of Irish immigrants then entering, 99; formerly it was 448. In 1965, 5,378 Irish men and women immigrated to the US. In the first six months of the new law, 696 entered. At the same time, total immigration to the US increased 23,677 over the previous year. We invited all organizations of people of Irish extraction to unite with us in working for fair changes in the new law. We indicated on the hand-out, that we were willing to process and advise those who desired to enter the US. An address and telephone number was provided as well as a list of the sponsoring groups. This was also a means of thanking those who contributed as well as prodding those who had not.

Judge Collins's description of the forming of the committee and the birth of its campaign would be familiar to many. A few dedicated people, office space, a phone line and, something quite novel at the time, an answering machine. The committee was up. Now for the running. A good deal of the committee's work would involve spreading the word to the dizzying array of Irish organizations, some of them, like the Ancient Order of Hibernians (AOH), divided into divisions and operating in different states.

Collins would write that by the time the seven years of AINIC's existence had passed, 'I never wished to sit on a dais again. I never wished to eat in public on a platform again and I never desired to eat a mid-morning breakfast of chicken, potatoes and peas.' Each set of remarks, he recalls, had to be separately crafted to fit the audience and to satisfy time limits. The idea of a time limit was somewhat fanciful. Some functions involved speechifying deep into the night in a manner that would have left the Lincoln–Douglas debates in the shade. Collins writes:

A few of the early engagements stand out in memory. At the installation of a new president of the UICA [United Irish Counties Association], I was one of the many speakers at the Henry Hudson Hotel Ballroom on West 57th Street. I took at least fifteen minutes to speak my piece, well over the allotted amount of time. Afterwards, I mentioned to Judge Comerford that I had spoken too long. He said, 'Not at all. If you have something important to say, don't worry how much time you are taking. Never mind that you exceed the time limit that those in charge have imposed.' It was good advice that I never forgot.

Often the dinners and lunches did not start on time. Sometimes we operated under Irish country time.

Nevertheless, Collins contends that these gathering allowed the immigration committee to get its message across, sometimes to large audiences. 'Often there was a report of the meeting or dinner in the Irish papers, which provided added publicity for the cause.' The largest dinner was the New York GAA gathering, with as many as 2,500 guests seated in the Grand Ballroom of the Statler Hilton Hotel. Grabbing and holding the attention of such a crowd, out for a good night, wasn't easy. Collins recalls:

> If the toastmaster began without obtaining attention and silence, all was usually downhill and the noise accelerated as the speeches progressed. There were two exceptions. One was the former Governor of New York, Malcolm Wilson, who often addressed the dinner. He never began until he obtained silence and he always got it for the duration of his speech. I learned a lot by watching his operation. I was the other fortunate speaker exempted from the noise. In my case it wasn't due so much to technique as the content of the message. The audience was interested. The subject deeply affected them.

Fr O'Callaghan, being a priest, had an advantage over Collins the jurist. In his structured messages, 'which were always extemporaneous', O'Callaghan told his listeners that if the 1965 law was not changed, the GAA organization, being composed of many new immigrants, would be the first to go, followed by the United Irish Counties Association, and then lastly the Ancient Order of Hibernians.

At times, the importance of a gathering was less about the host organization than about who might be on the guest list. The Irish Institute dinner in the spring of 1967 was one such occasion. An important event, certainly, but made more important still by the guest of honor, Senator Robert F. Kennedy. It was to be held in the Grand Ballroom of the Hotel Commodore. Collins recalls how the committee 'sought permission to have four or five of our immigration committee information cards placed on each table at the dinner', but this was rejected on the grounds that it appeared AINIC was being critical of the Kennedys for their role in passage of the 1965 act. 'This suggestion was to arise again over the years. We tried to make it clear that we were not attacking the Kennedys', Collins asserts.

As it turned out, an intervention by a labor leader whose union was buying lots of tickets for the dinner reversed the initial block on table cards:

> In short order, we received an answer from the Institute that the cards would be more than welcome on the tables and that it was important that I attend the dinner. I was to be given a complimentary ticket for one of the tables. I attended and during the pre-dinner festivities someone fetched me from the common folk, took me to an ante-room, and asked me to pose in a small group photo with Senator Kennedy.
>
> At that stage of our work, I was not yet brash enough to question the Senator about immigration on such an occasion. I was never to see him again as he soon after was assassinated.
>
> The whole experience provided a lesson, one of many that we would receive.

It will never be known what Senator Robert Kennedy might have said to Judge John Collins. Any and all responses on behalf of the Kennedy family would, after Robert's death, be left to the last surviving Kennedy brother, Edward.

CHAPTER 28

The Road to Washington

Sooner or later, New York would not suffice. Neither would Boston, Chicago, San Francisco, Philadelphia or any city where the Irish could muster numbers. Washington, DC beckoned. But before the nation's capital, there would be the Bronx. The road to New York City's northernmost borough would be paved with words, spoken and printed. Newspaper articles, statements, interviews, and letters to politicians and government agencies, an endless stream of them.

The American Irish National Immigration Committee was well equipped for words given its leadership.In its early days, according to John Collins, American Irish National Immigration Committee's (AINIC's) protagonists were 'blamers'. He would write:

> We were more than ready to place blame on any agency that was preventing Irish entry to the US. We placed blame on the US State Department and the US Embassy in Dublin and told them so in writing. Our letters generated return letters which in turn generated more letters by us. The State Department was more than willing to share blame with the Immigration and Naturalization Service [INS], part of the US Treasury Department which processed immigration cases in the US. Naturally these agencies were sensitive to criticism.

As often as not, the INS would hear it from a member of Congress who had been contacted by AINIC. Raymond Farrell, a Rhode Islander, was commissioner of the service. He was something of a standout as he had risen through the ranks to his leadership post.

Collins contends that Farrell would become 'desperate' to seek out AINIC – to find out what it was, and what it wanted.

Once necessary questions had been answered, INS Assistant Commissioner Tom Gibney, Irish American like his superior, was sent on a mission to find the leaders of what was becoming an Irish American insurgency. The mission would lead to a dinner table in the Bronx. Matters were explained and the response was sympathetic.

As Collins, O'Callaghan, and their colleagues dug deeper into the immigration issue, they found themselves dealing with a particular problem affecting the Irish. The new immigration law required that so-called non-preference immigrants required special certification by the US Labor Department. The certification process ruled out certain jobs being open to non-preference immigrants, which described nearly all Irish immigrants.

Jobs denied to the Irish included bartender, janitor, painter, bus driver, laborer, domestic day worker and elevator operator. Jobs like these were, more often than not, the first kind of work that most Irish arrivals had traditionally obtained prior to the 1965 act. Collins writes, 'The labor restrictions to the 1965 Law caused us to rail all the more. We wanted to go to Washington to protest.' That mission was preceded by Father O'Callaghan consulting with David Sullivan, a top labor leader based in the nation's capital.

Sullivan was an immigrant from Cork. He had been in the IRA. After arriving in the US in the 1930s, he set about organizing workers who maintained office and apartment buildings. He began Local 32-B of the Service Employees Union and would become vice president of the American Federation of Labor and Congress of Industrial Organizations (AFL-CIO) and president of the Service Employees International, with a membership of 540,000.

In 1965, Sullivan would lead the New York St Patrick's Day Parade as its grand marshal. In May 1967, Collins and O'Callaghan met with Sullivan in the Sheraton Hotel at La Guardia Airport. Collins describes the occasion:

> For about two hours he listened to what we had to say. He knew Fr O'Callaghan for years but it was the first time I had met him. He spoke clear thoughts with little left of his native

Cork accent. He had a certain dour appearance but it was obvious that he knew the ways of Washington and sincerely wanted to help us. It was clear to him that our summation of the problem was far from crystal. He wanted us to think it out. We did. Much involved technical matters.

The meeting with Sullivan identified for Collins and O'Callaghan 'five problems' now facing the Irish. One of them was a new requirement in the 1965 law requiring a definite job offer before entering the US. This was an issue not only for the Irish but was, Collins and O'Callaghan concluded, 'an impossible burden' for immigrants, the Irish included.

The fact that the Irish tended to emigrate from their island as individuals also resulted in obstacles in the new rules favoring family reunification. Overall, the Irish were facing often-insurmountable hurdles. But a question arose as to whether or not the White House, Congress, the Immigration and Naturalization Service, and relevant government departments were aware of this.

There was only one way to find out. Collins, O'Callaghan and John Kerry O'Donnell headed for Washington and another meeting with Dave Sullivan, this time in his DC office. The meeting that followed might not have been possible for every national group, but the Irish could still manage it. Present at the meeting, Collins would record, was Thomas Donohue, Assistant Secretary of Labor and, as it happened, a former aide to Dave Sullivan. Another top, Labor Department official, Lawrence Rogers, also attended. 'They were there to help us,' Collins would recall.

The meeting lasted four hours, and out of it emerged a range of ideas, strategies and plans. One idea was to place 'constant pressure' on congressmen and senators. Another was the production of a 'comprehensive brochure' outlining the issues and the possible solutions. Seven hundred letters to members of Congress followed, and the committee began producing releases for a press that would have mostly assumed the Irish were on easy street when it came to immigration.

On September 20, 1967, Collins and his colleagues were back in Washington, this time for a meeting with Dale DeHahn, a staff assistant to Senator Edward Kennedy. De Hahn told his guests that a number of senators were hoping to introduce a bill aimed at ameliorating some of the effects of the 1965 law but that, meanwhile, there would be no delay in implementing the final provisions of the law. These provisions were to come into full force in the summer of 1968.

The Irish emissaries laid out their case to De Hahn, who responded by facilitating 'a brief meeting' with Senator Kennedy. Kennedy, seemingly not up to speed on the nature of Irish immigration in most recent years, asked why the Irish could not take advantage of the family reuniting preferences provided for in the 1965 act. 'We easily answered his query', Collins would later write.

The visitors had a number of meetings on their agenda that day. They also had an agenda – part of it being a bid to delay full implementation of the 1965 act from the designated time in July 1968 to some point in 1969.

A meeting with officials at the State Department brought a reminder that it was not just the Irish who were up in arms but also the Germans and Dutch. As Collins would later record, one official told the visitors that 'England and Germany' would also be drastically affected after July 1968, 'but they will be killed before they know they are sick. Ireland realizes she is sick and will die after July, 1968.' This rather startling assessment may or may not have been an expression of sympathy for the Irish position.

The State Department, specifically its visa office, actually agreed with the idea of delaying changes until 1969 by way of an amendment to the 1965 act. Collins and O'Callaghan were given the impression that the delaying amendment had been an idea floated by Congressman Arch Moore, a Republican from West Virginia. Moore had been in Ireland not long before. Somebody, perhaps, had whispered in his ear. In the meantime, July '68 it would remain. The visa office officials estimated that after that point in time the Irish would be confined to somewhere between 500 and 1,000 visas annually.

More meetings followed – with the Immigration and Naturalization Service and the Labor Department. The former was informed that the desire of many Irish to come to America was such that some Irishmen were volunteering for service in Vietnam in order to secure legal entry. 'Apparently the Immigration and Naturalization Service had no objection', Collins writes.

All of these meetings took place in one day and were followed by the return trip to New York. Collins would recall, 'We did our best. What was clear was that what we had been telling the Irish community was quite correct. Immigration from Ireland was near an end unless something could be done. Everyone we visited in Washington had made this clear.'

Collins, O'Callaghan and their fellow committee members were campaigning on multiple fronts. Part of the campaign was directed at the Irish American community, part of it at the Johnson (and later Nixon) administration, Congress and, in a less overt way, the Irish government – the political part of it and its apolitical diplomatic representatives in America.

The Irish government was at times hard to read. For some years there had been a clear desire in Irish political circles to retain as many people 'at home' as possible – to foster desired economic expansion. At the same time, politicians were all too aware that they could find themselves in a squeeze play between an economic downturn and restrictions on immigrating to America. England could take only so many Irish and, besides, the United States was a far bigger draw for a great many Irish with ambitions stretching beyond the home island. Collins records:

> It was clear to us, from the start of our work that we would not be receiving open support from the Irish government. In this regard, we were in a different position than the Italian Migration Committee. The Italian Ambassador to the United States and his government openly sought additional US Immigration benefits on behalf of Italians.
>
> Our committee made it abundantly clear that we were not encouraging young Irish men and women to leave Ireland and emigrate to the US. We approached the issue as Americans. We were seeking only that the Irish receive benefits equal to that of any other nationality group.
>
> While the Irish government never took any official position, we do know that the Department of External Affairs (now the

Department of Foreign Affairs) prepared a twenty-four page analysis of the issue.

Though the Irish government didn't take an 'official' position, it certainly took interest from afar – and more closely by means of its diplomatic outposts. The analysis referred to by Collins would conclude:

> there is no hope of a return to the days when the Irish emigrant entered the United States almost at will because of his privileged position by comparison with other would be immigrants; he may derive from educational background or special skills – or the help of friends in the US – in identifying job opportunities ... There is some prospect of an amendment by legislation but at present the pressure being exerted on the Labour Department by the Irish organizations to amend its regulations seem to offer most hope of success alleviating the position of would be Irish immigrants.

And indeed it was more a case of hope than prospect. AINIC and other Irish organizations were wearing out shoe leather and knocking on doors. Irish representatives in the US were sympathetic and helpful, and Collins and his colleagues were provided by Irish diplomats with names and contact details for potentially sympathetic and helpful individuals and organizations across the continent.

One Irish entity in particular rendered nuts-and-bolts assistance to Collins and his fellow campaigners. A cynic might contend that Aerlínte Éireann, or Irish Airlines (later Aer Lingus), had a vested interest in transatlantic Irish migration, but a realist might respond, against the backdrop of direct assistance to AINIC: so what? 'I can't sufficiently emphasize the importance of the assistance they rendered', Collins would write of the airline's public relations team at the time, most especially Thomas Kennedy, Carl Sugrue and William Maxwell. The airline's outside advertising agency was put at the disposal of the committee. The result was an ad proclaiming 'No One Need Apply', which appeared on St Patrick's Day in the *New York Times*.

The New York St Patrick's Day Parade would host an immigration marching unit led by AINIC. Collins would recall, 'We needed sashes with the names of Ireland's thirty-two counties. Irish Airlines designed, ordered and paid for all these as well as a banner stretching the width of Fifth Avenue with the word "A Fair Immigration Law for the Irish."'

Help from a business, even one as prominent as a national airline, was one thing. Help from a government was quite another. Collins states:

> It is unfortunate that we could not develop the same vigor from the Irish government in Dublin. The strongest position taken by Dublin was in the spring, 1968 when the Irish Government called on the America Charge d'Affaires (there being no US Ambassador at the time) and told him that they did not approve of the current US Immigration policy and had no opposition to a bill (HR 16593) then pending before the US Congress. If the government had taken a strong stand on the immigration issue, over the year, success might have been achieved.

Perhaps. But the United States was on a course – one that would take it into, and through, 1968, a year of strong stands the world over for and against all manner of issues. It would easily be possible for even an ally government's concerns to be lost in the tumult. Very easy indeed.

CHAPTER 29

To the Hill

Every year of the twentieth century is a contender for the title of standout. But 1968 is a clear title-holder. CNN, for one, saw fit to screen a four-part 'docuseries' in 2018 to mark the passing of half a century since 1968. It was billed as the exploration of a year 'marked by seismic shifts in American politics, social movements, global relations and cultural icons that changed the modern landscape'. Things shifted in Ireland too. And Irish America, being linked to both countries, took heed of the transatlantic shifting – for the most part not happily.

The American Irish National Immigration Committee (AINIC) began to shift too – out of its initial New York confines and early forays as far as Washington, DC. And there had been a fair few of those. 'They made so many trips to Washington', Patrick O'Leary recalls of Judge Collins and Fr O'Callaghan.

O'Leary, for many years an officer with the New York Police Department (NYPD), was one of many Irish Americans and immigrants who flocked to the AINIC banner, eager to help its campaign. That campaign, in its early days, was indeed centered on New York City and its immediate surroundings. Collins and his colleagues realized that a national campaign was imperative. That entailed a lot more than zooms up and down Interstate 95 between the nation's largest city and it capital.

And so began journeys intended to set up committee chapters that took the jurist and cleric to Boston, Philadelphia, Pittsburgh, Detroit, Chicago, Cleveland, Baltimore, Buffalo, Providence, San Francisco, and – forays into next-door territory – New Jersey and Connecticut.

Meetings were held with local Irish and Irish American organizations, politicians and Catholic clergy. Local AINIC branch committees were established in some instances and alliances forged with Irish American groups, not least the Ancient Order of Hibernians which, more than any other entity, had a national organizational base. Beyond Irish America, the AINIC leaders would reach out to other ethnic communities, not least German Americans, as represented by the likes of the Steuben Day Parade Committee in New Jersey.

Coverage would be sought in local Irish media outlets. Sometimes reports would be sent back to New York from locally based correspondents. The *Irish Echo* had a few of those, Pat Hennessey in Chicago being the most prominent. Hennessey, an immigrant from County Kilkenny, had been campaigning on immigration as well as writing about it. He also worked for the Daley administration. In baseball terms, he was covering all bases, though when it came to sports, his greatest passion was for hurling. Hurling is often described as the world's fastest field game. The AINIC campaign was now speeding up to a hurling rate.

In due course, the campaign rolled into Cleveland, Ohio – long a destination for immigrants from County Mayo and Achill Island in particular. Cleveland was also the base of operations for Congressman Michael Feighan, chairman of the House Subcommittee on Immigration. Feighan's Irish link went back to Achill. That connection had not prevented his support for the 1965 act, but neither had it blocked support from numerous other Irish American legislators who did not view the bill as a measure of specific exclusion directed against the Irish.

Collins and O'Callaghan arrived in Cleveland on February 9, 1968 in search of a meeting with Feighan and intent on setting up a local committee. The meeting with Feighan took place in the congressman's downtown office – 'impressive in size and grandeur', as Collins would recall.

The visitors explained their problems with the new immigration law. Feighan listened and indicated a desire to help. Collins, however, was uncertain, later writing, 'Feighan always appeared to me like a cat with a sneaky smile.'

The congressman with the allegedly feline smile would subsequently turn up at a meeting in the John Glenn Room of the Hilton Hotel organized by the visitors from New York. Indeed, Feighan, an old school-style politician, had arrived before the hosts and was working the room when Collins and O'Callaghan walked in. For the course of the meeting, the New Yorkers had to be ever-vigilant with regard to Feighan, who was in full election year mode. Indeed, Collins told Feighan that he could not be in a group photo at the end of the meeting because he and O'Callaghan were not in Cleveland to support any particular candidate.

Writing a half-century after 1968 was seared into the history books, Niall O'Dowd, a publisher and immigration activist, would take critical aim at Congressman Feighan, an 'obscure Ohio politician', but one who had changed American immigration forever and all but ended Irish immigration to the United States. 'It was Feighan, an Irish American, who shot down merit visas and European quotas and insisted on family reunification in the Johnson/Kennedy immigration bill, which utterly changed America.'

In their effort to pass the 1965 act and give substance to President Kennedy's dream of a changed immigration landscape, President Johnson and Edward and Robert Kennedy had all, according to O'Dowd, recognized one stumbling block: 'the head of the hitherto obscure immigration subcommittee'. That head, Feighan, 'wielded enormous power and Johnson knew he had to get the congressman onside to pass the bill'. O'Dowd points out that Feighan had initially opposed the '65 bill.

The 51-year-old Feighan was elusive. He had a history of catering to conservative groups and was very cool to the new proposal. His backers wanted to essentially retain the European quota and then add in some family reunification, a course of action that Feighan initially backed. 'Then came an unexpected hitch.' O'Dowd writes:

> In the 1964 election Johnson won in a landslide at the head of the ticket, but Feighan just barely scraped in against Ronald Motti, a Czech American who accused Feighan of treating immigrants from countries outside the chosen few as second class.

Motti was mostly referring to Eastern bloc countries like his own Czechoslovakia, whose citizens were desperate to escape the Soviet Union.

Motti made immigration his major policy point.

Feighan's instincts were to keep quotas from Europe and bring in some unification of families. Following the election results he realized he had to be more liberal towards families from outside the European charmed circle.

President Johnson took political advantage of Feighan's desire to be re-elected.

Looking at Feighan's close shave, Johnson, the ultimate political persuader, swung into action.

He knew Feighan would now have to agree to accept some new form of an immigration bill. He hounded the congressman, cajoled and browbeat him. He was good Johnson dispensing favors one day, bad Johnson the next, warning him of dire consequences.

Johnson had Feighan travel on Air Force One and stop by the Oval Office. He assigned a staff member full time to him. He wanted Feighan to sign off urgently. Johnson didn't have the word 'no' in his vocabulary.

When Feighan still dithered, Johnson put it about that he was running a candidate against Feighan in 1966. Finally, Feighan caved ...

On June 1, 1965, Feighan submitted his substitute immigration bill. Instead of merit visas, he chose family reunification.

Feighan's congressional career came to an end after the 1970 House election – not at the hands of a Republican, but a fellow Democrat who had defeated him in a primary. He would die in 1988 at 87 years of age. The headline of the *New York Times* obituary would describe Feighan as the 'Architect of the '65 Immigration Law'.

The *Washington Post* would note that Feighan had been chairman of the House immigration and naturalization subcommittee who had been a vocal anti-communist and protector of America's borders. 'For years he blocked efforts to liberalize US immigration policy before being convinced by President Johnson that reform was needed.' Actually, he might not have been fully convinced. In fairness to Feighan, facing into the headwind of a full force Lyndon Johnson was an unenviable situation for any politician. The man from 'County Cleveland' would not be the only member of Congress to cave to Johnson's towering powers of persuasion.

If Feighan was an uncertain ally, Congressman William F. Ryan would be a certain champion. Collins outlines the need for a champion as follows:

> Early in our committee's existence we recognized the need to attach our struggle to the name of a Congressman. We needed someone to offer legislation as a solution to the immigration problem. Preferably the person should be a known senior Congressman of Irish American extraction. He or she should be Democrat rather than a Republican as that was the party in power and that party represented the majority of our adherents.

Feighan was out of the running as 'he seemed satisfied with the then current law'.

Congressman (Peter) Rodino of New Jersey, the next ranking Democrat, 'understandably was a supporter of the 1965 law and ethnic wise would be responsive to the Italian Migration Committee'. Italians were much more likely to immigrate in complete family units as opposed to as individuals, which was the dominant Irish trait at the time. Rodino would come into the picture again in the 1980s when a great many individual Irish turned up at America's closed door. Judge Collins writes:

> Various names from other states were suggested but it appeared that we would have to reach them as there were no volunteers. In New York, a Congressman reached out to us – William F. Ryan. Judge Comerford told Father O'Callaghan and myself that he had been approached by Bill Ryan, who offered to help us. The Judge and Bill Ryan lived in the same neighborhood.

Congressman Ryan was aligned with the reform wing of the Democratic Party. His congressional district, a swathe of Manhattan's Upper West Side, was home to some of the most liberal voters in the country. Collins and O'Callaghan would have been more comfortable with a centrist, but Ryan had made the move and they could not afford to be too choosy. Collins would write:

> When his name was first mentioned to us, I was convinced that the only thing he and I had in common was prior employment as prosecutors in the office of New York County District Attorney Frank S. Hogan. Ryan had served in the office some years before my appointment. Father O'Callaghan and I decided to take the plunge and 'go' with him for better or worse. As it turned out, it was for the better. No man could be more dedicated to our cause. As the years rolled on, he earned the respect and honor of the Irish community.

Ryan was indeed a man for the moment. Before too long had elapsed, he contacted Collins by phone and told his former colleague that he wanted to set up an ad hoc committee of Congress members who would be interested in the immigration problem facing the Irish. The committee quickly took form and held its first meeting on April 1, 1968 in the House Judiciary Committee hearing room in the Rayburn Office Building. Twenty-one House members from seven states attended and, as Collins would note, they included lead actors in the immigration debate on Capitol Hill, including Congressman Emanuel Celler, chair of the Judiciary Committee, Michael Feighan, Peter Rodino, and a member from Massachusetts by the name of Thomas P. O'Neill.

At this juncture, the committee led by Collins and O'Callaghan had achieved a notable success. The hearing might have been ad hoc, but it had the potential to be *ad astra* in political terms. In addition to the Congress members, the gathering was attended by officials from the US Labor Department, the State Department, and the Immigration and Naturalization Service.

As Collins would record, Congressman Celler stated that he saw 'no reason why', within ten days, a provision couldn't be made 'for the entry of five to six thousand Irish a year'. This was heady stuff. Congressman Feighan, however, seemed non-committal in the eyes of the AINIC visitors. Congressman Rodino proposed a plan to help all nationals but it would result in the entry of an additional 500,000 immigrants a year. Collins writes, 'We were pleased to hear Celler's remarks. We didn't think Rodino's plan would have much chance of success. It sought the impossible.'

After the meeting, Congressman Ryan moved fast. On April 10 he introduced a House bill, HR 16593, aimed, as Collins would put it, 'at remedying the Irish question'. The bill attracted twenty-three co-sponsors, a couple more than had attended the ad hoc hearing.

The bill proposed that for three years those countries whose immigration was reduced by the 1965 law – Ireland, Germany and Britain – would receive additional visas. Collins wondered about the three-year limit but was reassured by Ryan. What Washington passed on a temporary basis tended to become permanent. As Collins would record:

> The Ryan formula established a floor under immigration. In any fiscal year after June, 1990, if the visas issued to any country fell below seventy-five per cent of the number issued during the ten years 1956–1965, additional visas would be issued in the following fiscal year to make up the difference between the number issued in that year and the seventy-five per cent of the ten year base period. In effect, this would mean that if in fiscal year 1969 visas issued to Irish applicants was 1297, and if the Ryan formula was in effect in 1972, the Irish would be entitled to 4,003 additional visas, the difference between 1297 and 5300 – 5300 being seventy-five per cent of the ten year average for Ireland. No labor certification would be required for these additional visas.

Collins, O'Callaghan and AINIC members around the country began campaigning to secure a hearing for Ryan's bill, which would have to take place before July 5, when Congress would go into summer recess.

Some things still appeared normal in 1968 – things such as the idea of a summer holiday. In glaring contrast, there was the Tet

Offensive in Vietnam and the assassinations of Dr Martin Luther King Jr. and Robert F. Kennedy – the latter event sending a particular shudder through the psyche of Irish America.

Through it all, AINIC kept its eye on its prize. A hearing on Ryan's bill was set for July 3. Clearly it would be a short engagement. The next day was the Independence Day holiday and Congress was heading for the hills on July 5. This was a *carpe diem* moment in the literal sense. After all that they had argued for – after all the miles they had traveled – Collins and O'Callaghan were up for a little seizing. July 3 would be their *diem*.

CHAPTER 30

The Swinging Door

The doors of Congress opened to the Irish in July 1968. The doors of America had just closed. The hearing on the Ryan bill took place two days after the Immigration and Nationality Act came into full force. In his testimony to the House Immigration Subcommittee on July 3, John Collins would state that Irish immigration in America had come to an end three days previously, on June 30, 1968. Thus, the starting point for his argument was an ending.

The July 3 hearing would see testimony from five individuals, with John Collins top of the list. Ward Lange, national chairman of the Steuben Society of America, also testified. But while German immigration would be represented by Lange, and Congressman Peter Rodino was de facto representing Italian immigration, there was little doubt, based on the list of testifiers and submitters of written statements, that the predicament of the Irish was the primary reason for the hearing taking place (it would adjourn and resume for another day on September 18).

The hearing was chaired by the not wholly sympathetic figure of Ohio Congressman Michael Feighan, who was flanked by Congressman Rodino from New Jersey and representatives Arch Moore from West Virginia, William Cahill from New Jersey and Clark MacGregor from Minnesota. Feighan and Rodino were Democrats while Moore, Cahill and MacGregor were Republicans.

Feighan kicked off, his words suggesting that he didn't view the hearing as being altogether necessary. He stated:

> The Immigration Act of 1965 became fully effective on Monday, July 1, of this year. In those countries which previously had

reserved numbers that were more generous than their needs required will have to compete with the rest of the world in getting one of the 170,000 numbers. This hearing will give an opportunity to representatives of organizations who believe that the Immigration Act of 1965, which became fully effective on July 1, has created and will create inequities for nationals of certain countries which previously had enjoyed what might be considered favored treatment.

The abolition of a national origins quota system has been met with almost universal acceptance and even praise. Now, the question of problems presented is how remedial steps may be taken in order to afford the nationals of such countries an opportunity to compete on an even basis with nationals of other countries who have filed petitions previous to July 1, 1968.

It is my personal opinion that the concept of the national origins system should forever be abolished. The question again presents itself, how we may maintain the principle that every immigrant applicant should be treated without consideration of his place of birth, color of his skin, or political or religious affiliation and at the same time provide a minimum number of immigrants from each country that previously did not use the full numbers allocated to them.

Congressman Rodino responded by stating that he wholeheartedly endorsed Feighan's words. Rodino, whose name would be prominent in the Watergate hearings, and again in the immigration debate of the 1980s, referred to the 'urgency of the problem', and a problem that was 'complex and complicated'. Nevertheless, he said that 'we may be able to come up with an equitable formula which will eliminate the discrepancies which now exist in a law which we certainly intended to be just and fair'. He continued:

We believe on the whole it is just and fair, though in countries such as Ireland we do find that some difficulties have arisen. Mr Chairman, I want to commend you for having the foresight to call together this urgent meeting and I hope our colleagues on

Emigrants leaving from Scotts Quay, Queenstown (Cobh), Co. Cork, Ireland, *c*.1890s.

Passengers and crew on board the immigrant ship SS *Gallia*, near Queenstown (Cobh), Co. Cork, Ireland, 22 July 1895. © Getty Images.

Immigrants awaiting examination on Ellis Island, New York, *c*.1910s.

The inspection room on Ellis Island, New York, *c*.1910s.

This photo from the *Irish Echo* archives is of a young man on the Blasket Islands in the 1930s. He is holding a broadsheet copy of the *Irish Echo* to the camera. Given the time and where he was from he quite possibly emigrated, perhaps to the *Echo's* home city of New York, or another American destination.

A descendant of emigrants returns. President John F. Kennedy makes a historic address to both Houses of the Oireachtas, 28 June 1963. © Irish Photo Archive.

Cadet Michael McGrath shaking President Eamon de Valera's hand at Dublin Airport before the Irish contingent flew to New York and Washington, D.C. for JFK's funeral. Photo courtesy of Michael McGrath.

The Irish Army Cadets Rifle Drill Team in their final salute to President Kennedy at Arlington National Cemetery. Michael McGrath is at the end of the second row. © Associated Press.

President Lyndon Johnson signs the 1965 Immigration and Nationality Act into law on Ellis Island. Senators Edward and Robert Kennedy are standing to the right of the president. Photo courtesy of the Lyndon B. Johnson Library Collection/Yoichi R. Okamoto.

President Johnson addresses the gathering on Ellis Island with the Statue of Liberty as a backdrop that seemed appropriate but, ultimately, and for sure through Irish eyes, could be seen as ironic. Photo courtesy of the Lyndon B. Johnson Library Collection/Yoichi R. Okamoto.

Sean Minihane of the Irish Immigration Reform Movement.

As a congressman, Brian Donnelly opened America's door to thousands of Irish. Pictured here, second from left, he is being honored at the 1988 Cork Association dinner dance in New York. Also pictured (l–r) are immigration reform campaigners at that time, and for decades into the future, Siobhan Dennehy, Mae O'Driscoll and Dan Dennehy. On the far right is Irish immigrant and Hollywood legend Maureen O'Hara.

Bruce Morrison telling it how it was.

The various iterations of Kennedy–McCain and McCain–Kennedy were debated between 2005 and 2007. McCain's name in the lead made the immigration proposals more palatable, it was hoped, to Republican legislators.

Senator Charles Schumer and Ciaran Staunton of the Irish Lobby for Immigration Reform.

Senator Edward Kennedy and Taoiseach Bertie Ahern. Kennedy's office was always open to the Irish. His death closed a Capitol Hill door like no other.

Judge John Collins (center) is presented with an award by the Ancient Order of Hibernians for his contributions to Irish America. On his right is Joseph Doherty, an attorney who worked for Judge Collins as a law clerk, and on his left is Martin Galvin of the Ancient Order of Hibernians. Photo courtesy of Kevin Kennedy.

Irish immigration campaigners from around the United States gathered in Washington, D.C. for briefings and meetings. They are pictured in front of the White House in January 2010, one year into Barack Obama's first presidential term.

Irish Ambassador to the United States Dan Mulhall (far side of the table with glasses and glancing to his right) hosting a meeting of Irish immigration advocates at the embassy in Washington. Photo courtesy of the Irish Embassy.

the committee will endorse whatever legislation is necessary to deal with the problem.

Feighan responded that he was 'quite confident' that a proper solution could be found. John Collins, with a solution very much in mind, was now called upon to testify. Casuistry was about to be employed by the future judge.

At the outset, Collins acknowledged that US immigration law prior to 1965 had been 'unfair to many nations', and that the United States had been 'more than generous' to Ireland over the years, hence the lack of protest from 'the American Irish' when the US sought to 'correct the discrimination against other nations'. That was then, however, and now it was evident that the new law 'in attempting to cure the discrimination of the old law has now saddled Irishmen – and quite possibly other nationalities – with an inequitable and unfair US immigration policy'. Collins stated, 'US immigration is on the rise. One country's immigration to the United States increased by 200 per cent in one year alone. Meanwhile the number of Irish permitted to enter the United States continues to decline not because the Irish don't wish to come here, but because they are barred from entry.' At this point, Collins stated AINIC's goal:

> The American Irish, all 30 million of them, are not seeking to encourage Irishmen to come here. But they do seek as American citizens and voters that those Irishmen who desire to come and settle in the United States be given that opportunity subject to reasonable regulations, and they do seek the same equality of opportunity in immigration that other nations now share in. To this end, the American Irish National Immigration Committee was formed. Having headquarters in New York and chapters throughout the United States, it seeks a fair, just, and equitable US immigration policy.

Since the new law had gone into effect, Collins said, Irishmen, 'literally by the thousands', who wanted to come to the US and formerly would have been able to do so, were being deprived of visas. Collins quantified a future flow of Irish visas. He spoke of 'less than 400 a year'.

At this point, he took his listeners into the legislative long grass in a point-by-point analysis of the components in the new law that were throwing up obstacles to Irish immigration. Being a lawyer, Collins was on natural ground. Collins would refer to Ireland as 'she' and 'her', and in the course of his testimony, challenge 'various rumors' that the Irish government was in favor of the law generated by the 1965 act and against the changes contained in Congressman Ryan's bill. He stated:

> I tell the distinguished members of this committee today that those rumors are false, they are despicable rumors. We have it on good authority from the Irish Government that the Irish Government is not in favor of the continuation of the present US immigration policy and it has no objection whatsoever to the passage of H.R. 16593. The chargé d'affaires in Dublin, Ireland, was so informed by the Irish Government last Friday morning, and the Irish Ambassador to the United States was so instructed by his Government in Ireland.

Collins conceded that the terms of the 'old law' had been unfair to some other nations but this 'did not justify solving the problem with new terms unfair to Ireland'.

And then the emotive bottom line:

> Ireland's sons and daughters have for decades contributed to the building and growth of this Nation in every conceivable area of endeavor. The quota which was given to Ireland under the old law was in part a small recognition of these contributions. Recognizing that the Irish have no monopoly on these contributions, nevertheless, the present law in its effect on Ireland is a sad commentary in this area in that the sweat and blood of the Irish working class has easily been forgotten … The situation now existing with regard to Irish immigration must be remedied and the American Irish community cannot be satisfied until it is remedied.

Collins concluded by asking the committee – that being the entire judiciary panel represented by the subcommittee – to approve HR 16593.

Congressman Rodino expressed reservation, stating that the Ryan measure would, if implemented, effectively continue the policy of national origins cast aside by the 1965 law. Speaking directly to Collins, he stated:

> Now I support what you want to do and I want to support a proposition that is fair, but I cannot possibly in good conscience go back to anything that is in any way a continuation of the system of national origins which intended that certain people from certain countries be treated as though they were preferred over people of other countries. I think that this would be undemocratic. I think this would not be in keeping with the high principles which every American intends to preserve. Now, after this statement I want you to know I will vigorously support any proposition that is fair, any adjustment that we can bring about in the law, but I would want you to think seriously of the endorsement you give to this kind of formula set forth in H.R. 16593.

Collins fought his corner and disputed the assertion that Ryan's bill 'in any way' was a return to the national origins system.

Ground was opening up between those giving testimony and the members of the subcommittee. Any notion that the hearing would be a slam dunk for the Irish witnesses was out the window – figuratively, as there were no windows in the room.

Congressman Cahill backed up his fellow New Jersey representative, Rodino, when he said to John Collins, 'It seems to me what we are up against now is whether we want to undo what we did in 1965.' Cahill, like his colleagues, was sympathetic, but pointed to a 'legislatively impossible situation'.

Impossible or not, the committee members were hearing, verbally and by way of written submissions, from members of AINIC from around the United States: as far from Washington as 3,000 miles, as Collins would point out to Chairman Feighan. Those written statements were duly entered into the record and added to the verbal testimonies delivered by John Collins and four others. The subcommittee also took on board written statements of support for HR 16593 from congressional co-sponsors.

Congressman Ryan, speaking in support of his bill, said he was 'encouraged' by support in Congress for an 'equitable solution to the unforeseen consequences of the Immigration and Nationality Act of 1965'. Ryan would note that twenty-three members of Congress had joined in co-sponsoring his bill and that eleven other members had introduced identical bills. He said:

> Only two days ago, on July 1, 1968, the provisions of the 1965 Act went fully into effect. Unless that Act is amended, the result will be to drastically reduce – perhaps by as much as 90% – the traditional level of immigration from nations which historically have provided much of our immigrant stock. My bill would prevent such catastrophic declines, without in any way penalizing nations which have gained immigration places, and without increasing the world-wide total of immigration to the US by more than approximately ten per cent.

Ryan said that before discussing his bill in detail he wanted to take a few moments to review the intent of the 1965 act, 'and some of its unintended consequences'. In specific relation to the Irish, he stated:

> In the case of Ireland, for example, the Congress was assured by the State Department that Irish immigration could be expected to level off at about 5,200 annually when the Act was fully in effect. This compared with an annual average of about 7,200 during the previous decade and was almost equal to the actual level of Irish immigration in 1964, the year prior to the enactment of the Act. Since Ireland was a formerly privileged quota nation, a level of 5,200 yearly seemed equitable even though it was significantly below the former quota of 17,756.
> In fact, however, Irish immigration has already declined well below that estimate during the three-year transition period when the Act was not fully in effect. Between 1965

and 1968, any immigrant who could qualify under one of the preference categories, could gain entry so long as his nation's former quota for the year was not exhausted. In other words, until July 1, 1968, there has been no world-wide competition for preference places.

But even with the partial protection of the former quota, the number of immigrant visas issued by the American Embassy in Dublin has declined from 4,619 in 1964 to 4,004 in 1965, to 1,741 in 1966, to 1,809 in 1967. There has been a slight increase in the first six months of 1968 because the Embassy has widely publicized the fact that beginning with July 1 of this year, when Ireland no longer has her former quota, it will be extremely difficult for Irish to qualify. It has been estimated by the State Department that the rate of Irish preference immigration during the next year will be only about 600.

Ryan again emphasized that his intent was not to restrict immigration flow from nations newly benefiting from the 1965 act. His concerns were rather over the 'near eclipse' of immigration from many nations 'whose sons have built America, which was certainly never the intent of Congress'.

Written submissions were added into the hearing record from half a dozen Irish cause contributors who could not be accommodated by virtue of time constraints. Also added into the record by way of a congressman, Andrew Jacobs Jr, was a telegram signed by three leading members of the Ancient Order of Hibernians who proclaimed that the Irish of Indianapolis and Indiana were 'greatly disturbed at the apparent discrimination against the Irish'. Telegrams could be tricky things. The intent of the communication was to support the Ryan bill, but it stated that Congressman Jacobs' support was being sought by the Indiana Hibernians 'to prevent the Ryan bill to come to the floor for a vote in this current session'. Unintended, certainly, but the committee members doubtless got the gist.

They got more than that from the written submission of Fr O'Callaghan, listed as vice chairman of the American Irish National Immigration Committee and delegate of the National Board of the Ancient Order of Hibernians. Fr O'Callaghan took the scatter gun approach, treating the attending subcommittee members to a broad outline of the contribution of the Irish to America over the course of the nation's history from the Revolutionary War, through the Civil War (both sides) and up to and including the Second World War. Beyond the military aspect, O'Callaghan sketched out the Irish contribution to the labor movement and, most ecumenically, the 'various churches'. It was a fair bet that the listeners were not overly familiar with the 'Nuns of the Battle Field' monument in the very city that was hosting the hearing.

And if Fr O'Callaghan had a battle cry for the occasion, it was, as he penned in his submission, 'We are not Johnny Come Latelies'. The Irish had certainly come early to America. But had they now arrived too late at the legislative table?

CHAPTER 31

A Stunned Loudness

'America Closes The Door; No Visas To Irish In July'. There was no way around a headline like this one. It ran double-barreled across the top of page one on the September 14, 1968 issue of the New York-published *Irish Echo*. The subhead read, 'Full Effect of Immigration Act Is Felt In First Month of New Law'. The first word in the report set the tone. It was 'No'.

The *Echo* reported that no visas had been issued to Irish applicants in Dublin seeking to immigrate to the United States during the month of July. The paper told its readers that this was the first month in which the Immigration and Nationality Act of 1965 was fully operative. The report stated:

> John P. Collins, national chairman of the American Irish Immigration Committee, released the startling figure last Monday in New York. Mr Collins received the information in a report from the American Consul in Ireland, George J. Peterson. In July, 246 Irish men and women made preliminary inquiries for visas. No visas were issued since none of the applicants qualified under the preference or non-preference categories of the new law.

The Collins visit to the embassy had taken place in early August. He had met with top officials and had been briefed on the stark new reality.

The *Echo* report added that, 'in another development', the US Department of State had handed down a decision on the new law. The decision had been prompted by a case taken by Frank

O'Connor, an attorney who also happened to be a longtime *Irish Echo* columnist. The State Department had ruled that immigrant visas were 'presently not available' to beneficiaries of fifth preference visa petitions with a majority date later than January 1, 1968 who were chargeable to the allotment for Ireland.

In effect, according to O'Connor, this precluded the admission of Irish brothers or sisters of US citizens at any time in the foreseeable future. This was due to countries such as Italy, Greece, Portugal, China, Poland and others with prior petition filing dates. Countries who had benefited from quotas under the old law, Ireland among them, would now have to take their place in a line behind these prior-filing-date nations. Already, it was estimated, there was a ten-year waiting list for visas, with Ireland very much at the rear of the line.

The State Department decision, opined O'Connor, almost completely excluded anyone under the professional categories such as doctors, teachers or engineers from moving to the United States from Ireland. It also excluded all Irish under the sixth preference. This covered skilled workers such as nurses and the unskilled who had made up the bulk of Irish immigrants. Indeed, O'Connor pointed out – with more than a degree of certainty that he would generate a reaction – the State Department ruling placed a bar in the middle of the Atlantic that would mean near total exclusion from America of Irish nuns.

In the meantime, the *Echo* informed its readers that immigration from a range of other countries in Europe and Asia would 'soar upward' in the non-preference visa category. This category would be made up of mainly brothers and sisters, skilled and unskilled, and professional people. Their admissions, in turn, would make eligible their children and spouses, who would come under the second category as children of aliens permanently admitted – in other words, they would be family reunification admissions, which would now serve as an additional block against predominantly individual Irish visa hopefuls.

In the months that followed, the news would not get any better. This prompted organizers of the 1969 New York St Patrick's Day Parade, as parade historian John Ridge later characterized it, to highlight 'a new immigration law which effectively ended three centuries of Irish immigration to America with the stroke of a pen'. The 1969 parade would also reflect another news story seemingly growing by the day: the eruption of civil unrest in Northern Ireland. But while 'the North' would soon dominate the pages and airwaves of the Irish American press, the immigration story would continue to stoke the angst of Irish America – the broad community and its leaders.

With the Ryan bill stalled in Congress, the final year of a most tumultuous decade would see another hearing before the House Judiciary Subcommittee. That hearing into 'the effect of the Act of October 3, 1965, on immigration from Ireland and Northern Europe' took place on Wednesday, December 10.

The subcommittee convened in Room 2141 of the Rayburn House Building, again under the chairmanship of Congressman Michael Feighan. Congressman Peter Rodino was present at the outset, as was Congressman Thomas Meskill of Connecticut. Other members stopped by and were acknowledged before heading off for meetings elsewhere in the building. Congressman Feighan opened proceedings by stating that in repealing the national quota system it was not anticipated that the pattern of immigration then in existence would be so 'drastically changed' as the record now showed. This belief that patterns would not drastically change had been the general view before labor certification requirements had been included in the '65 bill. Feighan singled out Ireland and Germany, and natives of other unnamed Northern and Western European countries. He said:

> The large number of Congressmen who have cosponsored proposed legislation to restore traditional patterns of migration from Europe is indicative of the dissatisfaction with certain aspects of the 1965 act. Members of the Subcommittee are very cognizant of the results of the 1965 act with reference to the aforementioned countries.

Feighan noted that among the legislative proposals before his subcommittee was the bill introduced by his colleague, Mr Ryan of New York, now with the shortened designation of HR 165, and which had 'numerous cosponsors', and HR 10618, introduced by Congressmen Peter Rodino and William Cahill, both of New Jersey. Rodino, a Democrat, was the more active sponsor of the bill given that Cahill, a Republican, was about to leave Congress and become governor of New Jersey. Nevertheless, bipartisan backing for HR 10618 at its outset was an undoubted plus. Ryan's bill, Feighan explained, would guarantee each country of the 'Eastern Hemisphere' a number below which immigrant visas could not fall during any fiscal year. For Ireland and the other affected countries, the 'floor' would be computed at 75 per cent of the average annual number of immigrant visas made available during the ten-year period beginning July 1, 1955. It looked like a return to a form of the national origin quota system, and Feighan expressed the view that this was exactly what it was 'in some measure'.

HR 10618, Feighan said, would transfer 69,719 visas not used in 1968 to an immigration pool to be made available – one-half in 1970, and one half in 1971 – to those countries which did not use all the visas available to them in fiscal year 1968. Feighan said, 'These visas would be exempted from the 170,000 numerical limitation and would be exempted from the labor certification requirement. Personally, I view this proposal as a stop-gap measure not designed to face the issue which would still remain, or recur after such allocated visas would be used.' Clearly there were hurdles ahead for John Collins – again present in order to testify – and all those supporting the campaign for Irish visas.

Congressman Rodino did, however, open on a reassuring note – though Collins would remain wary. Rodino had backed the '65 act. Was he in fact a fox in the chicken coop? Collins would pose that question in his later records of the American Irish National Immigration Committee (AINIC) and its campaign. If he was a fox on this day, he would have been a concerned one. Rodino, addressing Feighan, expressed his concern over the decline in immigration from Ireland and other countries that had been 'high quota' ones before the 1965 act, 'I want to see the cause of this decline eliminated and I want to see the changes made as expeditiously as the Congress can move.'

Rodino then pointed to, and explained, three bills – two crafted by himself, and one made in collaboration with his fellow New Jersey legislator William Cahill. That bill, HR 10618, had come into being in April 1969. This, said Rodino, was a 'clean bill' designed to overcome the criticism directed at the operation of the transition period from the old national origins systems to the new first-come, first-served system.

As with the other bills, HR 10618 was a proposed way of directing unused visas from fiscal year 1968 into the hands of the Irish and others. Whatever about visas for the Irish, it was certainly raining bills with mentions of the Irish.

Rodino told Chairman Feighan that he was happy to state that the National Board of the Ancient Order of Hibernians (AOH) had studied the provisions of HR 10618 and had endorsed it. Rodino then submitted copies for the record of a letter and a telegram from Michael L. Delahunty, National President of the Hibernians.

The letter was supportive of HR 10618; the telegram was an explanation of Hibernian absence from the hearing and a plea for an adjournment so as to be represented at a resumption. In a later statement submitted to the subcommittee the following year, Delahunty acknowledged that an invitation had been sent to the AOH, but it was too late to allow the organization's designated representative to rearrange his schedule. That statement was dated July 31, 1970, and it dealt in some detail with Rodino's HR 10618, while suggesting some amendments. In the statement, Delahunty concluded:

> We appreciate this opportunity to submit our position to the Committee. We strongly urge that H.R. 10618 be approved as soon as possible. The precipitous drop-off in Irish immigration, caused by section 212(a) (14) if the Immigration and Nationality Act, as amended by the Act of October 3, 1965, must be ameliorated. We look in that direction and trust that the Members of the Committee will join with us in approving legislation to give the Irish a fair chance to re-establish a pattern of immigration to the United States.

That concluding line came close to eight months after Congressman Rodino had urged changes made as expeditiously as the Congress could move. Immigration was not an issue for the impatient or the easily discouraged. But it was an issue that could divide the Irish – or in this case, the Irish of two states.

The December 1969 hearing cast light on a batch of bills, but two of them – the Ryan bill and the Rodino proposal – were evidently at the top of the pile. Ryan was from New York, the home base for John Collins and AINIC. Rodino was from New Jersey, and he was backed by William Cahill, now heading for the governor's office in Princeton, and the AOH National President Michael Delahunty, who was based in Montclair, New Jersey.

Perhaps too much could be read into this possible Garden State-Empire State dividing line. After all, AINIC had its own New Jersey branch committee. Nevertheless, in his history of AINIC, Collins would call out articles in the *Irish Echo* critical of the Ryan bill and supportive of the Rodino proposal penned by Frank O'Connor, 'O'Connor had been to our early organizational meetings, but dropped from attendance thereafter. In April, 1969 he raised the issue of support for proposed legislation introduced by Congressman Peter Rodino (D-NJ). We knew at the time that the Italian Migration Committee had favored the Rodino bill in letters sent to fifty-one Congressmen.'

The Italians were now showing over the horizon. As, of course, were the Germans who supplied testimony to the December 10 hearing from the Steuben Society of America, the German-American National Congress and the American-German Immigration Committee of New Jersey, which, as it happened, was chaired by a gentleman by the name of Halsey T. Burke.

At the hearing, New Jersey Governor Elect Cahill nailed down his support for Rodino's bill. He also took a swipe at Ryan's bill, stating:

> My present feeling in reference to H.R. 165 is that its terms, which provide for permanent changes in the act, are harmful to any hope for the temporary adjustment which I have supported as desirable. Additionally, the permanent changes proposed by

the Ryan bill are of such a nature, in my judgment, as to be impossible of enactment in the light of the political realities of our time ... I find it difficult to view the Ryan proposal as other than a retrograde move in the direction of national origins favoritism. Whether intentional or not, that, in my judgment, is the way it would be viewed in Congress.

It looked like the Rodino bill or nothing, but John Collins, in a detailed testimony, lined up his forces firmly behind the Ryan bill, HR 165. He noted that 'seventy-eight Congressmen' from both parties and 'many different political persuasions' had co-sponsored the Ryan bill, 'They regard it, as do a number of labor unions, as a fair solution and so do we. If enacted it would provide a fair US immigration law for the Nation.'

Mention of unions was important and Collins was able to provide letters of support to the subcommittee from various unions, including those representing longshoremen and members of the Building Service Employees and the Brotherhood of Painters, Decorators and Paper Hangers of America. He also carried to the hearing a letter of support for AINIC and the Ryan bill from the New York City Central Labor Council, American Federation of Labor and Congress of Industrial Organizations (AFL-CIO) representing 1,200,000 members.

Collins spoke at some length, but if he had a battle cry it might have been these lines:

> Our committee is in existence for one purpose only, to right a wrong, to preserve the right of the Irish to enter the United States, not to encourage Irish immigration and certainly not to deny other nations the right to come here. To the chagrin of many it is still in existence and I assure all it will be until justice is achieved.
>
> Mr Chairman, Members of the Congress, we believe we're entitled to a better day and a better law. We regard each of you distinguished Members of Congress as being sympathetic to the plight of the prospective Irish immigrant. We beg you now to channel that sympathy into an effective solution.

Sympathy? Certainly. A solution? Well, the problem now emerging was that there were competing solutions.

Congressman Rodino responded by praising Collins for his eloquence and sincerity while at the same time pointing to 'some areas of disagreement' as to what the various bills proposed to do:

> we find ourselves at loggerheads, because there is an insistence that there is only one way, and that is the way expressed in this statement by Mr Collins. I refer to the Ryan bill, which many of us take seriously because it refers again to the old national origins concept which I know all of us, including Mr Collins, oppose.

This was a shot across the bows from a congressman who, in the not-too-distant future, would chair the Watergate hearings. Peter Rodino was not a man to easily ignore. John Collins was not a man to easily disregard.

Collins stuck to his task. He disputed Rodino's view that the Ryan bill would see a return to the national origins system, 'We again categorically reject national origins ... We want to see it dead. We don't regard the Ryan bill as being a return to national origins any more than we would regard your proposition, the Cahill–Rodino bill, as a return to national origins.'

The argument was increasingly focused on a return to something rather than forward progress towards something new. And the argument looked set to continue. Congressman Feighan adjourned proceedings promising additional hearings in the following year. 'I want to make this clear,' he said, 'there is no intention to have this be a marathon.'

Intent or not, the battle for Irish visas was looking like more of a long-distance process than a legislative sprint. There were competing bills in Congress, promises of more hearings, and, most critically, an increasingly apparent rift between leading advocates for Irish visas. Some would call it a classic Irish split.

Any split apart, the battle was facing, as New Jersey Governor Elect Cahill had put it, the political realities of the time. These added up to sympathy on Capitol Hill, but also antipathy and outright hostility. And there was the massive political *fait accompli* that was the 1965 act. In the face of all this, absolute unity in Irish ranks was a minimum requirement. But it simply wasn't there.

CHAPTER 32

Peaks and Fallows

At a New York gathering of Irish Americans on a spring evening in 1992, presidential hopeful Bill Clinton entered a Manhattan hotel function room hosting that year's Irish American Presidential Forum. The first person in the audience that the former governor of Arkansas sought to shake hands with was Paul O'Dwyer.

O'Dwyer, an iconic figure in the city's Democratic Party, was a man who boldly symbolized the power and potency of the Irish immigrant story. Twenty-four years earlier, as a Democratic Party nominee for the US Senate, O'Dwyer – known widely as a 'liberal lion' – found himself and his son Brian battling the effects of tear gas fired by the Chicago police during the street demonstrations embroiling his party's 1968 National Convention. Many of those police officers had Irish names. As did the mayor of America's second city, Richard J. Daley – a political lion for sure, but not in the O'Dwyer mold. Mayor Daley, as once described by an aide, viewed affirmative action, a concept that O'Dwyer wholeheartedly embraced, in very clear terms. 'Nine Irish guys and a Swede' was as far as Daley was willing to go.

Paul O'Dwyer's family roots were in County Mayo. Daley's were in County Waterford. The distance between the two counties can be covered in a few hours by car. The political distance between O'Dwyer and Daley, two sons of the Irish diaspora and both members of the Democratic Party, could be measured in light years. Together, however, they illustrated the fingertip to fingertip breadth of the Irish American political presence in American life.

In the last year of that tumultuous decade, the Daley concept of diversity reached new heights, albeit non-political ones, and only in a figurative sense. When Apollo 11 blasted off for the moon, it carried three astronauts: Neil Armstrong, Buzz Aldrin and Michael Collins.

Armstrong was for the most part Scots-Irish but had family connections to County Fermanagh. Collins, as his name suggested, had roots in County Cork. Aldrin, whose mother's family name was Moon, traced his family lineage to Sweden. So two Irish guys and a Swede. The Irish of America, in a multitude of respects, had reached Olympian and now cosmic heights in the closing years of the 1960s. One of those heights, unfortunately, was a peak in immigration terms. And as the decade gave way to 1970, the situation for Irish visa advocates was looking decidedly like a tumble down the reverse slope.

It was also a divided tumble. In his rendering of the work of the American Irish National Immigration Committee, John Collins would write of 'a fifth column in our midst'. More precisely, perhaps, a fifth columnist, 'After we were about one year into our campaign, newspaper columns critical of the Ryan bill began appearing in the Education Column of the *Irish Echo*. This was a feature written by Frank O'Connor, an attorney.'

In April 1969, O'Connor had penned a column indicating support for the Peter Rodino bill. On the topic of O'Connor's column, John Collins writes:

> We knew at the time that the Italian Migration Committee had favored the Rodino bill in letters sent to fifty-one Congressmen. At first, O'Connor's columns were only tangentially critical of us but as the months wore on, the criticism seemed a bit harsher. O'Connor and I never had any quarrel, indeed I hardly knew him. I inquired of others as to why he might be writing such material in opposition. Was it that he disliked Congressman Ryan and what he stood for? Ryan was a liberal, active in the anti-Vietnam War movement and was the first member of Congress to introduce a bill seeking the impeachment of President Richard Nixon.

Regardless of O'Connor's reasoning, his columns, according to Collins, were not helpful to the American Irish National Immigration

Committee (AINIC), 'they presented to the Irish community a picture of a divided community on the immigration issue. This was so, even though O'Connor only spoke for himself. To the Irish community, however, O'Connor's columns were presenting a confusing picture. Was he right or were we right?'

Still, Collins and his colleagues were not overly concerned, at least not initially:

> The editor of the *Irish Echo* newspaper – the Irish American newspaper then having the largest circulation – was John Thornton. The owner and publisher were the Grimes family. In an unofficial way, Thornton was a firm supporter of our committee. He provided extensive coverage of our work and his editorials were masterpieces. He, as we, recognized the right of O'Connor, as a columnist, to express his free opinion. Also, O'Connor did not write each week on the issue of immigration and two other columnists at the *Echo*, Sean Maxwell and Pat Hennessey of Chicago, were writing columns in the paper favorable of our work.

Concern, however, would grow as AINIC's work proceeded over time. The election of New Jersey's Michael Delahunty as National President of the Ancient Order of Hibernians (AOH) (succeeding Walter O'Leary of Massachusetts) would result in the appointment of the *Echo*'s O'Connor as AOH National Immigration Chairman. O'Connor, as Collins would put it, now had not only a voice by way of his column but 'stature and power as well'.

Delahunty was also close to Congressman Rodino, with whom Collins and AINIC were familiar by way of the 1968 and 1969 congressional hearings. Rodino's bill was aimed at helping the Irish cope with the negative effects of the 1965 act, which Rodino had supported. But the bill, as far as Collins could determine, was put together at the behest of Delahunty:

> To us it was akin to getting the fox to mind the chicken coop.
> We analyzed Rodino's proposal and found it to be far inferior to the Ryan proposal which had been in the hopper

for some time. Now before the Congress we unfortunately had a battle between two Irish groups rather than a battle with the existing immigration law. The Irish chain had been weakened, and by Irishmen.

Collins wasn't shy about expressing this view. He did so at a New Jersey Hibernian dinner in Newark where he told guests, Delahunty among them, that the work of his committee was being destroyed for no real reason and only 'our own people' would suffer.

Delahunty, according to the Collins account, was not happy with the light in which the Hibernians were being cast on the immigration issue. Rivalry and intrigue would now bedevil the campaign for Irish visa relief. Delahunty, an immigrant from Kerry, was presumably acting with pure motive and had the same aim as Collins: access to America for the Irish. But they were coming at the issue from opposing angles and backing different congressmen. Regardless of a shared goal, the rivalry was all too real and a blow to any chance of a united front.

Rodino, too, was acting out of genuine concern for the Irish. In a letter to AINIC in July 1968, he stated the belief that the '65 act had provided that no country would receive fewer visa numbers than it had previously received under the national origins system. 'As it turned out', Rodino writes, 'the intended generosity only served to handicap countries such as Ireland.' So, an unintended consequence.

Even as they sometimes concurred, at least on paper, the main backers of two political initiatives remained on seemingly close, but distinctly separate, tracks. According to Collins:

On May 12, 1969, Delahunty upped the ante by inviting Congressman Rodino to a closed session of the AOH National Board. Fortunately, we had good informers who kept us abreast of the situation. Delahunty permitted no questioning of Rodino and advised all Hibernians to withhold money from our committee until the National Board made up its mind as to what bill to support. They were also advised that Congressman Rodino planned a trip to Ireland. On learning this, we cabled and advised the Irish Foreign Minister Frank Aiken and Major Vivion de Valera, the President's son and publisher of the Irish Press, of the situation.

Back in New York, Collins and his allies were alarmed by the fact that the O'Connor column in the *Irish Echo* was now 'spouting the line that we, in essence, were meddlers who were preventing the ultimate solution. The situation was most disheartening for us, particularly since we had invested so much personal time and effort. We now had to spend as much time explaining the split as we did fighting Washington on the immigration issue.'

The argument over which bill to support went back and forth through 1969 in Irish American newspapers and on radio shows. Collins was deeply frustrated by Delahunty's stance, but even more frustrated by the fact that, despite the support of many Hibernians, including members of the National Board, it was Delahunty, the National President, who commanded the bully pulpit. Collins would coin the term 'the Delahunty Hibernians'. And it was this perceived grouping that brought forth, as Collins would describe it, 'the apogee of insults'.

The insult came in the form of a full-page ad in the *Irish Echo* taking issue with AINIC and supporting the Rodino bill. Collins got wind of the planned ad and took out a full-page ad of his own. He later recorded, 'The Delahunty group got a hell of a land when they opened the *Irish Echo* and found our ad facing their ad. We were beginning to have the last laugh but at much unneeded expense. The fifth column was beginning to fade and flounder.'

The fading and floundering reached its denouement when Delahunty's term of office came to an end. Collins records:

> He was succeeded by Edward Fay of Pittsburgh who was a great supporter of our work. As his delegate and liaison for immigration, he appointed former congressman John Costello of Los Angeles, who was a member of our committee.
>
> In time, we came to develop a new and healthy relationship with both Congressman Rodino and the Italian Migration Committee. It was on our own mutual terms and there was

respect on both sides. By 1972, our committee had earned the good graces of the Congressman. In a letter dated November 13, 1972, he stated: 'there is no doubt that your confidence in me gave the campaign the momentum to make it one of the most successful in my years of public service.'

Time had passed and time was passing. The immigration issue would remain front and center for America's Irish. In 1973, a third hearing would take place on Capitol Hill chaired by Congressman Joshua Eilberg, a Democrat from Pennsylvania. This hearing would focus on illegal aliens, a term not especially familiar to the Irish in the early 1970s, but one that would have far greater resonance a little over a decade later.

John Collins and his committee had not secured a new deal for the Irish by 1973 but they had raised the issue of Irish exclusion from the immigration rolls to a degree that could not easily be ignored. Along the way, they had gathered the support of Irish American organizations and numerous individuals in the Irish immigrant and Irish American community. Many politicians had offered support and possible legislative solutions. Unions had come on board with statements of support.

So what of the churches, most especially the Catholic Church, which represented the great majority of immigrant Irish? Collins writes, 'Almost from the outset, it became clear that we were not to have the active support of the institutional Catholic Church. The one exception was an effort to obtain immigration status for religious – nuns and brothers.'

The Church line relayed to Collins and the non-institutional Fr O'Callaghan was that while the Church was sympathetic it could not support what it perceived as a request to return to the national origins system. As Collins notes, the US Catholic Conference of Bishops had supported the 1965 law, which had increased immigration from Italy, and Central and South America – parts of the world that could, of course, send far more Catholics to the United States than Ireland.

The 1965 law, Collins acknowledged, promoted the equality of peoples at least as far as immigration to the US was concerned,

'In our view, of course, this so-called equality was misguided and not grounded in reality.' Collins was of the view that the bishops' conference simply didn't comprehend the 'true effect' that the new law would have on countries such as Ireland.

As they reached out to the Church for support, Collins and O'Callaghan would come face to face with entrenched positions, notably among influential lay Catholics, that shaped attitudes to Irish immigration. These positions could be traced to the Irish Civil War, and even the neutrality of the Irish Free State during the Second World War. And in one instance it seemed that the Irish were viewed first and foremost as outsiders, foreigners – because of the way they spoke English. Collins writes:

> One illustration of this was vividly described in California. Cardinal McIntyre, the Los Angeles Archbishop – a son of New York and those earlier generations of Irish – needed priests in the 1960s. Dr Lucey, the Bishop of Cork, offered five or six. The Cardinal accepted but required the Irish priests to attend school 'to learn English'. They, understandably, were offended. So was Dr Lucey – so much so, that he told the Cardinal that no further priests would be sent if the Cardinal insisted on the 'schooling' requirement.

The Catholic Church was becoming a mirror image of Capitol Hill. There were prominent individual clerics supportive of AINIC and its goals, but not enough of them. The Church as a single body, for a variety of reasons, was keeping its distance.

Something similar was happening with union support. Individual unions and their members in cities provided 'tremendous support', according to Collins, 'With few exceptions however, the international unions and the AFL-CIO [American Federation of Labor and Congress of Industrial Organizations] headquarters did not approve our efforts.'

But it would be the lack of full support from the American Catholic hierarchy that would leave an especially sour taste in John Collins's mouth. And he would not be alone in this. He would recall:

Individual bishops and priests supported our work but the organized political arms of the church never supported us. To some of our committee workers, this left a bitter taste. The US Church at the time seemed willing to support the projects of just about every nationality, except one that had given it stability, power and finance. Father O'Callaghan was fond of saying, 'Eaten bread is soon forgotten.'

Interestingly, and certainly ironically, one of the strongest supporters of AINIC wearing a clerical collar was a Methodist minister from Belfast by the name of James Trew. He would become an invaluable liaison between AINIC and non-Catholic members of Congress, many of them of Ulster Scots heritage. Collins writes, 'In the work for a fair immigration policy, Jim by his mere presence, reminded so many Senators and Congressman from the US southern states of their ancestry. He represented that our committee was engaged in work that passed beyond the confines of the Catholic Church.'

Unfortunately, reminding wasn't always followed by persuading.

CHAPTER 33

A Measure of Success

The American Irish National Immigration Committee's (AINIC) work was invariably a balancing act. In political terms, it was a self-proclaimed neutral entity. It supported Democratic congressman Bill Ryan at every twist and turn. This was an easily understood quid pro quo. Ryan's immigration bill offered the American Irish National Immigration Committee (AINIC) the Promised Land of a restored status for would-be Irish immigrants. Support for Ryan apart, it proved difficult at times to sit on the fence. Other forces would pull AINIC off it and into unwanted political battles.

Sometimes this was without AINIC leaders being aware that they were in a scrap. Congressman Feighan in Cleveland was never going to attract Ryan-like support from the committee. Joseph Sweeney, a rival for the congressional seat, did attract such support, though this was supplied quietly and behind the scenes by the local AINIC committee. Feighan, nevertheless, defeated Sweeney in a primary.

On occasion, John Collins would contend, AINIC was 'used'. An example from his perspective was when Congressman Emmanuel Cellar of Brooklyn, as chair of the House Judiciary Committee and running for re-election, took out an ad in one of the Irish American newspapers in which he mentioned AINIC and his efforts to help it. 'He hadn't lifted a finger, ever, to help us,' Collins would later state. AINIC concluded that nothing could be gained by going after a politician whose name was attached to the 1965 act, so it let the matter drop.

The one constant in this turbulent political sea was Congressman Ryan and his bill. Ryan was both legislator and facilitator. On the day that the US House of Representatives was voting on a bill authorizing construction of the DC Metro, Ryan arranged a meeting between John Collins and John McCormick, Speaker of the House of Representatives. Another meeting arranged for Collins was lunch with future speaker Tip O'Neill. Speaker McCormick, Collins would record, told his visitor that Congressman Feighan was difficult to deal with. Collins didn't need to be told this, but neither did he have to dwell on it, as Feighan was defeated in the 1970 election.

But as much as there were members of Congress not overly inclined to get behind AINIC's agenda, there were inanimate legislative hurdles. One of these was the 'rule'. For a bill to move for a floor vote in the House it had to be granted a 'rule' by the House Rules Committee. Collins writes, 'It was becoming increasingly clear that the Ryan bill would not receive a "rule". It is easy to get a bill introduced in Congress. It is far more difficult to get a vote.' He continues:

> It was possible that the Rodino bill could get a 'rule'. It was being offered by a committee chairman. However, no doubt, Rodino saw what might happen on the House floor during any debate and vote. Ryan could offer his bill as an amendment. The chair would rule that out of order. The appeal on the chair's ruling would then be voted on. After a debate Congressmen would be forced on the record, if they so voted, to signify opposition to the Ryan Bill. Our Congressional sponsors would not be willing to do that. Hence a stalemate. So it was suggested to us that if the best of both bills could be included in a new Ryan Rodino Bill – a compromise – we had a chance.

Congressman Ryan, at least at first, wasn't overly enthusiastic. 'After all,' Collins would record, 'there was a question of pride of authorship and he had put enormous work into the project, but so had we. We persuaded him that half a loaf was better than none at all.'

In March 1971, the compromise bill was introduced with the designation HR 9615. The House Judiciary Committee voted on the bill in August and it passed muster quite comfortably. It would be November before the required 'rule' was injected into the process and a full House vote given the go-ahead.

As the House pondered HR 9615, AINIC worked to forge alliances with Italian and German equivalents. A joint committee was formed with the Italian Migration Committee; the new alliance even had its own stationary. The joining together made sense, not least given the fact that the compromise bill was the work of an Irish American and Italian American legislator. Collins would record:

> The Congressman managing our compromise bill in the House decided that the best day to bring the bill to a vote would be March 16, 1972, the eve of St Patrick's Day. The debate on the bill on the floor of the House lasted two and one-half hours, after which the bill passed. Great publicity followed. *The New York Daily News* carried a major article. Of course, we had to inform our troops locally, nationwide and the Irish Government of the actions we had taken and why. All seemed pleased.

Congressman Ryan hailed passage of HR 9615 as follows:

> The action of the House in approving the legislation, without amendment, is truly a victory for all who have fought so long to correct the inequities of the 1965 amendments which drastically curtailed Irish immigration. It is a tribute to the dedicated efforts of the American Irish Immigration Committee under the leadership of John Collins and Father Donald O'Callaghan who presented persuasive testimony before the committee and organized support around the country for legislative change.

This legislative change, as envisaged in the House bill, would make additional visas available for four years under a prescribed formula. If the bill was fully in effect in 1972, this would mean 4,003 additional visas for Ireland. This would be on top of the actual 487 visas allocated to Ireland that year. Collins was now looking ahead:

> Spurred on by our victory in the House we were confident that the Ryan–Rodino Bill would pass in the Senate and then

be signed by the President. At the time, one and one-half years remained in the session of Congress.

Already Senator Hugh Scott, Republican of Pennsylvania, and Senator Clifford Case, Republican of New Jersey, had offered similar types of bills in the Senate. Robert Taft Jr., Republican Senator from Ohio, had submitted the Ryan–Rodino bill under Senate No. 2877.

Of course, the key once again would be the chair of the Judiciary Committee. This time in the Senate it was James Eastland of Mississippi. We had no solid contact with him and had to depend on Senator Ted Kennedy to exercise the necessary persuasion and pressure.

Back in January, AINIC had secured a meeting with Kennedy. He had assured the committee that he would 'earnestly work' to see that an approved House bill was adopted in the Senate.

Kennedy would be duly reminded of his pledge by means of postcards sent to his office in the late summer of 1972. AINIC members and supporters sent 12,000 postcards, and as best AINIC could determine, Kennedy, or at least his office, had replied to all of them by November of that year.

Letters, a couple of hundred of them, were sent to Senate Majority Leader Mike Mansfield, a Democrat from Montana. The man to write to above all else was Senator James Eastland, though that would have been a fool's errand. Eastland wrote something himself – a letter to John Collins in which he indicated that S.2877 was not going to be taken up and would be allowed to die as the session of Congress expired. This was not altogether to surprising in a presidential election year. Congress punts more than it even pontificates in such years.

But there was a new Congress at the outset of 1973, and by May, Congressman Rodino had brought back his bill under the designation HR 4973. Congressman Joshua Eilberg was now chairing the House Immigration Sub-Committee. Eilberg, by September, was indicating that he would not be acting on HR 4973.

It was back to Ted Kennedy who, contrary to the expectations of some, produced a Senate bill in the year's final month. Much of its content was drawn from the old Rodino–Ryan House bill, so to Irish eyes it looked good on paper. By now, however, those Irish eyes were becoming somewhat jaundiced, as explained by Collins:

> By January of 1974, we began to question whether the Kennedy bill was a political ploy to save face or instead was an earnest action. By now, we knew well how easy it was to introduce a bill destined to go nowhere.
>
> In February, 1974, our friends at the American and Citizenship Conference petitioned Senator Eastland to hold hearings on the Kennedy bill. Eastland did not. By September of 1974, Kennedy was telling us that he was 'still hopeful'. Not long after, the session of Congress came to an end – a new session to begin in January 1975. Two more years had passed with no action. Once again, we would have to begin all over again.

Collins, however, would not begin all over again. Much had changed since he and Fr O'Callaghan had started their journey, not least the fact that O'Callaghan, 'my partner in the struggle', had passed, as had Congressman Ryan. Collins writes:

> I had since married and now we had a young son. I had changed jobs in the interim. I could no longer contribute the necessary energy and carry the workload of a new campaign. I was no longer sure that our various chapters could be kept engaged for a longer period. I offered my resignation to the committee and Tom Feeney, the Vice Chairman, agreed to soldier on for the near future.

Words and terms like 'struggle' and 'soldier on' about summed up the situation. They applied to the members of AINIC, Collins and O'Callaghan to the fore, and also, indeed, to Congressman Bill Ryan, who had died in September 1972, and of whom Collins would later write, 'There was no end to the man's energy and motivation. Our committee suffered a tremendous blow by reason of his death. He was a man of wisdom, compassion and love, who touched our lives.

He could disagree without being disagreeable. We sorely missed Bill Ryan.'

There can be no underestimating the level of energy and commitment required to get the United States to change its mind when it is not so inclined. America, as it is so often said, is a nation of laws. Once a law is set it can take heaven and earth to move it. So it seemed, from an Irish American perspective, with regard to the 1965 immigration law.

Irish America, of course, could be energetic and forceful once enough of it was focused on a specific issue. But by the early 1970s, much of Irish America was increasingly focused on a specific issue. It wasn't immigration and visas; rather, it was the storm clouds over Ireland, and especially Northern Ireland.

All was changing, changing utterly. And what would be born of it was anyone's guess.

CHAPTER 34

Troubles Behind, Troubles Ahead

A month after the *Irish Echo* reported on its front page that 'America Closes The Door', the front page led with a headline pointing to a new and very different story: 'Nationalists, Police Clash in Derry Weekend of Protest'.

The *Echo* is a weekly, but not a Sunday publication. That is to say, its focus is on hard news, weekday style. As such, it would prominently report the big stories of the week from Ireland during the years of the Northern Ireland Troubles. There would be a lot of years – too many of them. And a lot of stories for the front page and the inside pages too. As the streets of Belfast and Derry burned, immigration would largely be consigned to Irish America's backburner.

That is not to say that grievances over the door closing following the 1965 immigration act were pushed entirely into the shadows. It was more a case of being put on hold. The immigration story would return to the *Echo* front page, and other front pages, well before the Troubles gave way to the Good Friday Agreement and the peace process.

But the full-frontal assault on the 1965 act by Irish American activists had come up short. The law remained in place. Yes, criticism of the act continued. In the *Irish Echo*, Chicago-based columnist Pat Hennessy, an immigrant himself, would regularly lament the consequences of the act. And while the American Irish National Immigration Committee faded from the front lines, there was a formal Irish presence maintained in the argument through a group called the Irish Immigration Working Committee. It was primarily Irish American in its ranks, with unions well represented.

In the ten years from 1971 through 1980, a total of 11,940 visas were issued to the Irish so exclusion from the United States was not total. And for a time it seemed as if even the drastically reduced level of visa allocation might be sufficient to satisfy Irish demand. For one thing, economic recession in the US during the 1970s was enough to deter some who contemplated an Atlantic jump. And the Irish Sea, as ever, was a much easier barrier to traverse. Besides, the Irish economy was growing – or at least there were promises of growth emanating from politicians.

As P.J. Drudy wrote in his introduction to *The Irish in America: Emigration, Assimilation and Impact*, during the 1970s 'there was a substantial net in-flow of population'. At the same time, Drudy noted that the phenomenon was a temporary one due to increases in unemployment in Ireland. Maybe, just maybe, the closing of America's door would prove to be an economically neutral occurrence, perhaps even an irrelevant one.

Then again, even if the legal obstacles were in place, and the American economy was sputtering, that same economy could still generate a powerful pull effect on top of the push generated by Irish joblessness. A recessionary America offered more than a recessionary Ireland. And for many young Irish in the late 1970s and early 1980s, there was also the prospect of quick money, often cash, and potentially earned off the books. America need not be a permanent option but a temporary Plan B, with a return to Ireland, pockets stuffed with dollars, as the intended climax of the adventure.

There was one problem with Plan B. It could be snuffed out if Plan A began working beyond expectation. The Irish migration to 1980s America, Ronald Reagan's America, began to pick up in numbers around 1982–3. Those early arrivals were to discover something that their ancestors had also identified: that it was possible to settle in a new and unfamiliar place. What they were also to learn was that it was possible to do so even without the security of legal status.

And so the numbers of 1980s Irish began to grow. In 1984, President Reagan, a descendant of more traditional Irish immigrants, made his much-ballyhooed visit to Ireland in search of his roots in Ballyporeen, County Tipperary. Some of the local kids weren't around to wave at the Gipper. They were back in the United States giving his immigration agents the slip. Eluding the attention of the Immigration and Naturalization Service (INS) wasn't something to treat lightly. But it was a relatively easy task in those barely computerized pre-9/11 years when I-94 visa slips had a habit of falling out of passports.

The east to west migration picked up steam in 1985 and '86. Stories would drift back eastwards of a cousin or friend pulling in hundreds of dollars a week. It was financial catnip to a generation that had been promised a lot more than their parents – who had access to much more than them in terms of education and creature comforts but felt that daily life in Ireland was still falling short of all the promises.

It wasn't long before the new Irish were being noticed, though not necessarily by the Immigration and Naturalization Service (INS). Their fellow Irish, already ashore, and legally so, could not but be aware of the new arrivals. The reaction was twofold: say little or nothing in the hope that the newcomers would be able to live and work under the radar; or take another hard look at the reason why all these young Irish were settling in (or trying to) as illegals – or, to use the less charged term, undocumented.

Going back to the early 1800s, the Irish in America had reported on themselves with newspapers. The 1980s would add a monthly glossy, *Irish America Magazine*, founded by a new Irish arrival, Niall O'Dowd. *Irish America*, in an October 1986 editorial headlined 'No Irish Need Apply', fired one of the first salvos at US immigration law on behalf of O'Dowd's newly arriving fellow Irish, who, for the most part, were heading for undocumented status after six months on US soil. The law facing these 'new Irish' was quite simply 'a disgrace', the editorial stated. The same issue also cast light on a long-suspected but largely unseen hand in the perceived origins of this disgrace: the 1965 reform act.

House Speaker Tip O'Neill, the veteran Massachusetts legislator, recalled in an interview that as the debate over immigration reform had reached a climax more than twenty years previously, the Irish ambassador in Washington at the time (O'Neill couldn't actually recall his name during the interview, but it was William Fay) had paid visits to the leading Irish American politicians on Capitol Hill, urging them to vote in favor of the reform act. The idea behind this ploy was noble enough in intent, at least from the Irish government's perspective. O'Neill said:

> The Irish ambassador came around to our offices and asked us to vote for that bill because there was a tremendous brain drain out of Ireland and they wanted to stop it. That's why we voted for it.
>
> I can remember people in my neighborhood coming up to me, saying furiously they wanted cousins and relatives to come over here. And I told them, 'Listen we're doing this because we have been asked by the Irish government to help stop the brain drain.'

It would subsequently come to light that the Lemass government had also opposed a special exemption for the Irish to be built into the '65 act, something that several Irish American political leaders, Ted Kennedy among them, had drawn up.Two decades on, in *Irish America*'s view, this had been entirely the wrong approach. The magazine opined that the Lemass-led government had been 'short-sighted in the extreme', that Irish citizens had been held back for 'an-all-too temporary economic renaissance', and that the Irish government, 'with the subtlety of a sledgehammer and no thought for future generations', had 'actually acquiesced in the closing of the American frontier, perhaps for ever, to their own people'.

At first glance it looked as if any action prompted by such an editorial might be a replica of what had occurred during the campaign by the American Irish National Immigration Committee in the 1960s and '70s. In other words, another full-on drive against the '65 act's consequences for the Irish, intended or otherwise. But the 1980s would prove to be a different kind of battlefield. For one thing, the lack of visas and their attendant green cards was not proving a deterrent to the Irish. The American frontier, though legally closed to most, was still, for the most part, physically open. And the Irish were pouring across it.

On top of all this, the '65 act would be overshadowed to a degree by new and comprehensive immigration legislation that would favor some Irish, even as it frustrated far more. And as was the case with 1965, the Irish would respond by joining ranks in an organization dedicated to tackling inequity, real and perceived.

History wasn't precisely about to repeat itself. But a new generation of Irish immigration reform warriors was about to take up a fight that the previous generation had fought. This time around, the front lines would be a staging ground for the rhetorical fire and fury of newly arrived Irish. And a broad swathe of established America would find itself having to pay attention.

CHAPTER 35

The Boys from Massachusetts

The 1980s would have its Congressman Bill Ryan. That would be Congressman Brian Donnelly. The 1980s would have its version of the 1965 Immigration and Nationality Act. That would be the 1986 Immigration Reform and Control Act. And, of course, there would be Senator Edward Kennedy, who would add a third decade to his activity on the immigration issue.

It was in 1986 that there would be a riposte to the deliberations and resulting law in 1965. Some Capitol Hill legislators had never fully accepted the idea of immigration being based primarily on family reunification. The demands of a diversifying labor market and increasingly technical skills required by many employers were drawing fire from critics of the status quo such as Senator Alan Simpson, a Republican from Wyoming, and Brian Donnelly, a congressman from Massachusetts whose district was centered in one of Irish America's heartlands, Dorchester.

The 1986 act, signed into law by President Reagan on November 6, was a double-edged sword. It had first emerged above the legislative horizon in 1983 and its prime backers would be Simpson, Democratic congressman Peter Rodino from New Jersey – whose name was well familiar to the Irish as a result of the campaign by the American Irish National Immigration Committee in the 1970s – and Democratic congressman Roman Mazzoli, whose name could easily be associated with New Jersey or New York, but who in fact represented a district in Kentucky. The eventual act, also known as the Simpson–Mazzoli Act, carried in its lines an amnesty for undocumented immigrants who had entered the United States before January 1, 1982 – this, assuming those arrivals met a range of mandated requirements. The new law additionally introduced a number of stiff new labor requirements with serious penalties for employers who knowingly hired undocumented workers.

Later estimates for the number of immigrants who qualified for the bill's amnesty provision put the number at over three million. The problem for the Irish was that there were very few of them in that grand total, because the great bulk of the Irish wave in the 1980s occurred after the 1982 cut-off date. The number of Irish who secured legality under the amnesty, it was generally agreed, could be counted in the hundreds.

But the '86 law had a green lining for the Irish. And it would come courtesy of Congressman Donnelly. With the number of Irish arriving in the US now sufficient to prompt alarming headlines back in Ireland, the pressure was mounting on both Irish politicians and diplomats. And it was diplomats based in Boston who would encourage Donnelly to do something – anything.

And so a device called the NP-5 visa program was born. Its arrival in the world would accurately reflect the nature of the United States Congress in the era of Reagan and O'Neill – a time when deals could still be struck and nudged over the legislative finish line. The NP-5 would give the world, or at least thirty-five countries in it, the so-called 'Donnelly Visas'. Ireland would be one of the thirty-five, and something of a first among equals when it came to divvying up a great stack of green cards.

The countries to benefit from the program – most of them European – were deemed to have suffered the greatest disadvantages as a result of the 1965 reforms. There would be 40,000 visas made available over a five-year period from 1987 to 1991. But there nearly weren't any visas at all.

Not surprisingly, many if not most of the fast-arriving and mostly young Irish were planting their feet in traditionally Irish corners of America. If all of them had headed for, say, Utah, there might never have been help forthcoming from Capitol Hill. But they would descend in great numbers in places such as the Bronx, Queens, Upper Darby in Philadelphia and Dorchester on the outskirts of Boston.

Dorchester was in the heart of Brian Donnelly's congressional district, which he would represent from 1979 to 1993. It was no surprise that he would hear of the newly arriving Irish and their difficulties in settling into a legal American life. Donnelly was one of those legislators who believed that the '65 act did have unintended consequences for the Irish and was effectively discriminating against those who wanted to follow the traditional, legal route to a new life in America. Donnelly wasn't an expert on immigration, but he was an expert politician who could quickly draw deductions from the stories he was hearing from concerned Irish American constituents – and sometimes directly from the newly arrived Irish. He would later say that he had 'bullied' his way onto the House Judiciary Subcommittee on Immigration, Refugees and International Law which was, in the run-up to passage of the 1986 act, chaired by Congressman Mazzoli.

The legislation being crafted by Mazzoli, Rodino, Simpson and others proposed to deal exclusively with illegal immigration. The argument to exclude legal immigration from the pending reform was based on the view that to pass a bill at all it would be necessary to focus entirely on illegal immigration. The amnesty would be a one-off, and the rest of the measure would be a crackdown on illegality by making it hard for undocumented and illegals to find work.

Brian Donnelly was having none of it. He drew up an amendment that would offer visas to many people in many countries but, most particularly, the undocumented Irish of Dorchester and Massachusetts. Tip O'Neill would famously say that all politics was local. Donnelly was bearing witness to that prescient assertion. He had an amendment lined up. It contained the Donnelly Visas. But did the visas have a chance? Donnelly was far from certain. He was being made promises that more or less came down to 'next year Brian, maybe'.

So the Simpson–Mazzoli–Rodino measure proceeded through various committees and both the House and Senate. It passed through the House-Senate Conference procedure before returning to the House for what was anticipated as a final *pro forma* approval. Donnelly had other ideas. 'The vote began', he would later recount, 'with mostly green lights of approval. But I had worked things out with other Irish American representatives. The train was leaving the station and we needed to force through the amendment. We decided to vote against Simpson Mazzoli.'

And so Donnelly and his allies determined to vote against final passage for a bill that they fundamentally agreed with. As Donnelly would later recall, 'Tip [O'Neill] would be counting on us, we knew that. But we would save our votes until the last minute and hit the red lights together. That's what we did. The bill came crashing down. We killed it.'

O'Neill could read a room and figured that Donnelly had to be the cause of this stunning upset. Donnelly was summoned to the Speaker's bench. The gentleman from the 11th District unloaded his mind quickly, before the gavel came down, figuratively, but not entirely short of literally, on his head.

'Mr Speaker, they are refusing to include my amendment,' Donnelly said. O'Neill asked Donnelly how he could get him and his rebel group to vote for the bill. 'Include my amendment', came the reply. Donnelly remembers the moment as pure O'Neill – a dash of political theater that would become increasingly rare in Congress as the twentieth century proceeded to its close, 'He said to me, "everyone thinks I'm dressing you down Brian." He winked at me and said, "I'm going to stare at you and look very stern. But don't worry, we'll look after the Irish."'

Donnelly went back to his seat, looking serious but trying not to smile. O'Neill went off to discuss the unforeseen failure of the bill with the House Rules Committee. He came back the next day with promises that a Yes vote from Donnelly and his gang would be followed by the attachment of Donnelly's amendment. Thus, the Donnelly Visas came into the world.

'This was one issue on which Irish American legislators were unanimous', Donnelly would recall years later. 'It was the first time in my generation that Irish Americans united on one issue. We could never get that with Northern Ireland.'

Donnelly's assessment was both critical and positive. It also highlighted what was something of a unique moment in political time. The moment would stretch for a few more years, but the Donnelly Visas would see the coming together of an Irish American political trio that would not be replicated in any of the years to come. Speaker Tip O'Neill and Congressman Donnelly would hand over to Ted Kennedy in the Senate. It was like a slick passing move, with a goal at the end of it. The *Washington Post* would later assess it as follows:

> In 1986, Rep. Brian J. Donnelly (D-Mass.) proposed an amendment to the Immigration Reform and Control Act that would provide 10,000 visas on a first-come, first-served basis for nationals of countries 'adversely affected' by the 1965 changes. Sen. Ted Kennedy (D-Mass.) filed similar legislation in the Senate. Then-House Speaker Tip O'Neill – yet another Irish American Democrat from Massachusetts – ensured that the amendment passed.

The Donnelly Visas would also reveal a high degree of Irish American community readiness and organization. As the *New York Times* would later report, the Donnelly Visas were awarded on a first-come, first-served basis, 'The Irish, who were well organized, submitted 200,000 of the earliest applications, winning just over 40 per cent of the first 10,000 visas, and were expected to do well for the rest.' The percentage secured translated into 4,161 visas – no small number for a country the size of Ireland when competing with so many others of far greater size and population.

Impressive though the number was, it was not sufficient to meet the needs of the steadily growing number of undocumented Irish within America's borders – this, in addition to the many more Irish now eyeing those borders. The gap between promise and fulfillment in 1980s Ireland, for all too many young citizens, was, as Yeats might have put it, a widening gyre.

But leaving Ireland was not the end to all problems. While America, at first flush, seemed like a great adventure, the lack of legal status would mean that, over time, the walls began to close in, even in a land thousands of miles wide. There was nothing else for it. The walls would have to be pushed back. And the way to do it was to band together, speak with a single voice and join forces under the banner of a dedicated organization. The Donnelly Visas were an encouragement. Visas were on offer, but more of them were needed and it looked glaringly obvious that they would have to be fought for.

To carry the fight, a handful of Irish arrivals and sympathetic Irish already living legally in America spoke to each other and came up with an idea that would take a name: the Irish Immigration Reform Movement.

CHAPTER 36

To the Banner Born

It was, admittedly, a bit of a mouthful. But the task ahead required a *nom de guerre* with more than a hint of gravitas. The Irish Immigration Reform Movement (IIRM) matched the mood of the moment. And the 'Irish' part of it was to attract the attention of the non-Irish mainstream American media. That was the idea.

If 1986 had delivered the Donnelly Visas, 1987 would confirm for many that one visa program would not bring an end to a story that was generating more and bigger headlines on both sides of the Atlantic. Unemployment in the Republic of Ireland was approaching 20 per cent and the North's Troubles were hardly an incentive for the young to hang around its six counties. So the youth of the island scattered, and more and more of them were turning up in American cities. It was only a matter of time before they organized in protest against what they had fled and what they were now facing.

This was altogether different to what had developed after the 1965 act and its effective bar on the Irish. Relatively few Irish had jumped the fence in the immediate years following the act's implementation. The 1980s Irish were jumping over it in droves, and this would be noticed by the Irish and Irish American community, politicians, and the aforementioned media.

Within Irish America there was disagreement over how precisely to react. Some wanted the growing phenomenon of the undocumented Irish – the illegal Irish – to be kept under wraps as much as possible while the community quietly helped by providing jobs. Others wanted the clearly deteriorating situation to be confronted head-on. And that would mean creating a political stink. It wasn't too difficult a task to create that stink, especially after the *New York*

Times discovered the strange new tale of Irish people living in the legal shadows. Ireland's political leaders now had no choice but to rouse Irish America from its slumbers on behalf of the new Irish in their midst.

On February 11, 1987, Taoiseach Charles Haughey, in the face of escalating press coverage on the crisis across the Atlantic, delivered an election eve campaign promise of a 'major initiative to secure legal status for the large number of young Irish emigrants in the United States who have not got such status at present'. Haughey pledged his Fianna Fáil party to 'use every diplomatic and political means available to us to secure legal status for all these young Irish people'. This would entail mobilizing Irish American opinion in order to 'bring the maximum political pressure to bear on Congress and the White House'. It was unclear precisely what that maximum might actually amount to, but there was no doubting the growing prominence of the story surrounding 'all these young Irish people'.

On April 17, the *New York Times* upped the ante for everyone – the undocumented Irish, Irish America and politicians back in Ireland – with a story about one undocumented Irishman named Patrick. The report was headed: 'Invisible Aliens: Irish Fear Effect of New Immigration Law'. Patrick, reporter Marvin Howe told the paper's readers (Patrick Hurley's surname was withheld), lived in the country illegally and resented being called an undocumented alien. Howe writes:

> His grandfather was an American who fought with the United States Army in France in World War I. One sister is a nurse in the United States Army in England and is married to an American. Another sister works on a horse farm in New Jersey; a brother has a job in a warehouse in Connecticut. His American relatives include a retired Army colonel, an F.B.I. agent and a Boston police officer.

If family connections were a hand of cards, this would have amounted to a royal flush. But Patrick found himself playing the role of joker. And he didn't like it.

Howe had spoken to the Immigration and Naturalization Service (INS) and had uncovered some interesting statistics. In 1986, for example, a mere 1,839 Irish had been admitted to the US as permanent residents but 98,188 had entered the country with temporary visas. 'Officials,' reported Howe, 'noted recent research showing that the Irish are one of the leading nationalities that tend to overstay the terms of temporary visas.' From this a *Times* reader could quickly conclude that a significant proportion of the 98,188 were still, temporarily, somewhere in the fifty states. The *Times* story also revealed that all these Irish were doing a fairly good job of not attracting INS attention. Only eight Irish illegals had been deported in 1985, as opposed to 3,034 Salvadorans and 11,368 Mexicans.

Ironically, one of the reasons for relative Irish invisibility was that, unlike Latin Americans, they tended not to congregate in large numbers in work activities such as agriculture, despite the fact that they had fled a country which touted itself in a TV commercial at the time as 'the world's greenest dairy land'. The streets of New York, Boston, Philadelphia and other cities were not exactly green, but they were increasingly home to young Irish whose family roots were deeply entrenched in the greener parts of that dairy land.

The Irish Immigration Reform Movement would be the handiwork of a number of people, but Patrick 'Pat' Hurley and Sean Minihane, his boyhood friend from Skibbereen in County Cork, would become the public voices for the organization. The former was illegal, the latter was legally living in the US. They literally straddled the issue they were championing.

And it was in the kitchen of Minihane's New York apartment that, on a Saturday morning in early May 1987, that the two came up with the name of the new Irish organization and its war cry, 'Legalize the Irish'.

A few days later, on May 20, the IIRM held its first full meeting in the Queens meeting room of the Cork Association. Mae O'Driscoll, a legal immigrant from Skibbereen – who had experienced the August 1969 hijacking of TWA Flight 840 by Leila Khaled and fellow members of the Popular Front for the Liberation of Palestine – recorded the minutes of the gathering.

The immediate and substantial aid given to the nascent IIRM by a well-established Irish organization such as the Cork Association would prove invaluable. And it would mirror the assistance given to John Collins and the American Irish National Immigration Committee by the Limerick Association and others two decades previously.

Collins, now a judge, spoke to the Cork Association of his experiences leading a reform group and his view of prospects for the 1980s undocumented Irish. He would later write that his message was not a positive one. The US economy was not in the best of shape and he was concerned that labor unions would be wary of immigration law changes that would adversely affect the US labor force. Still, he was supportive of the IIRM's goals and purpose. These goals and this purpose were outlined at the first meeting, which the *Irish Echo* reported under a somewhat understated headline: 'Immigration Reform group gears up'.

Pat Hurley, for one, was revving up. At the May 20 meeting, he had delivered an impassioned address that had held the room spellbound for thirty minutes. And he had also penned a letter, no less informative and impassioned, to the *Echo*. Hurley's letter was a call to political arms. It was headed 'Plea from an undocumented alien' and was signed 'Patrick, an undocumented alien from County Cork'.

The idea of an Irish immigrant being described as an undocumented alien was something new and puzzling to most of the paper's readers. In the letter, Hurley drew an outline of economic conditions in Ireland – conditions that were, by 1987, so bad that various Catholic Church agencies had started distributing 'emigration kits' in secondary schools. Hurley wrote:

> It is estimated that over 100,000 of us Irish are now working and living illegally in the US. For us the hour of decision approaches, before the full force of the recently passed immigration act is brought to bear.
>
> Our choice is one of two unattractive options – to return to poverty and hopelessness in Ireland, or to remain on here, in the hope that employment opportunities will not be

completely obliterated, and in apprehension of being hunted down and ultimately deported. For the vast majority of us, return is out of the question. There is no future for us back in the 'old country'.

Hurley's words came across as dramatic, but those who knew him never doubted that they were written from the head as well as the heart.

He wrote of not standing idly by and 'allowing ourselves to become a lost generation, destined to wander a world that is no longer made up of wide-open, welcoming continents'. He spoke of a 'right of sanctuary' for the Irish in America – a right 'earned by the committed contributions of countless Irishmen in the building of this great country'. And addressing a large portion of the *Echo*'s readership directly, Patrick, the undocumented alien, delivered his bottom-line appeal:

> We are no different in nature to you immigrants who came before us. We cherish the same hopes and dreams that you once cherished. However, it seems that, for us, this welcoming sanctuary no longer exists.
>
> Immigrants of the past, do not forget us. Do what you can to help us in our plight. Help us regain a necessary refuge in this country, not only for ourselves, but also for those who will follow. For remember, if you deny us, you deny that from which you came.

And just for good measure, Hurley offered a vision of what he hoped lay ahead, 'And maybe on a St Patrick's Day in better times to come, we will proudly march side by side. We, proud that we did not fail and that we won through against the odds, and you, proud that you did not forget the "old country," or your people, in their hour of need.'

Hurley, in what amounted to a declaration of both independence and dependence, could easily have been accused of laying it on a bit thick. But it didn't seem so to his fellow illegal Irish, each of whom were living every day as either their first of a new life in America, or their last. Besides, laying it on thick was catnip for journalists, and Hurley and his IIRM comrades were well aware that escaping from the shadows would require light to be cast into those same shadows. That's where the media and, beyond it, the politicians came in – but more than just the Irish American media and, down the line, more than just Irish American politicians.

The *Times* story, of course, was as good a start as you could hope for, and at the May 20 rollout, its beneficial effect was clear in the room. Not only was the 58-year-old *Irish Echo* and two-year-old *Irish America Magazine* on hand, but also the *New York Times*, the *Village Voice* and the *Daily News*. Irish radio show hosts Adrian Flannelly and Dorothy Hayden Cudahy were also present. Congressman Tom Manton, the most powerful Democrat in Queens, sent a representative, as did the Irish Consulate in Manhattan. Niall O'Dowd, well advanced in his plans for a new Irish American newspaper aimed squarely at the new immigrant arrivals, reported the meeting for the *Irish Press* newspaper back in Dublin.

The meeting required a fair bit of reporting. It lasted for three hours. Out of it all there would emerge, over time, an IIRM that was politically charged and in hot pursuit of as many political connections as it could muster. The months following the organization's founding were filled with meetings, fundraisers, and attempts to attract positive and useful publicity. The preferred kind of attention came from sympathetic journalists and politicians. The Immigration and Naturalization Service did not fall into this category, but the government's immigration enforcers seemed to be keeping their distance, at least for the time being.

The press coverage rolled on and the politicians rowed in behind it. One among them was Mayor Raymond Flynn of Boston, whose adviser on Irish affairs, Frank Costello, told the *Wall Street Journal* that the city was missing out on the talents of all the new Irish arrivals because they couldn't start their own businesses. Nevertheless, Boston was ready to take in the Irish, any which way, and certainly as fully legal immigrants, legal guest workers, or American citizens by way of military service. That was what was stated. What went unstated, but was understood, was that the city that saw itself as

America's Irish capital wasn't going to fret much about the precise status of so many of the new Irish arrivals.

The IIRM, meanwhile, wasn't confining itself to Queens, or indeed New York City, and began setting up branches in other urban outposts. There would be press releases, buttons, T-shirts and banners – one of them, eventually, and after some debate, finding itself in Pat Hurley's dreamed-of St Patrick's Day Parade, though a parade still awaiting the arrival of those better times.

Before 1987 was to pass, Niall O'Dowd's new immigrant-focused weekly, the *Irish Voice*, would hit the streets. Its first headline was a gauntlet on the ground: 'We'll Never Return – Young Illegals'. Not only were the young illegals determined not to return to Ireland. They were still arriving.

CHAPTER 37

Numbers Up, Numbers Down

Between 1871 and 1921, about 2.1 million Irish men and women had immigrated to the United States, 'roughly a third of the estimated entire exodus of 6.5 million who crossed the Atlantic after 1607 to settle in what eventually became the American republic'. So recorded Kerby Miller in the opening paragraph of his contribution to *The Irish in America: Emigration, Assimilation and Impact*.

Apart from the numbers, which are significant and impressive, the two words that stand out for special consideration are 'roughly' and 'estimated'. Irish migration to America will forever be a rough count. There were periods in the evolution of the new nation during which officialdom was able to more or less accurately count the number of immigrant arrivals from Ireland who would ultimately put down new roots in that same new nation. And there were times when they couldn't accurately count, failed to count or lost count. The latter half of the 1980s veered into such territory.

Regardless, the argument at the time was always going to be dominated by numbers, and often conflicting ones. Pat Hurley had already posted a number for the Irish who were temporarily in the United States while longing for permanency. That number was 100,000. With the dawn of 1988, and as the Irish Immigration Reform Movement (IIRM) campaign rose higher above the political horizon, that number would be on the way to 250,000. This was, of course, entirely without foundation. But it grabbed attention. And attention was key if any kind of success was to be attained.

In the opening days of the New Year, Congressman Brian Donnelly got to work again on behalf of the Irish with a new bill in the House of Representatives. Senator Edward Kennedy penned a companion for the Senate. In truth, neither man required an inflated number to spring into action. Indeed, they were wary of extra zeroes flying around the place. Actually getting a bill passed would be easier if it didn't look like a response to an outright Irish invasion.

Immigration and Naturalization Service (INS) spokesman Duke Austin was keeping an eye on the numbers. And not just the Irish ones. 'If you call Kennedy and Donnelly they'll tell you it's not an Irish immigration bill, but if you look at the world situation you'll say it benefits the Irish,' he would opine. 'Once you start becoming internationally specific you run into all sorts of problems. You've got two million people waiting to immigrate to the United States from the Philippines, India, Mexico and Korea.'

Ireland was small, even as the IIRM was significantly raising its profile. And the INS man wasn't exaggerating with his two million. Indeed, the number of people arriving in the United States at the moment the IIRM came into being – from any one of the countries named by Austin – was enough to shove the Irish off the edge of the map. More than 27,000 Indians, 35,000 Koreans and 50,000 Filipinos arrived in 1987 alone. Mexico was a country with enough of its people eyeing the US to keep the INS working overtime all by itself. An official study on immigration presented to Congress once described illegal immigration from Mexico as nothing less than a 'geometric progression'.

So how was it that the Irish, with their far smaller numbers, could see to it that flustered INS officials had to keep answering questions from reporters about thousands of Irish as opposed to millions from all over the world? There were several reasons, not least the fact that the Irish were English-speaking, educated and, as a result, an easily understood story for journalists to report. The Irish didn't appear to be 'foreign' to the average American – many of them with Irish heritage themselves. The Irish, then, were accorded the privilege – and it was certainly a privilege – of being described in national or ethnic rather than racial terms. This helped when it came to tapping into the very tangible goodwill factor afforded by those Americans who considered themselves at least part Irish. And there were millions of them.

The presence of many Irish Americans in the national media was a factor too. There were, quite simply, a lot of Irish Americans producing and directing the news segments, speaking to cameras, assigning the reporters, writing the stories, editing them and placing them into prime spots on page this or that. Added to all this there were the ready and willing Irish American politicians, particularly in the House of Representatives. Individuals such as Brian Donnelly, Bruce Morrison and Joe Moakley were to attain prominence as Irish boosters. And, of course, there was Teddy Kennedy.

The IIRM was like a fishing trawler with a huge net scouring a goldfish pond. When it came to grabbing attention, it couldn't miss. But beyond initial attention, there was the deep sea wherein lurked the machinations of Congress. You needed friends in the place – big friends. Kennedy was very big, but with the arrival of all the young Irish he found himself facing a consequence of his own work two decades previously. How would Kennedy react to the pleas – no, demands – of all the newcomers as voiced by the IIRM and their supporters?

Those supporters were growing in numbers – as were the arriving Irish. By the spring of 1988, an encounter with a young Irish person would most likely mean an encounter with a young Irish person who was undocumented. Even for the more cautious in the engaged Irish American community, it was becoming ever harder to maintain the argument that the situation should be kept under wraps and jobs dispensed on the quiet. For one thing, the IIRM wasn't interested in this whistling past the graveyard approach and neither was its initial de facto sponsor, the Cork Association. The association placed an ad in the Irish American weeklies with a big headline – an old familiar: 'No Irish Need Apply.' Don Martin, a corporate lawyer in New York and an early days supporter of the IIRM, viewed the situation facing the Irish as 'a living, breathing indictment of American immigration policy'.

So Martin drew up his own indictment in the form of an open letter to President Ronald Reagan. It was proclaimed to the world in a paid-for ad in the *Irish Echo* of March 12, 1988. The letter was a blatant pitch to broad Irish American sentiment, which, up until now, had largely taken a back seat to the newly arrived upstart cousins. And of course it was addressed to a president who was more than a little sentimental about his Irishness. The letter wasn't signed by Martin himself but rather by 'The Irish Immigration Reform Movement'. It informed Reagan that the 1965 act had made Irish immigration to the US 'virtually impossible'.

Martin had an idea that the Gipper could easily identify with heroes, real or mythical. And he was right. The ad included a 'Roll of Honor', naming the 257 Irish-born immigrants at the time who had won the Congressional Medal of Honor, the nation's highest award for military gallantry. Martin's concluding paragraph was almost Lincolnesque:

> Mr President, we do not think it requires any wild inference on our part to assert with confidence that these men would argue most forcibly and strenuously for their fellow countrymen, if they were able to do so. Indeed, we feel that in a very real sense they argue for us now, with a silent eloquence that will not go unheard.

Ted Kennedy was determined not to go unheard. With Senator Alan Simpson, his ideological rival though legislative ally, Kennedy had been busy putting distance between himself and his own handiwork in 1965. On March 15, 1988, days before the annual extravaganza of all things Irish that was St Patrick's Day, Kennedy and Simpson engineered an 88–4 Senate majority in favor of a bill – their bill – that would widen the gap between contemporary law and the family reunification emphasis of 1965.

Included in the Kennedy–Simpson bill's lines were 55,000 annual 'independent immigrant' visas that would be awarded on a points basis. Points would be awarded for English language skills, educational level, occupational demand and work experience. Kennedy commented that the bill would facilitate immigration from countries in Western Europe that had fared badly since the 1960s. Whatever about Capitol Hill and its oft-coded language, there were no prizes for guessing which particular corner of Western Europe was foremost in the mind of the man from Massachusetts.

The *Irish Echo*, in an editorial, hailed passage of the bill as 'wonderful news'. The Senate, the editorial stated, had said yes to immigration reform and a debt of gratitude was owed to Kennedy and Simpson. Passage of the bill was the first legislative highlight of the IIRM era. The *Echo* was correct in suggesting that the House of Representatives' version of Kennedy–Simpson, being propelled along primarily by Brian Donnelly and Brooklyn Democrat Charles Schumer, faced 'tougher sledding'. It would.

One of the biggest ruts along the way was expected to be Congressman Peter Rodino, chairman of the House Judiciary Committee. Rodino was planning to quit Congress after forty years. With the '88 elections looming, Rodino was the worst kind of politician to have blocking a path. He no longer needed votes. The *Irish Echo* editorial concluded with, 'We hope that the gentleman from New Jersey, who has fought the good fight over the years, will make the immigration reform bill his last best fight.' These were words more rooted in hope than expecation.

Still, hope and expectation were combining to fuel the IIRM's expanding campaign. And expand it did – not just in terms of manned outposts in various cities but also in terms of outreach to politicians at every level: city, state and federal. As it became seemingly bigger and certainly louder, a critical difference between the IIRM and the American Irish National Immigration Committee (AINIC) from the 1960s and '70s came into starker relief. One columnist, the *Irish Echo*'s Mike Devlin, likened the IIRM, largely led as it was by young immigrant Irish, to an Irish government in exile. And there were times when US politicans, such as New York Mayor Ed Koch, seemed to be treating the group as if it was a quasi-government.

This did not settle well with the actual Irish government in Dublin, and there were publicly aired differences, most especially over money and an IIRM request for Irish government funding for an office in New York. That request being denied, the IIRM let fly. It's response came after two heated meetings in New York between IIRM representatives and the visiting Frank Fahey, 'Minister for Youth and Sport' in the Charles Haughey-led Fianna Fáil government. The IIRM verdict on the Fahey visit was summed up in a post-meetings statement. The visit was, the statement said, a 'useless, cosmetic public relations exercise and a waste of the Irish taxpayer's money'.

This was heady stuff. Charles Haughey visited the US a few weeks after Fahey. Haughey met Cardinal John O'Connor in New York and huddled with Ted Kennedy at his family compound on Cape Cod. The taoiseach gave the IIRM a wide berth.

Meanwhile, the IIRM was realizing that it would have to be in for a longer haul than some of its more optimistic members might have believed. The reason for the group's existence was the amnesty contained in the 1986 Immigration Reform and Control Act. The amnesty was aimed at immigrants who had arrived in the US before January 1, 1982. Most of the now-undocumented Irish had arrived after that date. The amnesty was set to expire on May 4, 1988. There was an effort to extend it, especially by big city mayors, but the expiry date remained in place. Not that this mattered all that much to the Irish. The 1982 date was by far the more pertinent.

The Kennedy–Simpson bill was still the most pertinent bill on Capitol Hill, but it was no longer alone. It had made the crossing from the Senate to the House. The United States Senate has 100 members, the House of Representatives has 435. Not surprisingly, hot-button issues could easily prompt more bills in the latter than the former. And that's exactly what was happening as the warm days of spring gave way to hot days of summer.

CHAPTER 38

Like Summer Leaves

By the early summer of 1988, there were several immigration bills floating under the Capitol Dome and a heightened expectation that the Irish might end up with 10,000, 14,500, even 15,000 visas when all was said and done. That was if all was said and done.

The House Immigration Subcommittee heard testimony at the end of June from several congressmen pushing their own proposals. Joe DioGuardi, a New York Republican, made clear his view that a bill he was sponsoring was good for the Irish and good for America. His bill would allow for a 'new wave of Irish immigration that will again result in a better United States'. Subcommittee chairman Roman Mazzoli was cautious in his reaction to such enthusiastic testimony. He said he was more in favor of immigration reform than against it. Hardly a ringing endorsement, even for the pack-leading Kennedy–Simpson measure.

July 4th came and went. Successful congressional legislation, more often than not, takes its time to reach maturity amid an array of distractions and events, holidays and recesses. The calendar for 1988, a presidential election year, was especially crowded, what with party conventions and the need for Congress members to get back to their states and districts to address bread-and-butter issues while buttering up voters. Peter Rodino, on his road to political retirement, didn't have to butter up anybody. So Irish eyebrows were indeed raised when, in late July, Rodino offered a bill of his own on the House floor, in partnership with Roman Mazzoli.

Rodino, seen as an impediment if not an outright enemy by the Irish, was now proposing an extension of the Donnelly Visa lottery. The Rodino–Mazzoli proposal was a near mirror image of Kennedy–

Simpson but with even more potential for the Irish, combining as it did Kennedy–Simpson's independent category visas along with extra Donnellys.

Rodino's change of tack wasn't only a result of the Irish tugging at his sleeve. The 79-year-old legislator was also coming under severe pressure from groups representing Hispanic and Asian immigrants. As a result, Rodino's bill also proposed what the *Irish Voice* described as a 'stunning' 800,000 visas for family reunification. Rodino's bill also took a dig at its Senate cousin. There would be no points for speaking English. Nevertheless, the *Irish Echo* reported that the Rodino proposal emerged after the congressman had been paid several visits by Ted Kennedy. Jerry Tinker, Kennedy's senior aide attached to the House Subcommittee, said that Kennedy continued to press both Rodino and Mazzoli for a positive response, 'He kept plugging ahead and was very determined. He spent a hell of a lot of time on it behind the scenes as well as publicly.'

All the plugging eventually paid off. The Rodino–Mazzoli bill was now set to be discussed in hearings staged by Mazzoli's Immigration Subcommittee on September 7. Time was short though. The one hundredth Congress was to adjourn less than a month later on October 3. And between the hearing and adjournment there were only eighteen working days listed. The window of opportunity for the Irish was narrow. But Rodino had some words of comfort borne of years of last-minute wheeling and dealing, 'It is expected that the Judiciary Committee and the Immigration Sub-committee will review this proposal and proceed to mark-up in an expeditious fashion.' This was music to Irish ears. And words that could just about be believed. The 1986 reform act almost died at the last moment but was saved by a filibuster on a defense issue that kept Congress detained in Washington longer than planned. Then again, defense was something of a sacred cow. Did anyone in Washington have the energy or commitment to launch a filibuster on behalf of one specific group of illegal aliens? Some had their doubts.

In an internal briefing memo drawn up in early September to coincide with a visit to New York by Tánaiste and Minister for Foreign Affairs Brian Lenihan, Irish officials stated that all advice received led to the conclusion that 'a specific amnesty for the Irish would be impossible to achieve because of Congress's deep attachment to the principles of non-discrimination in the immigration area and the opposition of other ethnic groups'. Asian groups were singled out in the memo for having particular problems with the anticipated reduction in family reunification visas and the new emphasis on English-language skills if Congress passed a bill similar to Kennedy–Simpson. The memo concluded:

> In view of these difficulties, both real and potential, the embassy has been in close and continual contact with Congressman Peter Rodino, a senior and influential Congressman from New Jersey, who is the Chairman of the House Judiciary Committee and is due to retire this Autumn. Congressman Rodino proved very sympathetic to our approach and promised to see what he could do to help. However, he warned that there was no chance of the Kennedy/Simpson bill getting through the House this session. Following a meeting on July 27th between himself and Senators Kennedy and Simpson at which Senator Kennedy indicated he disagreed with Congressman Rodino's assessment, the latter has now introduced a Bill in co-sponsorship with Congressman Mazzoli who is Chairman of the House Immigration Sub-Committee. Before the measure was introduced, the Tánaiste's office rang the Congressman's office to make known the Tánaiste's appreciation for his efforts.

Such was the way things worked. The Irish Immigration Reform Movement (IIRM) was also running up its phone bills in preparation for the Washington hearings. But as the Lenihan briefing memo made clear, there were no warm and fuzzy phone exchanges between Dublin and IIRM leaders – at least those in New York. The memo stated, 'On legal reform there is considerable interest among the Irish community in the present debate in Washington. Except for the IIRM, relations between the Consulate and the leading Irish American groups are excellent.' The IIRM, it seemed, had attained its own version of American exceptionalism. Some of those favored

Irish American groups and the out-of-favor IIRM (relations between Irish consulates and IIRM branches in cities other than New York were generally better) were by now heading to Capitol Hill for what turned out to be a memorable exercise in pumping up emotions and cranking up legislative machinery that was otherwise winding down in anticipation of the November House elections.

The September hearings before the Immigration Subcommittee were staged over two days, one week apart. The opening session on September 7 was held in the full Judiciary Committee hearing room. This was Pat Hurley's opportunity on Ted Kennedy's stage. Chairman Roman Mazzoli proceeded cautiously at the outset, posing the question to his attentive and expectant audience as to whether or not the door to America was 'open too narrowly, too widely, or just right'.

Kennedy went to work on familiar ground, telling the assembled House members that there was a 'timeliness' about the proposed immigration legislation. Timing, as Kennedy well knew, had as much to do with an election as reform. He knew what buttons to press, and when and where. He proceeded to the issue of fairness, pointing to the imbalances in immigration numbers that had inadvertently arisen in recent years. Nobody present was being blamed, but they were being presented with an opportunity to be impartial and caring legislators.

Kennedy threw statistics at the subcommittee. Only 1,852 Irish applicants qualifying for visas in 1986, even though the statutory ceiling for Ireland was 20,000. The Irish were simply missing out because they were not qualifying under family reunification rules. An 'excessively restrictive force' had been in operation since 1965, Kennedy said. In this regard, the man from Massachusetts was speaking virtually *ex cathedra*.

Alan Simpson hammered away at the whole notion of basing US immigration law on reuniting families. This was not in the national interest and was failing to meet the demands of the labor market. Kennedy and Simpson had rather different motives for testifying, but their arguments were merging somewhere in the middle.

The politics (heart) and statistics (head) had been thrown into the ring. The emotional fire was added by Tom Flatley, a Mayo native and hugely successful Massachusetts-based businessman. Flatley had arrived in America in 1950. He had earned his American citizenship by way of service in the Korean War. He was a model success story – Irish and American, an older version of the kind of people, he told the congressmen, who were now being almost entirely excluded because of the 1965 act. Apart from stating that the situation was 'simply wrong', Flatley the businessman pointed to what many were saying was Ireland's best-educated generation ever. All this talent was potentially being lost to Europe, Australia and other places. At this rate, he was telling his listeners, there would be no more Tom Flatleys, ever.

The hearing gave the Irish advocates a chance to size upon the opposition. And there *was* opposition – or at least sides with potentially opposing priorities. The hearing was far from being a save-the-Irish rally. Testimony was delivered by Asian and Hispanic representatives, labor leaders, government officials, representatives from Jewish groups and the Catholic Church. Those from the Catholic Church, while undoubtedly sympathetic to the mostly Catholic Irish and happy enough to see more NP-5 Donnelly visas made available, were also making it known that the idea of reuniting families could not be entirely sacrificed to the demands of the market.

Significantly, the Commissioner of the Immigration and Naturalization Service, Alan Nelson, signaled the Reagan Administration's wish to see some reform. Nelson expressed the administration's liking for the Kennedy–Simpson bill in particular. He felt that the issue of reform should be bipartisan. This was both a hint and a nudge.

The first of the two hearings presented the Irish campaigners with their first close-up view of Congressman Howard Berman of California. California was the immigration cockpit of the day, as New York had been a hundred years previously. Berman's concerns were prompted mostly by Asian and Hispanic lobbyists, but he was aware that both coasts would have a say in any final determination. He announced a bill of his own, with increased numbers of family reunification visas but also a 50,000-visa annual lottery for the young and single brigade, Irish and otherwise.

Berman seemed like a potential ally, and outside the hearing room he was uttering reassuring words to Irish ears. But, for the record, he sounded a warning, 'I will strenuously oppose any backsliding to the days when the United States had a notion of which countries were the source of the most desirable immigrants.'

Some groups, particularly the Asian Pacific American Legal Center and the National council of La Raza, tried for a delay of game. They suggested pushing the issue on to the next Congress or establishing a panel of experts. Congressman Barney Frank, well aware of how things could be killed off by panels and committees, wondered aloud if these organizations were merely fearful of a bad result.

Outside the hearing room, in a familiar corridor of power, Ted Kennedy held court. Looking tanned and a little large for his suit, he was offering hope laced with caution to a small knot of Irish activists and reporters. The key thing was to get the Kennedy–Simpson bill into the House and Senate conference phase. In other words, the horse-trading part of the process. Kennedy's bottom line was clear. If conference was attained, there would be a result, one way or the other.

The Irish in America – and not least in Kennedy's Massachusetts – had earned a reputation for working things out behind closed doors. Irish political deal-making depended heavily on eyeball-to-eyeball negotiation, *quid pro quos* laced with a whiff of tobacco, and a shared sense that everybody should benefit but first and mostly us, ourselves, the Irish. Kennedy was an heir to much of that Honey Fitz and James Curley mystique. In one sense, the modern Congress member was little-different to the old-style ward boss. Behind all the Beltway trappings there was more than a hint of the smoky room political horse-trader. In the end, it all came down to the deal.

Edward Moore Kennedy represented different things to Irish Americans. He was at once a hero and a villain. Just being a Kennedy was reason enough for simultaneous worship and resentment. He was a hero to many liberals and an arch-villain to numerous conservatives. Not a few Irish American Catholics viewed him as a fallen angel who was still falling.

But on that early September day in Washington, and in the eyes of those clustering about him in the air-conditioned corridor, Ted Kennedy was Santa Claus in a summer suit. And this, at last, was surely the season of giving for the visa-hungry Irish.

CHAPTER 39

Christmas Postponed

'The Irish are doing this all wrong. They are just getting other immigrants' backs up.' Rick Schwartz of the National Immigration, Refugee and Citizen Forum was not so much unsympathetic to the Irish as he was sympathetic to a picture that had more than just the Irish in its frame.

The Irish Immigration Reform Movement (IIRM) was certainly intent on getting backs up, and the degree to which it was successful at doing so inevitably blunted its more subtle and sensitive tactics, such as they were. But the IIRM had to be careful. The perception that Congress was cooking up a bill for the Irish alone had the potential to bring everything crashing down. Getting the balance right was difficult, if not impossible. So backs up it would be. Hopefully there would be enough of the right ones.

As for the congressional cooking? The Kennedy–Simpson bill looked very green indeed. And the Peter Rodino-inspired House equivalent was loaded with extra Donnelly Visas. Neither bill was being warmly embraced by Asian and Hispanic lobbyists, although the House measure did include a family reunification component. The Irish, meanwhile, were grasping at both. It was now a case of any port in a storm.

Part two of the Immigration Subcommittee hearing was set for September 16, and the IIRM was listed to speak. The speaker might have been Sean Minihane or Pat Hurley. Each was an obvious choice, though their styles would have been in sharp contrast. But the IIRM opted for a pinch hitter, an American voice: Don Martin, the corporate attorney. It would be a smart move. Martin spoke with eloquence and barely restrained passion. He argued for greater numbers of legal immigrants from those countries shut out by the 1965 act. He urged a compromise between the two bills before the subcommittee, one that would keep family reunification laws intact even as an extended NP-5 program took care of the current crop of Irish visa hopefuls.

But Martin didn't stick with just the nuts and bolts of immigration law. He went straight for the committee's heart, all the while hoping that it actually had one:

> If all the men who have served in the uniform of the United States since 1861 were to parade before this Congress today it would constitute an army of millions.
>
> Yet, in all that number just 3,349, or about a brigade, would wear a blue ribbon signifying the Congressional Medal of Honor. Of that brave number, 257, or about a company and a half, were immigrants from Ireland. If those immigrants could speak to you now, we are certain that they would argue for fairness and for diversity. Indeed, we believe they argue for us now with a silent eloquence that will not go unheard.

It is likely true that some other national groups in the room, not to mention those from organizations that wanted all immigration curbed, were silently gagging. But Martin's unvarnished appeal to stars-and-stripes sentiment seemed to have some effect. Chairman Mazzoli said, 'I'm glad to see that this generation of Irish Americans are as eloquent as those who went before them.'

Another member of the subcommittee did not say anything to match Mazzoli's words, but he would later remember sitting bolt upright in his chair as Don Martin unfurled his Irish roll of honor. Congressman Bruce Morrison, a Democrat from Connecticut, was a relatively junior member of the Judiciary Committee and its immigration offshoot. 'I remember Martin testifying about the Medal of Honor winners', Morrison would recall some years after that September hearing. 'That particular moment crystalized it for me. It was a very important moment for me.'

It would prove to be a very important moment for thousands of Irish down the road, but even after Martin's stirring words, it was still unclear what the way ahead was for Irish visa hopes. Jerry Tinker, Ted Kennedy's point man on immigration, suggested what it might be. What lay ahead now, he told reporters, was 'akin to pulling a legislative rabbit out of the hat'.

The Subcommittee had heard the arguments. But despite the importance of the issues to all sides and the emotion of the moment (courtesy of the IIRM's Martin) it took no vote. Clearly, there would be discussions among the members away from the hearing room, the advocates and the reporters.

Not all the advocates had been in the room, as it turned out. Brian Lenihan, Ireland's foreign minister, was in Washington and engaged with all relevant congressional leaders and anybody else who cared to listen, including Secretary of State George Schultz. It seemed as if something was coming down other than the first falling autumn leaves. But what?

The question was to be answered many times in the following few weeks but never quite accurately. Rumors flew and hopes were raised only to be dashed. The politicians seemed to have their minds on only one thing: elections. There was talk of unofficial meetings involving Kennedy and Rodino. There was word that a stop-gap bill with NP-5 visas galore, mainly for the Irish, was only days away. But a truly definitive headline remained elusive, and a settling feeling in the Irish camp was along the lines of being grateful for anything that came the Irish way.

Whatever was taking shape, it wasn't looking like a comprehensive reform package, although more Donnelly Visas for the Irish was being spoken about with rising frequency. Merely extending an existing visa program only required passage of amendments to existing legislation, not an entirely new act. Congress was now due to rise on October 15. It was coming down to the wire, as a headline in the *Irish Voice* signaled.

And then, on the day that September was poised to surrender to October, there was a huge breakthrough. The phones began to ring. It was Friday afternoon, only a few weeks before the elections. Members of Congress were planning weekend voter blitzes in far flung districts. But the numbers generating excitement in the ranks of Irish immigration campaigners had nothing to do with the latest opinion polls. Rodino's Judiciary Committee had unanimously approved the House legislation that proposed extension of the Donnelly program. As many as 30,000 green cards now appeared destined for eager hands – many of them Irish – and over the coming two years. The first batch of 15,000 would be offered to applicants who had gone on a reserve list after already applying, but failing, to secure a Donnelly.

The 15,000 visas would be applied immediately to the same number of applicants who constituted the 'immediate reserve list'. Of this number, 9,866 were Irish. Another 15,000 would follow in fiscal year 1990, which would actually start on October 1, 1989, exactly a year away. Again, these visas would be issued to people who had already tried, but failed, to secure a visa. Their names were resting in stacks of mail bags in Washington.

The Judiciary Committee-approved bill was a compromise. It was neither the Kennedy–Simpson nor the Rodino–Mazzoli version. It was a reduced and simplified measure tagged with Roman Mazzoli's name, although there were effectively many fingerprints on its pages. Charles Schumer's hand, for one, was clearly evident. Its official title was 'Amendments in the Nature of a Substitute for H.R. 5115', or more simply, 'Immigration Amendments of 1988'. It didn't sound especially historic, but few Irish cared. Also announced was a new 20,000 visa lottery for late 1990 and 1991, put together by Howard Berman. It was aimed at countries that had been securing fewer than 5,000 legal immigrants a year. Ireland qualified, although it was quickly suggested that a Donnelly windfall could push Ireland over the Berman limit. But no, the Berman proposal even contained a provision that would exclude Donnelly Visas being counted against the 5,000 limit.

It was a clear victory, 50,000 visas in all. Yet it was not seen as enough. Adrian Flannelly, the New York Irish radio show host, who had personally delivered thousands of Donnelly applications to Washington the previous year, was speaking for many, 'While this legislation is a breakthrough, we must not rest on our laurels. There is a lot more work to be done for the illegals.'

Flannelly wasn't alone in his caution. The legislators themselves were delivering verdicts that fell well short of exultant. Roman

Mazzoli described his own handiwork as a 'narrow effort'. Rodino spoke with the experience born of forty years in the political trenches, 'I know immigration doesn't lend itself to quick fixes.' Brian Donnelly predicted a positive vote in the full House. A more expansive reform of legal immigration would take longer. The bill, he said, was 'the best result we can hope for at this stage'.

The Irish government, not entirely averse to even a quick fix, welcomed the bill. Brian Lenihan was awarded some of the credit for its success. The IIRM also welcomed the visas but took the view that visa lotteries could not cover all the undocumented Irish. The campaign for comprehensive immigration reform would continue. But, in the meantime, there was a vote to be won. All 435 members of the House of Representatives were about to receive telegrams from the IIRM advising them of the wisest course of action in the impending ballot.

It was left to Brian Donnelly to formally introduce the amendments bill on the House floor. It was approved unanimously on October 5 and passed on to the Senate. As was often the case, Congress went beyond its adjournment deadline. But it would take two weeks before House approval was tested in the Senate chamber. The bill was introduced on Friday, October 21, by Democratic Leader Robert Byrd. It was passed late that evening, again in a unanimous vote and without a roll call. Vice President Bush, now in full battle mode for his White House bid, revealed the Reagan administration's thinking when he praised the new legislation for restoring fairness and balance to America's immigration system.

The IIRM didn't see things entirely that way and described passage of the amendments as both a 'minor' and 'significant' legislative victory. Co-founder Sean Minihane said the amendments were 'a step in the right direction'. The effort to push through full-scale reform would continue in the next Congress. Ted Kennedy, standing for re-election on November 8, agreed, and so did Michael Dukakis, the Democratic Party presidential nominee. But as far as the amendments bill was concerned, all that was needed now was the current president's signature.

Ronald Reagan wore his Irish sentiments on his sleeve. But was he Irish up his sleeve too? The question was answered when reports surfaced that his fellow Republican, Senator Jesse Helms of North Carolina, had almost killed off the amendments bill in the Senate but was persuaded at the last minute by Reagan to look the other way. When it became known that Helms was going to be a problem, Irish diplomats phoned the White House. Reagan, in turn, phoned Helms and persuaded him to back down. It was a close call in every sense. The bill was approved by the Senate without a quorum. One dissenting voice would have killed it.

Reagan duly signed and virtually all the primary immigration players, with the exception of the retiring Rodino and a defeated New York Democrat, Congressman Joe DioGuardi, were returned to Congress in the elections. George Bush was on his way to the Oval Office after defeating Michael Dukakis; the incoming 41st president's heart seemed to be in much the same place as Reagan's.

All in all, matters seemed to be proceeding quite smoothly. That is, until the Immigration and Naturalization Service reminded one and all that there was still a long way to go. The votes were hardly counted when the Immigration and Naturalization Service (INS) raided a Boston nursing home and detained five Irish nurses. A sixth almost qualified for the Olympics by climbing through a ground floor window and sprinting across the grounds to safety. The US Secret Service, no less, followed this by busting a dozen illegal Irish in New Jersey in a phone-home scam involving stolen credit cards.

The year 1988 passed into the history books with the US Ambassador to Ireland, Margaret Heckler, announcing that interviews for Donnelly Visas would begin in January. Ted Kennedy was planning to re-introduce his bill in the first congressional session of 1989. The Irish government was, meanwhile, taking a bow, with Brian Lenihan telling the Dáil that he had 'lent his weight' to the compromise package that had emerged in Washington.

The 1980s were winding to a close. Christmas didn't deliver its biggest possible gift to the undocumented Irish. Still, 1989 could be the year that all issues and concerns would be resolved. Some were optimistic, some were cautious, some were pessimistic. All were hopeful.

CHAPTER 40

One Big Bust

The opening months of 1989 saw rising hopes for Irish success in the Berman Visa program. The Irish Immigration Reform Movement (IIRM) was, meanwhile, gathering itself for a long-haul campaign intended to steer the congressional immigration debate in as much of an Irish direction as possible. But there was a problem, and it was money or the lack of it. The American Ireland Fund (AIF), a private charitable entity, was inviting funding applications from Irish American organizations in a position to aid immigrants. The IIRM was one of them. Problem was, there were over four hundred other entities on the AIF list for a share of $50,000. IIRM eyes were now looking to Dublin, but Finance Minister Albert Reynolds was ignoring the US even as he set aside half-a-million pounds in the budget for immigrant welfare projects in Britain.

The IIRM was both angry and puzzled. Taoiseach Charles Haughey had previously instructed the Friends of Fianna Fáil fundraising group in the US to give $5,000 to the IIRM. So why was the group being snubbed now? No 'specific proposals' was the reply that came from the Department of Foreign Affairs in Dublin. Relations between the IIRM and the Irish government were still in deep freeze – and at the worst time possible.

The Irish government's own estimates were showing that emigration was still rising and, indeed, had reached a new peak in 1988. The 'net outflow' figure for the year was calculated as 32,000 – a rise of 5,000 over the '87 tally. The figures covered emigration to all countries, but another round of mutually antagonistic number-crunching between the government and the IIRM only added to the confusion. The government was working off a total net outflow figure to all countries from 1981 to the end of '88 amounting to 131,000. The IIRM was arguing that this estimate might even be falling short of the number of Irish who had come to the US. Regardless of the precise total number, not all of them were illegal and so could be counted with relative precision. An estimated 15,000 had migrated legally to the US between 1981 and '88. Roughly 7,000 more were working in America on temporary visas while as many as 5,000 were preparing to arrive for the summer of '89 on J1 student working visas.

St Patrick's Day 1989 saw just about all the undocumented – whatever their total number – applying for Berman Visas. Applications were being accepted by US authorities after March 1. The IIRM, again with a masterful eye for the emotional arm twist, had organized a 'Mass of Hope' for March 16 in St Patrick's Cathedral in New York. Despite financial worries, there was no shortage of publicity. The IIRM had been excluded from the New York St Patrick's Day Parade the previous year because the parade committee really hadn't a clue who they were. There were no such excuses now. The upstarts were included in the line of march for the '89 parade, due to be led by its first-ever woman grand marshal, Dorothy Hayden Cudahy. They were assigned the very last place in the roughly five-hour human chain along and up Fifth Avenue. But they were refused permission to carry a banner by the parade committee, always a stickler for precedent, rules and procedure. Still, this was progress of sorts. There was much joking about saving the best, if illicit, wine until last.

The *New York Times* ran another big story on the Irish newcomers, as did numerous other publications, including *Time* magazine, which splashed a report headed: 'The Re-Greening of America'. *Time* saw a better side to the undocumented story in the revitalizing of old and rundown city neighborhoods, but it paid particular attention to the political clout that the young newcomers were drawing to themselves.

The *New York Times* highlighted the IIRM's push for Berman Visa applications but stressed the clear difficulties: 20,000 visas, one application per person, 162 eligible countries and as many as 8 million applications expected. It was clear that the Irish, who had swamped the multi-application Donnelly program, were facing a veritable Mount Everest this time around.

But the Berman program, the IIRM's Pat Hurley told *Times* reporter Celestine Bohlen, was only part of the IIRM's long-term strategy. Hurley was photographed for the story but retained his nominal anonymity, being described in the caption as 'an Irish immigrant'. That he was – regardless of what his new country labeled him.

Charles Haughey arrived in Washington for St Patrick's Day festivities, but plans for the annual presentation of a bowl of shamrock to the president, this time Bush, were rather spoiled by the Immigration and Naturalization Service (INS), which, with uncanny timing, delivered a number of illegal Irish a St Patrick's Day greeting that they would not soon forget. Hours before Haughey's arrival, six young Irish women working in a Boston bar were led out of the premises in handcuffs. Four men, meanwhile, were detained on a construction site in New Hampshire. They ended up in prison garb before being placed, also handcuffed, on a TWA flight to London out of Boston's Logan airport. Had their hands been free, they could have waved at Haughey's west-bound flight somewhere over the Atlantic. It was all highly embarrassing for Haughey. The shamrock diplomacy was looking rather leafless as opposition politicians back in Ireland made hay with a vengeance.

Grim headlines spawned by INS raids apart, the Irish were still coming. The number of undocumented Irish varied depending on who was offering the estimate. But it would be possible to pinpoint the precise number of Irish who would get a pass into America be means of a Berman Visa. The signs were not good. By the end of May, over 3.2 million applications were stored in a warehouse outside Washington. The first three winners were from Pakistan, Iran and Kuwait. This was an indication of what would soon be starkly evident: the Berman Visa scheme was a bust for the Irish. In the course of what was a two-year program, only 205 Bermans were awarded to Irish applicants out of the twenty thousand in the pot.

Back in Ireland, Charles Haughey called an election for June 15. The IIRM resolved to make government financing of the reform cause in the US an issue at the polls. Election-inspired lip service was no longer enough. On the eve of the Irish vote, the US Senate Judiciary Committee approved a compromise immigration bill concocted by Ted Kennedy, Alan Simpson and Senator Paul Simon from Illinois. Simon had mounted a successful pushback on the English-language provision in the points system visas held over from the 1988 Kennedy–Simpson bill. Oddly, in the vote on English, Kennedy did not vote against Simon's move. The only negative in a 12–2 approval came from Simpson and Senator Strom Thurmond of South Carolina. The IIRM was disturbed and puzzled. A Kennedy spokesman explained that the English language provision had become a cumbersome obstacle to progress.

Cumbersome or not, the bill offered 54,000 independent visas in a points system based on age, education and special skills. Reform campaigners considered this a long way short of the Holy Grail. The Irish Consulate in New York was more sanguine, a spokesman declaring that the overall viability of the bill was 'considerably enhanced' as a result of the compromise. The independent category had remained untouched and the bill provided 'a review of the immigration system'.

On July 13, the bill was passed by the full Senate by 81 to 17. The Irish American newspapers were not so taken by the turn of events. One report described passage of the bill as a 'minor boost'. However, the final version approved was slightly different to that passed by the Judiciary Committee. A number of amendments had been inserted, including one with a distinct Irish imprint.

By this time, the IIRM had an extensive network of branches, with activists in virtually every major city. Chicago had one, and it made itself known to Senator Simon. Eugene Nestor, chairman of the Chicago branch, and the Rev. Dave Dillon buttonholed Simon at a fundraiser and persuaded him to meet them again to discuss the immigration bill. The meeting would take place in Chicago, in the rear seat of a chauffeured limousine. Simon was told that the bill was actually hurting the Irish – that the twenty points for English skills, deleted from Kennedy–Simpson as an impediment to progress, had raised the qualifying threshold way over Irish heads.

Simon was sympathetic. He admitted to a false belief that the Irish had done well under the amnesty provisions of the 1986 act.

Nestor and Dillon set his mind straight on that score. Simon didn't shower his Irish interlocutors with legislative candy, but he did make a couple of post-limo ride changes. The Senate bill allowed for 10,000 of the annual 54,000 independent visas to be distributed over a three-year period to the thirty-six so-called disadvantaged countries. This at least gave some Irish a slightly better chance of securing one. Additionally, Simon's second amendment would offer fifteen points to applicants with guaranteed employment in the US – a move that gave undocumented Irish a possible edge over likely applicants in Ireland itself, although there was now a diminishing number of those. Figures released in early September by the Irish government revealed that in the twelve-month period up to April 15, 1989, 46,000 people had quit the country. This was the highest annual emigration figure since the 1950s. It was enough to show up in the national demographics. Ireland's, the republic's, population was now falling. The government, however, expressed optimism that job-creation plans in the pipeline would arrest the decline.

Across the Atlantic, the IIRM was hoping for a decline in arrests. The House Immigration Subcommittee, now chaired by Congressman Bruce Morrison, met in early October to consider testimony from various advocacy groups, including the IIRM. Given the reaction Don Martin got from the now-chairman a year previously, it was fortuitous for the IIRM that they could call on Martin again to deliver testimony. As was the case with Morrison, Martin too had acquired a new title: IIRM Political Action Coordinator.

On behalf of the IIRM, Martin proposed a 'diversity' visa program that would last for at least a decade. Under the scheme, 60,000 visas would be allocated each year to the thirty-six countries hard-done by the 1965 act. An additional 20,000 visas a year would be set aside for countries deemed under-represented – Ireland being included in this category, at least at the outset. An additional 20,000 visas would be awarded to all remaining countries. The diversity visas would be given out on the basis of a points system, with points being awarded for age, education and, in a proposal clearly close to Martin's heart, knowledge of US government and history.

The IIRM wasn't finished yet. It proposed an annual allotment of 30,000 'replenishment visas' for the thirty-six countries that would not be tied to the points system. And, in a statement of its all-Ireland yet pragmatic character, it proposed a special allocation of 7,000 visas a year for Northern Ireland.

This was a series of proposals that, to say the least, were quite sweeping. If the Subcommittee wanted to know what the Irish shopping list amounted to, here it was in all its cheeky detail. By contrast, the various other groups testifying at the hearing pleaded largely for maintenance of the status quo, especially with regard to family reunification. Martin went so far as to promise rebuttal testimony against this position. The IIRM was showing its teeth to potentially powerful friends, or formidable enemies. It was a tactic not without risk.

'There appears to be a strong feeling in Congress that there's a need for reform to benefit independent immigrants,' Martin said after the hearing. With regard to the subcommittee chairman at least, Martin wasn't far off the mark.

Martin's new title was reflective of an organization that had shed its barricades image and was operating simultaneously in various locations and at a number of levels. The IIRM now boasted a national chairman in Sean Minihane. But if barricade polemics were required, Pat Hurley was always close at hand. A kind of minister without portfolio, Hurley shared Martin's emotional commitment to the idea of reform. The overall formula was seemingly working.

As Martin was testifying in Washington, two other IIRM 'leaders' – the group was loosely constructed in this regard – were heading for Dublin and a meeting with Bill Griffith, Head of Consular Affairs at the US Embassy. Jim Larkin, Connecticut-based North East Regional Director, and John Dillon, National Public Relations Officer, discussed the immigration situation with Griffith during a meeting that lasted almost three hours. Dillon and Larkin were presenting Griffith with evidence which, they said, backed up allegations that consular staff at the embassy were harassing Donnelly Visa applicants. Griffith vehemently denied this but did make the point that more than a few interviewees arrived at the embassy with something of an 'attitude'. The meeting went well enough, not least because there were no Irish with attitudes in the room. All three men were American, a fact that was not going unnoticed. The IIRM had clearly been successful in building a bridge to Irish America. As such, it could not now be ignored when it came calling on either side of the Atlantic. 'Our meeting created a tone of cooperation with the embassy', Larkin, whose very name carried some cachet in Dublin, remarked afterwards.

Back in New York, IIRM contacts with various congressmen were bearing full fruit. Representatives Eliot Engel and Charles 'Chuck' Schumer, from the Bronx and Brooklyn respectively, indicated that they would be introducing bills containing independent visa categories. Schumer said he was distressed that the Berman program hadn't done more for the Irish and that he wanted to see more Irish come to the US. Significantly, Schumer expressed his thoughts after meetings with a delegation from the now ubiquitous IIRM. Brian Donnelly, meanwhile, was proposing to extend the NP-5 Donnelly program for an additional five years.

In Ireland in November, Foreign Minister Gerry Collins was telling the Dáil that the US embassy had handed over 10,000 visas to Irish applicants during the year. In New York, two young Irish women were sitting in a US government car in handcuffs; they were being driven from the Bronx to INS offices in downtown Manhattan. One was in tears. She was sensitive by nature and crying came easily. But she was now possessed by another emotion: anger. She was, as she would later say, feeling 'madder and madder'. It was a collective feeling now among the new Irish. They were, to borrow a phrase, sick and tired, mad as hell and weren't going to take it anymore.

But things would invariably get worse before they got better. Before the year was out, seven young Irish were detained by the INS as they appeared in a court in the Boston district of Brighton. The seven had been arrested following disturbances at a Halloween party. But the arrival of the INS prompted allegations that the Feds had been tipped off by the local police. The complaint quickly found its way to Boston Mayor Raymond Flynn's office, where protecting the rights of the illegal Irish – as was the case in the office of Mayor Ed Koch down Interstate 95 in New York – possessed the status of a solemn pledge.

In San Francisco, three Irish illegals were reportedly detained at gunpoint by INS agents. There would later be denials by the INS regarding guns, but the agency was too slow off the mark – all INS statements now had to be cleared through Washington. The guns story took hold in the wider Irish American imagination despite the denial.

There was no Christmas package from Congress for the Irish that year. Indeed, House action on the various proposed bills had been put off until the New Year, or, putting it another way, the new decade.

The paramount Irish story of the 1980s, one that had sidelined even Northern Ireland in the Irish American press, was poised to spill over into the 1990s – the decade of Mary Robinson, her candle in the window and the diaspora for which it was lit; of Bill Clinton, Bishop Casey, Jack Charlton and Veronica Guerin. It came with the realization on the part of thousands of Irish that they owed their lives in America to a handful of well-disposed politicians and a band of amateur lobbyists who had long since passed the point of taking no as a final answer.

CHAPTER 41

The Morrison Express

Bruce Morrison was not, at first glance, your typical Irish American politician. For starters, he was Protestant – an Episcopalian. He was a Democrat and came from the north-east, yes, but not New York or Massachusetts. He hailed from Connecticut, a rather more Yankee locale. Morrison had first been elected to the House of Representatives in 1982. His interest in Ireland remained fairly dormant for his first couple of terms – this, despite his Ulster roots. But he traveled to Ireland in 1987 with a congressional fact-finding delegation. The trip was sponsored by the Irish American Unity Conference, one of Irish America's more consistently active lobby groups on Northern Ireland.

The North was the main focus of the visit, but in meeting with US diplomats at the embassy in Dublin, Morrison began to hear another story – one of an increasing flow of young, skilled Irish people who were heading for the United States and not coming back. They weren't all heading for Connecticut, but Morrison's district was in a state sandwiched between the next parishes of Boston and New York. He listened closely to the tale related by the diplomats. And it stuck.

For many of those young and skilled Irish in America, the passing of 1989 merely underlined the fact that they were entering the second decade of a contradictory life: being on the land mass of America while being legally locked out of a full American life. But there were sympathetic Americans ready to help, not least influential representatives of Church and State.

The Catholic Church, still heavily Irish American in the ranks of its clergy and hierarchy, was a natural source of sympathy and comfort for the new Irish arrivals. But some felt that more was required. Broadcaster Adrian Flannelly, the voice of record for the Irish community in New York since 1970, had been aware of the undocumented Irish since the beginning of the 1980s. By the middle of the decade, Flannelly, whose rather droll and world-weary commentary provided listeners with relief from the endless pep, pap and pop of mainstream radio, had found his prime guilty party: the Church. Flannelly told his listeners that the Church was forgetting the Irish in favor of what were now more numerous Catholic immigrant ethnic groups.

Flannelly's criticism of the Church's apparent failure to wield its crozier in defense of the arriving Irish could have been dismissed had he not put his sweat and toil where his words were. When the first batch of Donnelly Visas was being accepted in Washington, Flannelly drove south with his daughter Linda in a station wagon. In the back were 68,000 Donnelly applications from Irish hopefuls that were mailed into the Adrian Flannelly Show at the Mayo-native's urging.

Flannelly traveled as a journalist. The applications were being accepted from the stroke of midnight. When father and daughter arrived at the designated US postal facility, there was, as Flannelly put it, 'a line half-way around Washington D.C.'. Flannelly flashed his press identification and drove through the security cordon. Linda did the rest. The Irish applications were first into the mix. A number of lawyers were on hand and spotted Flannelly's caper. There was something of an uproar, and for a moment Flannelly feared a block on his operation – even arrest. But the Flannellys managed to bluff it out and escape into the night. It's impossible to accurately assess the precise effect of the midnight drive of Adrian Flannelly, but the Irish would ultimately look back on the Donnelly program with considerable satisfaction.

Flannelly maintained his criticism of the Church in his broadcasts. The position of the bishops was that the alien amnesty program in the 1986 act should be extended, family reunification laws should be preserved and there should be separate legislation to alleviate the plight of the undocumented, the Irish included.

Of course, there were many groups of undocumented, and some were dwarfing the Irish in terms of numbers. Nevertheless,

Flannelly's criticism had been heard and absorbed. The Archdiocese of New York reached out and a plan was hatched to bring over a number of priests from Ireland to work in specific parishes so that the new Irish – at least those still practicing their faith – might feel a little more at home. Beyond that, a new department would be set up in the archdiocese to act as a cushion for the Irish when they felt life was becoming impossibly hard. Thus, Project Irish Outreach was born.

The head of the archdiocese, Cardinal John O'Connor, would prove to be a sympathetic and active ally. O'Connor corresponded with both Taoiseach Haughey and President Reagan regarding the undocumented Irish and the obstacles they were facing. It was widely accepted that O'Connor could pick up a phone and pretty much dial direct into the Oval Office. He certainly had the president's address and a guarantee that his own written words would get all the way through. In one letter to Reagan, O'Connor 'invited' the president's attention to the undocumented Irish 'in a special way'. The cardinal, whose generally conservative outlook was close to that of Reagan, wasn't shy about asking for a favor. In the letter, he requested an 'Executive Order' granting amnesty to the illegal Irish.

Getting the Church onside with regard to the undocumented Irish was no small matter. The arrival in the US of immigrant chaplains from Ireland generated headlines on both sides of the Atlantic. Continued raids and detentions by the Immigration and Naturalization Service (INS) generated more. And there was now another headline. The Irish Immigration Reform Movement (IIRM) would finally be given financial assistance from the Irish government, which set aside the equivalent of $300,000 for Irish immigrants in the US, with some of it going to the IIRM. It wasn't much, but it was an acknowledgment that there was a serious matter to be addressed.

Bruce Morrison was also addressing a serious matter. Poised to introduce a bill of his own before the House of Representatives, Morrison was urging the IIRM to step up lobbying on behalf of Brian Donnelly's bill, which, by mid-February, had attracted only twenty co-sponsors in the 435-member House. Much of the IIRM's effort at this point in time was not so much lobbying Congress members but rather milking St Patrick's Day to the last drop.

The group's public relations officer, John Dillon, was intent on getting the IIRM's message across to 'fifty million people' through a combination of local and national media outlets. Dillon was taking particular aim at TV networks and newspaper editorial boards – contact had been made, over a period of months, with roughly two hundred of the latter. The main efforts were being concentrated in the districts of especially critical congressional legislators. The IIRM, for all intents and purposes, had a hit list.

On February 21, Morrison's Immigration Subcommittee met to hear submissions, mostly from government witnesses – including INS Commissioner Gene McNary. McNary was largely in favor of the Kennedy–Simpson Senate bill, but that proposed legislation was no longer alone in the world. Bills from House members Brian Donnelly, Lamar Smith, Hamilton Fish and Howard Berman were also in the mix.

Charles Schumer and Eliot Engel were also promising a bill while Bruce Morrison's proposal, the 'Family Unity and Employment Opportunity Immigration Act of 1990', appeared imminent. Morrison, who had now declared his candidacy for the governorship of Connecticut, wanted to see a unified bill marked up by the subcommittee by March 14. Naturally, he wanted it to reflect his own bill, which was offering something to everybody, including 25,000 visas annually for fiscal years 1992–4 to those who entered before January 1, 1990. These visas would be distributed between the now-well-known thirty-six disadvantaged countries.

Morrison's good intentions towards the Irish were genuine. But as he was now a leading power broker in the immigration debate while running a gubernatorial campaign, he was receiving support from, and listening to, not just Irish advocates but also Hispanic and Asian groups. Morrison had spotted, early on, what he believed was a flaw in IIRM strategy – what he would describe as an 'us and them attitude'. He would later recall:

> I talked about this with them over the years. By 1989 I was able to set the tone but at the beginning it was different. I told the IIRM that their presentation had a racial tone, that it was strategically flawed. There were enough anti-immigrant

advocates against everybody and the IIRM needed support from pro-immigration groups. I told them there were only two sides to the immigration debate, for it and against it. In the end, there was greater cooperation between the Irish and Asian and Hispanic groups.

The IIRM's Sean Minihane would put it more cautiously. It was, in his view, a case of 'to each his own'; 'Asians and Latinos were more interested in family preference. We couldn't object to that because we wanted to keep them away from what we wanted.'

What the IIRM wanted was best said in a banner which, after some wrangling with organizers, was about to be unfurled in the 1990 New York St Patrick's Day Parade. It would read, quite simply, 'Immigration Reform Now'. The IIRM's banner in the parade, which was duplicated and given to other marching contingents and a second 'Mass of Hope' on the eve of the parade, constituted the highlights for March. In Washington, meanwhile, Bruce Morrison's bill, HR 4300, was getting tied up in procedural wrangling and undergoing a number of changes. It was finally reported out of the subcommittee in mid-April by a vote of six to four. The new version proposed 75,000 visas for fiscal 1991–3 assigned to the thirty-six countries, plus a diversity visa program, the brainchild of Brooklyn's Charles Schumer, to follow.

The next hurdle to cross was the House Judiciary Committee, where opposition lurked in the person of Lamar Smith, a Texan, among others. Texas, however, was just a postage stamp away as far as the IIRM was concerned. In response to the favorable Subcommittee report, it was planning a nationwide write-your-representative campaign. Lamar Smith was to be singled out for particular attention. There a significant Irish American population in Texas, but as was the case throughout much of the south and west, it was far removed in both space and time from contemporary Irish Affairs. Still, it was always an option to invoke the Alamo, where the Irish and Scots-Irish had given fire and taken it in some abundance.

Bruce Morrison, running for governor and running much of the immigration debate, was praising the IIRM for having 'recast the issue'. The IIRM, he said at a May Irish American fundraiser in support of his gubernatorial campaign, 'had killed off the notion that giving an opportunity to the Irish or Poles is in any way contradictory with groups which favor family reunification'. This was the candidate speaking, and in retrospect it would appear fortuitous that Morrison was wearing two hats at the time. Other powerful immigration lobby groups were effectively feeding messages through him to the Irish. By hook or by crook, an alliance was forming, with Morrison at the center. Morrison, at the fundraiser, which was over the state line in New York, concluded with fighting words, 'Before I get to the governor's chair the buck stops at immigration reform, and I'm going to see that we get it and legalize the Irish.'

Getting it would take a while. The summer dragged on. Congress went into recess, came out and went into recess again with no action before the Judiciary Committee. Lamar Smith was getting a lot of mail with Irish names in the return address space but he wasn't budging. The Republican was becoming a prominent rallying point for the anti-immigration members – a counterpoint to Morrison. At the same time, twenty-six members of the House had now added their signatures to Morrison's bill. Joe Kennedy was the latest as Americans went into their own recess to celebrate Independence Day. July's main news would be that the deep well of hope provided by the NP-5 Donnelly Visa program was about to dry up. Whatever happened now, just about anything would be good for the Irish.

In early August, just before Congress adjourned for a month, Morrison's bill finally came before the Judiciary Committee, chaired by a not entirely unsympathetic Jack Brooks, a Texas Democrat. His fellow Texan, Lamar Smith, was not giving any clear ground despite the lobby campaign directed by the IIRM and now also the Ancient Order of Hibernians. But even against the efforts of opponents, the bill passed committee by 23 to 12 and was now headed for the House floor in September.

The IIRM, meanwhile, was already looking ahead to a successful passage. But that would not be the end of the tale. President Bush had the power to say yes or deliver a veto and it was known that he favored the Kennedy–Simpson Senate bill over the Morrison House version. With that in mind, the IIRM had launched 'Project One Million', an ambitious plan to cram the White House mailbox with a million postcards urging the president to lend his weight to the reform effort and sign any bill passed by Congress. The *Irish Echo* included the postcards in its August 8–14 issue. On the front page, publisher Claire O'Gara Grimes urged readers to send the cards, 'The significance should not go unnoticed that this year the Ellis Island Immigrant Museum will open its doors for our reflection and gratitude. Today that immigration station does not hold the key to the future. H.R. 43000 does. I implore all our readers to mail the IIRM's postcard.'

Not only George Bush was feeling the heat. One member of Congress – yet another from Texas – had caused a storm during the Judiciary Committee debate. John Bryant, a Democrat, had let it rip, even as the opposition's rampart was crumbling. 'Why do we have Irish amnesty in this bill? Is that consistent with the notion of diversity? Do we need more Irish people that look just like me, look just like Morrison, look just like Smith to encourage ethnic diversity in this country? I do not think so.'

These were pertinent questions. Bryant was, by his own description, Scots-Irish by descent. But he was a law and order man first. He described the proposed visas in the Morrison bill for Ireland and the other thirty-five countries as effectively an 'amnesty' for the Irish. 'These folks', he said, 'had come to the country illegally. They are working and because they have some friends in Congress they are going to get to stay here, and that is the only thing that is at stake; that is the only reason why that [the visa provision] is in this bill and that is not the way to make immigration policy.' The IIRM, aka 'these folks', reminded Congressman Bryant that Texas ranked number four in the country in terms of Irish-rooted citizens in its population and that he might be hearing from some of them next time he stood for election.

Against the flood of criticism, Bryant appeared to bend a little and conceded that he might not be in possession of all the facts. He said he would sit down with anyone who wanted to discuss the bill with him and was always willing to reassess his position if new facts warranted it. There were quite a few willing to sit down with

Congressman Bryant and bend his ear – not just Irish lobbyists but also Italians, Polish, Slavs and others.

As always, the line outside America's door was long and diverse. And the Irish were doing their best to be at the head of it. The Bryant kerfuffle was but one fight in a legislative war. The way things were shaping up in Washington, it was starting to look like 1988 all over again. So much to do, so little time before Congress rushed home for elections.

So what to do?

CHAPTER 42

The Train Arrives

September saw America's immigrant past celebrated in the reopening of a refurbished Ellis Island. There was much emotion on the island that day. In Washington, the prose was colder: talk of quotas, visas, labor shortages and points systems. It didn't quite match the hype and the shared sense of immigrant legacy swirling around in the New York Harbor breezes.

Three thousand miles away, the Irish government was drawing up a study of the situation as it now stood. Again, the language was terse, academic. But the report's conclusion revealed some sense of urgency. 'The Embassy at Washington,' it stated, 'will impress on our friends on the Hill our concerns regarding a relatively speedy passage of an agreed measure during this session of Congress.'

Agreement, however, was still proving elusive. The 101st Congress was back in session after its high summer hiatus. As well as John Bryant, Lamar Smith was still balking at a number of Morrison bill proposals, particularly the 75,000 green cards, which were now being dubbed 'transition' visas. If Ellis Island was a world away from Ireland, Texas was another world away from Ellis Island. A Smith spokesman said, 'While we accept as many immigrants as the rest of the world combined, we cannot accept everyone who wants to make a better life in the US.'

Bryant, still smarting from a torrent of criticism after his 'look just like me' remarks, was holding fast. His spokesman said, 'The congressman sees no reason to change his position on the bill. It's a logical position because the immigration system which would exist under Morrison's bill is not in keeping with public policy.'

By this stage, mid-September, there were thirty-one co-sponsors of Morrison's bill and about as many days to go in the life of the 101st Congress. As was the case a couple of years previously, an Irish foreign minister, this time Gerry Collins, arrived at the eleventh hour to lend Dublin's weight to the argument. Collins met with key legislators and emerged proclaiming the well-worn political line that was cautious optimism.

September turned into October and, like the first gale of autumn, the immigration debate blew full force in the House of Representatives on the second day of the tenth month. 'Why even waste our time on a bill that is going nowhere?' Congressman Gerald Solomon, a New York Republican, wasn't singing an Irish air when he delivered his view on HR 4300, known by now, more or less, as the Morrison bill. Solomon's wisdom was to be disputed, but he had blown away one prevailing view: that all the opponents of a bill favorable to the Irish came from south of the Mason–Dixon Line.

In a ninety-minute debate, everyone's knuckles were showing. The bill was good for America, bad for America, good for some, lousy for others. Amendments were offered, rejected and thrown out. At one point, Bruce Morrison paid tribute to Brian Donnelly and Donnelly returned the compliment. The Irish were hanging together for all to see. It was a red rag to the bill's opponents. The day's business came to an end but resumed the following day, Wednesday, October 3, when John Bryant pitched his flag, looked at Bruce Morrison and saw his Santa Anna.

Bryant offered an amendment that was simple and to the point: scrub every last line of the bill except the part dealing with family reunification. Bryant criticized HR 4300 for being a sop to Europe. It was nothing more than 'a patchwork of special interest pleadings'. But there were more than enough House members with special interests close to their hearts to defeat Bryant's last throw of the dice.

In the end, as it usually did, it came down to a vote. Morrison appeared confident. He knew the numbers. The bill was passed by 231 to 192 and went to the House-Senate Conference for reconciliation with the Kennedy–Simpson measure. Heading for the conference table were Transition Visas, Diversity Visas and

Employment Visas, and a few more Donnelly Visas for some who lost out to technicalities. It was pretty much all that the Irish had hoped for at the dying of the congressional year.

But in Congress it is never over until it is over. And even over isn't always the end. The conferees met on October 9 and 11. There was near total meltdown on several issues. Alan Simpson, for one, was proving to be difficult. Information was scant, but after the *New York Times* had reported joyous celebration in New York Irish neighborhoods, the *Wall Street Journal* and *Washington Post* put dampeners on things with reports suggesting that Simpson, from far away Wyoming, was applying the brakes to the reform bandwagon. The *Journal*, a consistently pro-immigration paper, lashed out at Simpson, accusing him of backing off his own proposals of just a year previous. Simpson struck back, accusing the *Journal* of being goofy and stupid. All the while, the adjournment date for Congress was being pushed back, first to October 19, and then October 23.

Regardless, a result emerged on October 19 – a perfect one from an Irish perspective. An agreed package came out of the conference that guaranteed at least 48,000 visas ending up in Irish hands – although only Irish hands from the Republic – over the coming three years. Northern Ireland hopefuls would have to fight it out with the other disadvantaged countries for 90,000 additional visas over the three-year period beginning in fiscal 1992, which actually began on October 1, 1991. The newly agreed visas for the Irish were not being called 'Transition Visas' any more, but few Irish cared. They were quickly dubbed 'Morrison Visas'.

All that remained now was formal ratification by the House-Senate Conference Committee, followed by rubber stamp votes in the House and Senate. Alan Simpson had rowed in after all and his support removed the fears of some that President Bush might wield his veto pen. 'Victory', the *Irish Voice* roared on page one. 'Irish Get Green Light', the *Irish Echo* trumpeted. The battle appeared to be over. But everybody had forgotten Murphy's Law. As Bruce Morrison would later recall:

> It was a touch and go conference. There were many moments when it seemed that Senator Simpson was going to get up

and walk away. But [Senator Edward] Kennedy was always there. He was very supportive. The bill could have fallen numerous times. John Bryant made an attack on one of the visa categories.

In deference to Simpson we gave him a stupid little provision to do with driving licenses with biometric information. It was related to the idea of identity cards only in a remote way. It seemed harmless.

It seemed. The provision allowed for a pilot program in three states. Drivers' licenses would contain personal information, including fingerprints, that could be used to meet work authorization requirements. Nobody really asked Simpson how seriously he felt about this matter. And it wasn't Simpson who reacted when the bill came back to the House and Senate. It passed the Senate 89–8 on Friday, October 26. The House was a different story. Morrison would recall:

> All of a sudden, out of nowhere comes Ed Roybal, a senior [Democratic] member from California. He launched an attack on the bill because of the drivers' licenses provision. Republicans had been voting no in the conference stages even though the White House was broadly behind the bill and their opposition was expected. But now we had liberal Democrats voting no because of Roybal's objection.

Roybal, a leading member of the Hispanic Caucus, was not acting alone. He was pulling in sufficient Hispanic and African American members behind his assault on the provision to ensure its collapse. The bill fell in the House amid near total confusion. Morrison was stunned. In one way it looked eerily similar to the last-minute rejection of the 1988 amendments – a coup engineered by Brian Donnelly. But the reason for failure then was a move in favor of the Irish. This latest shocker had nothing to do with them at all.

At this point, the House-Senate immigration bill conference had been permanently dissolved. There was no procedural way back. Any new bill could have been killed by filibuster, given that Congress was almost stampeding out the door and heading for the hustings. There was one chance left. Morrison approached Joe Moakley, a Massachusetts Democrat and chairman of the Rules Committee. Alan Simpson, meanwhile, was flabbergasted by the sudden turn of events in the House. In Morrison's view, Simpson was more goal-oriented than ideological, 'When he heard what had happened he almost chided us for putting this thing in and immediately agreed that it could be dropped.'

So what to do? It was in Moakley's hands. Irish luck began to cancel out Murphy's Law. Moakley was not badly disposed towards the bill, and that was a positive, but time was running out. Moakley, however, owed Morrison a favor. Moakley was concerned about the plight of refugees from the civil war in El Salvador. Morrison had approached him well before the latest crisis in that country and offered to help with the Salvadoran issue. The favor was now being returned by Moakley, and more quickly than Morrison had anticipated.

Moakley could resurrect HR 4300 from the grave by virtue of a concurrent resolution that presented the bill once more to both House and Senate, only without the former sop to Simpson. The resolution was approved in the early hours of a Saturday morning by a reconvened House-Senate conference committee. That afternoon, both chambers approved the resolution. The effect of this was that the bill, minus the offending line, could now be voted upon again. The Senate proved to be no obstacle, and after about an hour's debate, the House approved it 265–118, with support now from even the likes of Lamar Smith. The Immigration Act of 1990 had entered the world by virtue of a political C-section. Thousands of Irish who had made landfall in the 1980s were suddenly being offered a huge helping hand, assuming George Bush's own hand delivered the presidential moniker. Bush took his time, which did nothing good for Irish nerves. But the 41st president did eventually sign, in the White House Roosevelt Room, on November 29. The signing ceremony took all of ten minutes. It would change the face of Irish America. And it would change Ireland.

The Morrison Visas would only be offered to applicants from the Republic in the first year, but twelve months after they came into being, another bill opened them to Northern Ireland applicants in the second and third year of the program. The Irish border had never mattered to the Irish immigration lobby. Irish was Irish, no matter what the county or jurisdiction.

During the height of the battle for Irish visas, there was significant and public disagreement on the matter of numbers. How many illegal Irish were there in the United States? In attempting to attract political, media and public interest, the Irish Immigration Reform Movement (IIRM) had tended to go for higher numbers. When politicians started to take interest, it was felt necessary to scale back the estimates. It was always a balancing act. Too many Irish needing visas would put a scare into some legislators. Too few would mean that leaders in Washington would ignore a perceived non-crisis.

In the end, there was no arguing with the actual number of visas issued: 18,363 Donnellys and 51,714 Morrisons. Added to this were the 205 Berman Visas – which made recipients into something akin to human collectors' items – and a couple of thousand Schumer Visas. The total for all by the end of 1997 would be in the region of 72,000.

Another big number – many, many people – had put their shoulders to the Golden Door in the battle for Irish visas. There was an array of Irish American organizations – prominent among them, the Ancient Order of Hibernians. The US Catholic Church, when it recognized the issue, played an important role, publicly and behind the scenes. The Irish government and its diplomatic corps could lay claim to significant credit. But it was the IIRM that had led the storming of the ramparts. To it, the lion's share of the kudos that came with legislative victory. And there were the legislators themselves: Morrison, Donnelly, Schumer, Kennedy, Simpson, Berman and all the others.

The IIRM's warriors for reform would go their separate ways – their task, as far as was possible, complete. Bruce Morrison would be left to deliver a succinct valedictory: the IIRM, he said, 'benefitted from being political lay people rather than professional lobbyists. They stood out as real human beings.'

And that they were.

CHAPTER 43

McCain on McLean

It was April 2006, eight months before Senator Chuck Schumer would raise the rafters in the St Barnabas church auditorium against the backdrop of thunder and lightning. On this early spring evening, it would be another senator, John McCain, providing the polemical pyrotechnics.

McCain was a United States Senator from another state that looked to this crowd, for all intents and purposes, like another world. The church hall in which he stood straddled the line between the Bronx in New York City and Yonkers in Westchester County. McCain's home state, Arizona, straddled Mexico.

On this night, McLean Avenue had to stand in for, well, the Grand Canyon. But McCain was made to feel at home as he pledged his energy and influence to securing the kind of comprehensive immigration reform that would include relief for the undocumented Irish. And yes, sixteen years after the Morrison Visa triumph there were undocumented Irish in America, thousands of them, and all of them feared, at any given moment, an abrupt end to their American dream.

Speaking from a stage in the St Barnabas church auditorium, the Republican senator's gaze took him over the heads of a large and enthusiastic Irish crowd and out the front door onto McLean Avenue. Or was it, for a couple of rip-roaring hours, a thoroughfare called McCain? It might as well have been, because the rally, organized by the Irish Lobby for Immigration Reform (ILIR), was the biggest draw on the avenue at the end of another uncertain working week for the undocumented Irish of the Bronx, Yonkers and far beyond.

And it was on this line straddling the New York borough and the Westchester city that McCain delivered another verbal round in the fight for the kind of immigration law reform envisaged in the bill crafted by himself and a senator who was normally an ideological opposite, Edward Kennedy. Yes, Ted Kennedy, now in his fifth decade of fighting on the immigration reform front lines.

During his address to a crowd that, appropriately, waved as many American flags as Irish tricolors, McCain referred to his Democratic opponent as 'a lion in winter'. All those listening were hoping that McCain would be of a kind – a tiger in spring, perhaps. This assembly was primed and ready for a champion to step forward at what were – and always were – the closing minutes of the eleventh hour.

The champion was John Sidney McCain, a battle-hardened veteran in more ways than one. For an hour before McCain's arrival, the crowd revved itself for what would be a roof-raising welcome for a man whose ancestors came to America from Scotland and Ireland by way of County Antrim, and in a time when the Bronx and Yonkers were not much more than names on maps drawn up by Dutch settlers.

But McLean Avenue was a border between retreat and advance, every bit as much as the frontier that snaked across the arid terrain of McCain's home state. Advance meant staying here – legally. Retreat meant being gone from here. And for good. Judging from the energy released by the crowd, few among them, legal or otherwise, were planning on being easily gone.

By no means were all those present in the country illegally. The effort to secure lawful footing in America for the undocumented Irish had drawn the legal and undocumented wings of the Irish community together a good deal more rapidly than was the case with the Irish Immigration Reform Movement campaign, which had wound up fifteen years previously. This was in large part because many of the legal Irish community won their visas as a result of that Irish Immigration Reform Movement (IIRM) campaign. They understood what was at stake for their neighbors and friends.

Additionally, the ILIR campaign, in contrast to the IIRM campaign, had a significant advantage: the Internet. The ability to instantaneously reach out to many people, turning a room generally used for religious gatherings into what looked like a presidential campaign rally, was a vital asset to any group hoping to sway the agitated mind of Congress. McCain could not have been but impressed when he walked into a sea of smiling faces, ILIR T-shirts, placards and flags – not to mention a wall of sound that included, perhaps a little confusingly for the man, chants of 'Olé' and a good belting out of 'The Fields of Athenry'.

In the hour preceding McCain's entry, the crowd had been reminded why they were in the room in the first place. An undocumented young woman named Samantha spoke of a rising sense of pride as her despair turned to hope during the three months of the ILIR's existence. To cheers and applause, she extended 'a formal thank you' to all the Irish and Irish Americans who were now supporting people in her situation and 'helping to keep the Irish in America'.

The mood of the moment was well stoked by ILIR's Ciaran Staunton and Kelly Fincham, but politicians other than McCain were also allowed time to pledge their support for ILIR's campaign to legalize the Irish and, indeed, people of many other nationalities through the Senate's McCain–Kennedy bill. Congressman Eliot Engel said he was in the room because he loved the Irish. He was also clearly in love with his 'Legalize the Irish' T-shirt, because he all but pledged to wear it for the rest of his days. 'We will not allow the Irish to be kept out of this country,' Engel bellowed as the crowd roared back.

ILIR founder Niall O'Dowd said that no special deal was being sought for the Irish, just fairness in the allocation of green cards. 'We're going to have our green cards, I promise you,' O'Dowd said to more loud cheers. ILIR president Grant Lally, a Republican like McCain and head of the Irish American Republicans lobby group, said that ILIR had made history when it drew 3,000 people to a recent rally on Capitol Hill. 'We proved the pundits wrong,' he said.

It was left to Lally to introduce McCain. Lally's words were interrupted by thunderous applause at the point where he recounted McCain's refusal to be released from a North Vietnamese prison in advance of other American prisoners – this, because his father was a four-star admiral. The stage was set. The room was now well and truly in the hands of the senior senator from the Grand Canyon State.

In the hour or so that followed, McCain worked his way through a this-is-me speech, a focused pep talk and a series of answers to questions from the floor – one of them from boxer John Duddy, who almost brought the roof down when he introduced himself to McCain. McCain himself was a onetime Naval Academy pug.

McCain's address contained hints of possible things to come in broader electoral terms, but at no time did he stray too far from the fact that he was addressing a specific issue – one that, he believed, was critical to the American Irish of the present, even as it was additionally vital for the preservation of a future Irish heritage on American soil.

It was important, McCain said, that those in the room had taken the time and effort to support the cause of immigration reform. He spoke movingly of his years as a prisoner of war, when he had held fast to America's ideals while cherishing the honor of being a citizen of a country that was the last best hope of mankind. Irish immigrants in former times had suffered cruelty and injustice – a cold welcome. But they had risen above these challenges, he said.

Speaking on the issue of illegal and undocumented immigrants beyond the Irish community, McCain said he did not know how an estimated 11 million people could be rounded up and sent back to their native countries, 'And I don't know why you would want to.' Instead, McCain outlined a vision in which those illegals and undocumented could earn their legalization by meeting conditions set forth in the bill he had co-authored with Senator Kennedy.

With regard to the prospects for a bill that would rescue many in the room from their lives in the shadows, McCain said he thought there would be a bill 'for the president to sign soon'. At the same time, he was concerned over the House-Senate conference process, a matter alluded to in John Duddy's question. McCain said, 'Senator Kennedy and I worry that strange things can happen at conference, so we want it to be open and bi-partisan.' Getting an agreed bill through the Senate before the upcoming recess was critical, he emphasized. McCain added that President George W. Bush, meanwhile, was standing up for reform and deserved some credit for doing so.

'Sooner or later we will prevail. But in the meantime, how many people will suffer in the shadows?' he asked. The shadows had lengthened to darkness by the conclusion of what had been a warm encounter between immigrants in those shadows and a legislator from a sun-blistered state. But all were agreed that something important had been forged on the border between two cities – one with a name of Swedish origin, the other Dutch. But now both were homes to just about every nationality on earth.

The road to McLean Avenue that April evening stretched back across an ocean and through many years. But the organizers of the meeting could look back on just a few months of existence. The ILIR had come into being in the waning days of 2005. The ILIR saw itself as an heir to the IIRM, but it was also an advance, in a way. Whereas the latter had come into the world in a kitchen in Queens, the former's naissance took place in a function room in a midtown Manhattan hotel.

From the start, ILIR presented itself as a rallying point for Irish-American organizations as the argument on both sides of the immigration issue intensified in Washington. The inaugural ILIR gathering, at the Affinia Hotel on December 9, 2005, was addressed by a number of Irish community leaders as well as former congressman Bruce Morrison and Esther Olivarria, Senator Kennedy's general counsel on immigration.

The message delivered to the standing-room-only crowd in the hotel's Clinton Room was that the situation for the undocumented Irish was dire, the news from Washington was not especially encouraging, and Capitol Hill's battle for immigration reform was moving into a critical phase against the always-unpredictable backdrop of a midterm congressional election year.

Morrison told the gathering, 'It would be a shame to have a battle on immigration reform and have the Irish missing from action.' Being in action meant rallying Irish American opinion behind the bipartisan McCain–Kennedy immigration reform bill that was, at that moment, before the Senate Judiciary Committee.

That bill had been endorsed by an all-party motion in the Dáil and was generally viewed as being the nearest thing on Capitol Hill to a comprehensive reform measure. By contrast, there were expressions of deep concern at the meeting over a House of Representatives bill due for a vote within days. The Border Protection, Antiterrorism, and Illegal Immigration Control Act of 2005, or HR 4437, was aimed in significant part at undocumented immigrants. And, by the ILIR's estimate, there were as many as 40,000 Irish around the US who fell into this category.

Secure borders and national security were the top priorities for many members of Congress post-9/11. Comprehensive immigration reform was a live issue, too, but it was having to battle strong political headwinds that were still blowing after the events of a September day that had wreaked carnage just a few miles to the south of the ILIR's inaugural meeting place.

But politics could not be avoided. Niall O'Dowd, who chaired the meeting, said that it was time to rebuild the 'political clout' that had been so evident in the Irish American community during the IIRM years. Esther Olivarria had briefed the meeting, in detail, on various bills being pondered on Capitol Hill.

Bruce Morrison said he was 'sorry to have to be here for this battle'. Outlining the need for comprehensive immigration reform, Morrison said that while 'everything in the '90s was about enforcement', during this period 'the number of people out of status had gone up faster than any time in our history'. With the IIRM, he said, the Irish-American community had spoken with one voice and this was now needed again, 'We need to be organized and a part of this political fight.'

Being organized, said Niall O'Dowd, would necessitate the involvement of different groups and organizations, and the meeting heard pledges of support from representatives of several, including the Gaelic Athletic Association (GAA) and the Ancient Order of Hibernians (AOH). Michael Glass of the AOH told the gathering that the Hibernians would be 'pulling out all the stops' for comprehensive reform; the New York GAA president, Seamus Dooley, indicated that his organization was also ready to help.

Getting the ILIR message out, the founding meeting was told, would be aided by the setting up of a website – a tool denied the IIRM back in the days of faxes, landline phones and even the occasional surviving telex machine. And so the Irish Lobby for

Immigration Reform plugged itself into the wider world. It wouldn't be long before it was creating a buzz.

Its first public meeting would follow a few weeks later, at the end of January 2006. A full house packed Rory Dolan's, a popular bar and restaurant on McLean Avenue. It was just a short walk from the St Barnabas church hall, where a political powerhouse and self-described maverick would soon pledge himself to the cause of those Irish who were living in the political and economic version of Arizona's desert wilderness.

CHAPTER 44

No Going Back

If you were lucky enough to land a Donnelly, Morrison, Berman or Schumer Visa you were entitled to party like it was 1999 well before that standout year. But many Irish living in America during the final decade of the twentieth century didn't much feel like partying at all. While thousands of visas were issued, thousands of undocumented Irish could only watch as they went here, there and everywhere, but not into their eager hands. The visa programs were open to applicants in Ireland, too, and many green cards went east across the Atlantic. Not all of them were fully used. In some cases, they were put aside as migratory insurance policies.

The island of Ireland would undergo profound change during the 1990s. And Irish America would feel the effects. Young Irish immigrants who happened to be lesbian and gay made headlines around the world by attempting to secure a place in the line of march of the New York St Patrick's Day Parade, an iconic event in the Irish American calendar. The Irish American media, undergoing significant changes of its own, would be hard-pressed to keep up with the multitude of twists and turns in a growing variety of stories. And then, to top them all, along came Bill Clinton.

Clinton could have been a footnote in Irish history, but his winning of the presidency would lead to him leaving a rather large footprint in it. What he promised, at a 1992 presidential forum organized by Irish American Democrats led by John Dearie, a member of the New York State Assembly, would evolve into a hitherto unimaginable level of US involvement in the affairs of Ireland, and, in particular, the search for a peaceful settlement in Northern Ireland.

The immigration story did not completely vanish off the radar during the Clinton years, but it faded into a backdrop dominated by the nascent and then-emerging peace process. The undocumented Irish didn't vanish either but did their best to fade into the background, most especially when a new piece of immigration legislation, the Illegal Immigration Reform and Immigrant Responsibility Act of 1996, passed through Congress and made its way to President Clinton's desk.

The bill was enacted on September 30 of that year and became active on April 1 of the following year. It was anything but an April Fools' joke as far as the undocumented were concerned. It carried significant changes to immigration law, and most especially its enforcement. President Clinton lauded the act, stating that it strengthened the rule of law 'by cracking down on illegal immigration at the border, in the workplace, and in the criminal justice system, without punishing those living in the United States legally'.

Long before Donald Trump arrived in the Oval Office promising a big, beautiful wall along the US border with Mexico, the 1996 act – dubbed IIRIRA, ironically sounding like an acronym for some Irish grouping – gave the US Attorney General broad authority to construct barriers along the border between the US and its neighbor to the immediate south.

The Irish didn't have to concern themselves with a wall. They already had 3,000 miles of ocean to consider. But on the other side of this watery barrier, the land that had given so much of itself and its people to America was beginning to experience a growing prosperity that would, over time, amaze and even inspire envy among those Irish living in America, both legally and in the immigration shadows. The 'Celtic Tiger' would be both tease and temptation. Many green card holders would find themselves drawn back to their Irish point of origin. The undocumented, by contrast, could only watch, eyes ever wider, from afar.

Some Irish in the US, legal and illegal, felt intimidated by this strange new Ireland – its soaring property prices and changing demographics brought about by the arrival of a novel group of people: immigrants from other lands. Some would be asked questions by curious Americans. Often, the response was a shrug of the shoulders, a smile or a standard-issue response that sounded like it had been spat out by a government printing machine: young, best-educated, low corporate tax and all the rest.

The tiger roared on; the undocumented Irish soldiered on. And they did so inside an America that resembled a strengthening fortress. Congress was throwing up barriers aimed at the undocumented of all nationalities. By 1998, illegality would bring with it the risk of long periods of exclusion from the US in the event of apprehension – the dreaded 'Bars'. These Bars were rules imposing automatic exclusion: three years if an individual had overstayed by six months; ten years if the overstay exceeded a year. For the undocumented, America would become a continental-sized detention facility. A return to Ireland, even for the most celebrated and sacred reasons, would become all but impossible.

To make matters worse, an emboldened Congress and a House of Representatives being led by Republican Speaker Newt Gingrich did away with a hitherto obscure immigration provision called Section 245(i). The demise of 245(i) would mean that individuals could no longer adjust their status on US soil. They would have to return to their country of origin which, for the Irish, meant the imposition of the Bars. Being between a rock and a hard place could barely describe it.

To add to the growing feeling that the 1980s had not been that bad after all, pressure was being applied to the Schumer visa program, an Irish immigration lifeline. Congress trimmed it by five thousand visas a year before the end of its 1997 sitting. These changes took place, admittedly, against the backdrop of relatively little immigration from Ireland. So those voices raising early cries of alarm found it difficult to generate the sense of urgency so evident in the 1980s. At the same time, the emerging situation appeared graver than the 1980s, when being illegal might be tolerable so long as the individual could stay out of the physical clutches of the INS while visas were being fought for in Washington. By the close of the 1990s, the Washington visa spigot was all but tapped out.

Expression of concern and support for the undocumented continued to radiate from, and within, Irish America. Their plight was on the work-list each and every day for the growing number of Irish immigration support-and-advice centers located in major US cities. These centers had joined forces in 1996 as the Coalition of Irish Immigration Centres. Under the coalition's umbrella, what would eventually be fifteen centers were to be found in California, Pennsylvania, Washington, Illinois, DC, Maryland, New York, Massachusetts and Wisconsin. The centers could dispense legal advice and words of comfort, but they could not advocate or lobby at the political level. Yet their very existence was effectively a political beacon signaling the fact that all was not well for the undocumented Irish – indeed, the undocumented of all nationalities, given that their doors were wide open to all.

The first of these centers was the Emerald Isle Immigration Center, which was founded by Irish Immigration Reform Movement (IIRM) members in 1988 and based in an office in Woodside, still a heavily Irish neighborhood in Queens, New York. Emerald Isle was followed into the fray by an entity that was not attached to the future coalition, but rather the Catholic Church. Project Irish Outreach was an addition to the expanding immigrant pastoral operations of the Archdiocese of New York.

Again, though, the work being carried out in both Emerald Isle and Project Irish Outreach was, for the most part, behind the scenes – all involved were conscious of the legal complexities faced by the undocumented and the need for confidentially. There was no active lobby group operating beyond the doors of the advice centers – a void that was only highlighted by their ever-increasing workloads.

And so the century turned with the undocumented Irish reckoning that all the fuss over 'Y2K' was hardly top of their particular worry list. For many, the passing of the years since their first footfalls in America would be prompts for a lot of second guessing. What if they had stuck it out in Ireland and were now enjoying all the benefits of the Celtic Tiger? The question would go round and round and nowhere. There was no going back, and as the early days of the new century folded one into the other, there was no sign of being allowed to rest easy *in situ* with the blessing of Washington.

And then it was September 11, 2001. The surge of patriotism and patriotic fury that followed was just one of the forces unleashed. Another was an enhanced suspicion of outsiders – non-Americans.

And, of course, there were politicians ready and willing to harness such suspicions, fears and even outright xenophobia. Many things rose from the ashes of Ground Zero: heroism, nobility and sacrifice being just a few. But in the post-9/11 years, during which Ground Zero entered the American lexicon, the political and legal gradient leading to a fully accepted American life would become steeper for immigrants, the Irish included, as America embraced an edgier, more exclusive patriotism.

There was a sad irony in this. Ground Zero was where the World Trade Center towers stood and fell. Americans with roots from all over the world, and people from all over the world, had spent their working lives there up until the point that their lives were so barbarically taken.

America would change after 9/11. If it had been uncomfortable for the illegal and undocumented before it, the times would become increasingly fraught and perilous after it. For the undocumented Irish, the task of blending into the American mosaic was not as difficult a task as that faced by some other nationalities. But America would be a less sympathetic place for all those who were not fully legal parts of that mosaic.

The Irish needed relief – a way in. But who would advocate for them?

CHAPTER 45

Legalize the Irish!

You couldn't miss them. Whether on the still winter-tinged sward on Capitol Hill, in Philadelphia, Boston, or Queens in New York. In the spring of 2006, 'Legalize the Irish' T-shirts were sprouting faster than leaves and daffodils. The Irish Lobby for Immigration Reform (ILIR) was on the march.

ILIR drew a direct line back to its predecessor, the Irish Immigration Reform Movement (IIRM). And it could historically identify with the American Irish National Immigration Committee (AINIC) too. But there were differences. Critically, AINIC and the IIRM had come into being in the wake of major immigration legislation. ILIR came into the world in anticipation of legislation – specifically, the McCain–Kennedy Secure America and Orderly Immigration Act, which was introduced in the US Senate on May 12, 2005. ILIR, simply put, was trying to catch the wave. And hoping for a big one.

Years later, ILIR founder Niall O'Dowd would explain the timing of ILIR's arrival on the immigration reform battlefield:

As the Celtic Tiger began its spectacular collapse in the early 2000s the focus again rested on young Irish fleeing unemployment and bleak futures and coming to America. Not since the 1980s had such an exodus been experienced and it soon became obvious that it was not a fleeting phenomenon.

The Irish government in the US, through its diplomats, were feeling the pressure from back home and badly needed to create a coherent strategy to deal with the exodus.

I held successive meetings with Ambassador Noel Fahey and Consul General in New York Tim O'Connor with a view to creating an umbrella organization similar to the Irish Immigration Reform Movement, which had been very successful as an advocacy group in helping win the Morrison and Donnelly visas.

That generation had mostly moved on and I undertook to create a new group called the Irish Lobby for Immigration Reform providing two people signed up as leaders as well: Ciaran Staunton, a veteran of the IIRM who had done Trojan work in Boston and New York, and Kelly Fincham, who knew the story inside out, lived in a deeply affected neighborhood, and wrote frequently on the topic.

All was agreed and the first meeting took place in a midtown hotel on a wet night in December, 2005. A large crowd of about 300 showed up, many with heartbreaking stories of exile and hardship. We realized we had to mobilize on a massive scale and we did so.

There were chapters in the Bronx, Queens, Boston, Philadelphia, San Francisco and a group in Chicago that retained its name of the Chicago Celts for Immigration Reform.

The immigration debate at the time was focused on the Kennedy–McCain bill which President George W. Bush approved and had a decent chance of success. However, the House companion bill, introduced by GOP Congressman James Sensenbrenner, was a hardline enforcement piece of legislation.

We decided to take the case to Washington and buses from New York, Boston, Philly, as well as large numbers from Chicago and San Francisco showed up on the day. The estimate of canvassers for our first lobbying day was 2,500.

We had everyone wear a 'Legalize the Irish' T-shirt to distinguish us, which turned out to be a very smart move in terms of recognition.

We visited every congressman and senator and received a universally warm reception and linked up with a Latino group at a large public meeting to show it was everyone's fight. Many politicians and Latino activists had never thought of undocumented persons as an Irish issue.

We had our own event at which Hillary Clinton, Chuck Schumer, Ted Kennedy, GOP Senator Sam Brownback and dozens of others attended at a standing room only event. We made three trips in all to DC mobilizing new partners every time.

We had several such rally events over the following months including a spectacular event in the Bronx where 1,000 showed up to meet Senator McCain.

The rallies, to some observers, had an air of religious revival meetings. Politicians would drop by and say their piece to loud cheers and applause. At one gathering, Congressmen Joe Crowley, a New York Democrat, arrived with his guitar and proceeded to serenade the campaigners. Ciaran Staunton would tell those attending one meeting, 'You people have stayed the course. You come into these meetings as undocumented residents, but you're leaving as political activists.'

Numbers would be a big part of the ILIR story: numbers who turned up for rallies and volunteered their time; numbers of politicians contacted; the most important of all, the numbers on whose behalf the ILIR was waging its campaign. The immediate constituency was the undocumented Irish community. A precise count was all but impossible. ILIR settled on 40,000, though sometimes this estimate notched upwards to 50,000. For the island of Ireland, this was a lot of people. In terms of the estimated number of undocumented and illegals in the US when ILIR was founded, this was a comparative drop in the bucket. But it was an Irish bucket.

The McCain–Kennedy bill (Irish backers often dubbed it Kennedy–McCain, while some nicknamed it 'McKennedy') was an omnibus measure with three main parts: legalization, guest worker visas and border control proposals. To the ILIR, the AOH and other Irish organizations with a stake in the immigration issue, there was, in the early days of the bill's existence, a cautious degree of optimism and a feeling that a bill of some sort was finally due. After all, they seemed to have a habit of cropping up mid-decade. Added to this was the sponsoring duo – a blockbuster combination of arguably the most powerful Democrat in the Senate and certainly one of more significant Republicans. John McCain, of course, had the steeper hill to climb, because it was within the ranks of his party that most of the 'lock 'em up, throw them out' mindsets were to be found. Still, even the hard heads would have to listen to McCain – a maverick, yes, but also a war hero who was no soft touch when it came to national security.

They might have to listen to John McCain. But they didn't have to support his pitch for meaningful immigration reform. As McCain–Kennedy was stirring debate, McCain was casting an eye down the Mall towards the White House. Teddy Kennedy's White House dreams had long been set aside, though his mind was also focused on the 2008 election and the matter of lending his name and considerable clout to a fellow Democrat.

McCain's presidential ambitions would inevitably cause problems for his Senate activities. Once you raise your head above the presidential parapet, this is par for the course. McCain had allies in his own party. And enemies. This was on top of the normal dealings and machinations associated with an attempt to steer legislation through Congress – the political equivalent of running with the bulls in Pamplona.

McCain–Kennedy, in its original form, was destined for the congressional record but not a Senate vote. However, it did find reflection in two other pieces of legislation, the Comprehensive Immigration Reform Act of 2006 and the Comprehensive Immigration Reform Act of 2007. The existence of the latter spoke to the failure of the former.

The 2006 act was introduced in the Senate in April of that year by Pennsylvania Republican Arlen Specter. John McCain and Edward Kennedy were co-sponsors. It contained a legalization path for the long-term illegal and undocumented, many of whom were very long term indeed. The bill secured Senate approval on May 25 by 62 votes to 36. The House had its own bill, but Senate and House legislators failed to reach the compromise stage in a conference committee. This effort at reform died with the end of the 109th

Congress in the first days of January 2007. But all was not lost. The succeeding 110th Congress would consider the Comprehensive Immigration Reform Act of 2007, which also went by the title of Secure Borders, Economic Opportunity and Immigration Reform Act of 2007.

It was seen as a compromise between a path to legality for the now-estimated 12 million illegal and undocumented immigrants and enhanced border security, most especially on the border with Mexico. Compromise can be a difficult path to follow in the US political process. The bill was introduced on May 9, 2007 and was effectively consigned to the scrap heap by June 7. A similar Senate bill, S.1639, followed it into legislative oblivion on June 28. This bill was crafted by Ted Kennedy; it went down by 53 votes to 46, with one member not voting.

President George W. Bush expressed disappointment at the failure of Congress to pass meaningful immigration legislation. He wasn't alone in doing so. Kennedy was disappointed, too, but, interestingly, not just with Republicans.

In his interview with the University of Virginia's Miller Institute as part of the Edward Kennedy Oral History Project, Kennedy also took issue with his fellow Democrats. The segment was part of an interview process conducted over multiple days between 2005 and 2008, and in partnership with the Edward M. Kennedy Institute for the Senate in Boston. The segment was recorded on October 8, 2007 on Cape Cod. The sea air did little to temper the senator's criticism of Democratic Senate Leader Harry Reid, 'I've said at other times that the three issues that bring out the worst in terms of the functions of the Senate are civil rights, the debates on gay rights, and immigration.' And, to a significant extent, the failure of what would be Kennedy's last bid to fundamentally change US immigration law while providing a path to legalization for millions – and among them thousands of Irish – came down to functions.

He stated in the interview that Harry Reid 'was never really interested in it until the very end, and at the very end it was too late'. Kennedy accused Majority Leader Reid and other top Democrats in the Senate of looking at a broader picture in which Latino voters, increasingly sought after, would blame Republicans for immigration reform failure. Kennedy also took issue, more naturally, perhaps, with Republican Senator Mitch McConnell, who had 'absolutely no intention of doing anything but sinking the bill'.

As for John McCain, Kennedy said, 'In 2007, the second time we dealt with immigration, we had a group that included McCain, but he was running for President, so he was not around very much.' An up-and-coming senator who was mounting a presidential bid, Barack Obama, was 'somewhat interested'. Being somewhat interested wasn't going to cut it for Kennedy, who was known for having deep reservoirs of passion for the causes he espoused, 'Immigration starts out as reasonably sanitized, and then, as we have seen recently, in 2006 and 2007, basically deteriorates into racist amendments and racism on the floor of the Senate. It's been dressed a different way, but I've said that it's the same music we heard in the early '60s with different words.' What of President Bush, Kennedy was asked – 'Well, Bush wanted to get a bill, but he's completely ineffective in trying to influence people.'

At the conclusion of the interview, Kennedy summed his point up as follows:

> The interesting dichotomy on the issue of immigration with the undocumented is that you have two things. One is the politics, but there's a more substantive issue.
>
> In the House, all the Republicans were very strong anti-immigrant. In the Senate, it was divided between Republicans who aligned with the Chamber of Commerce, understood that the farmers and the growers and companies needed workers, we need workers for an expanding economy, and therefore we ought to bring more workers in the country. But they're temporary workers, so we're going to send them back, and that's fine. The Republicans in the House say, 'We're not going to have law breakers.' It's a values issue as well, divided between the Republicans who are interested in the economic benefit and who deplore immigration – at least they say, 'We're not going to be sympathetic to undocumented illegals.' But a lot of that is the racism.

The issue I see is on the one hand you ask, what are the values Americans really admire? They admire people who work hard. They admire people who look after their families and care about their families. They admire people who look after their parents. This is a big issue, particularly in this immigrant population.

Niall O'Dowd echoes Kennedy's overall view. Speaking of those early ILIR campaign days, he looks back with a mixture of pride and frustration, 'Once more, meaningful immigration reform was thwarted and one can only speculate how much less toxic the issue might have become if the 2006 or 2007 bill had passed. The Irish performed nobly, but the forces arrayed against immigrants in the Republican-controlled House were much too great.'

CHAPTER 46

McCain's Embrace

In the interview he gave in October 2007 (about eight months before he was diagnosed with brain cancer), Edward Kennedy was asked if he anticipated being able to have another go at immigration reform. 'Yes,' he responded. 'The fact is, these issues are not going to go away.'

And sure enough, immigration was swirling around the presidential campaign of 2008, which, when it eventually came down to two main candidates, was viewed by the Irish Lobby for Immigration Reform (ILIR), the Ancient Order of Hibernians (AOH) and other Irish groups as harboring strong possibilities for future immigration reform. After all, the Democratic candidate, Senator Barack Obama, was at least 'somewhat interested' in reform according to Ted Kennedy, who would cause shock waves in the Democratic Party by endorsing Obama over Hillary Clinton.

Meanwhile, the Republican banner was being carried by John McCain, and the Arizona senator was seen as being in the Irish corner on immigration reform. His April 2006 appearance on the border of the Bronx and Yonkers still resonated. But as 2008 dawned, 2006 became ancient history. Irish American community leaders were seeking to rekindle the presidential forum flame in what would be an open year – the White House not being home to an incumbent seeking a second term. 'There has to be a forum this year. This year is as important as any in the past that we have held one,' now-former New York State Assemblyman John Dearie, founder of the forum back in 1984, said.

The forum gatherings had been primarily focused on Northern Ireland – 1992 being the standout in that it secured pledges from Bill

Clinton that would be fulfilled with extraordinary results. By 2008, however, another issue was beginning to stake a claim to any forum agenda: immigration reform and what to do about the plight of the undocumented Irish.

Organizers offered presidential candidates a flexible roster that could mean multiple forum gatherings, in New York City or outside it. Invitations duly went out to senators Hillary Clinton, Barack Obama, John McCain and Mike Huckabee, the former governor of Arkansas and a Republican long-shot. Two of the four – Clinton and McCain – would make appearances, though not only in different locations and on different dates, but in two states – New York City in Clinton's case; Scranton, Pennsylvania in the case of Arizona's McCain.

The Obama campaign, meanwhile, would later respond to a series of questions presented jointly by the Ancient Order of Hibernians, the Ladies Ancient Order of Hibernians and the Irish American Unity Conference, a Washington, DC-based lobby group focused on Northern Ireland. The response came after Obama became his party's presidential candidate.

As it turned out, 2008 would be a standout year in that there were two forum gatherings – one in Manhattan attended by Hillary Clinton, the other in Scranton with John McCain. McCain was the first Republican candidate to ever physically attend the event. Clinton would not only attend a forum event; she would also hold a press conference for Irish and Irish American journalists organized by Brian O'Dwyer, a veteran Democratic Party activist, chairman of the Emerald Isle Immigration Center and, critically, a friend of the Clintons.

Hillary's interest in Ireland was taken as a given. Her need for Irish American support was considered crucial, not least because Irish America was riven and Ted Kennedy had declared his support for Barack Obama. John McCain's arrival on the Irish stage did not have such a party division as a backdrop.

Somewhat similar to the rather chaotic 1988 forum in New York, the Scranton gathering would be a Republican Party rally, but with a specific Irish wraparound. And by now, of course, McCain was his party's candidate. This rally with an Irish twist took place on September 22, less than two months before the election.

In the hometown of future Vice President Joe Biden, McCain acknowledged his pioneering status to loud cheers in a theater that was once the centerpiece of a Masonic temple. And in a delivery that crossed from general election issues to Ireland and back again, McCain addressed the immigration issue in a prepared speech that did not specifically answer the six questions in the Irish forum format but ranged over much of the ground that those questions covered.

Prior to his appearance in the packed theatre, McCain had met for a private discussion with the ILIR's Ciaran Staunton. He would leave that meeting with a very clear idea of how the Irish felt about what was a stalemate in the immigration debate on Capitol Hill – a situation that was brought about, in part, by the presidential election.

McCain was accompanied to the stage by fellow Republican senators Arlen Specter of Pennsylvania and Lindsey Graham of South Carolina. The former had loomed large in the immigration debate, the latter would loom larger as time passed. Also on stage – and he was given a huge cheer by the crowd – was independent Democrat Joe Lieberman from Connecticut.

During his address to the rapt audience, McCain praised the Irish who had contributed 'in literally every war this nation has fought' up to and including the present ones. He described this record of service as being 'remarkable' and a 'great heritage'. 'I'm proud to be the first Republican to appear,' he said in reference to the forum's history. 'I need the Irish American vote,' the Arizona senator concluded, while describing himself as the underdog in the November general election.

What would a McCain presidency have done with regard to the immigration impasse? This will always be a 64,000-dollar question. But regardless of who might do what, the air of euphoria that invariably surrounded a serious contender for the presidency did not entirely match the reality for the undocumented Irish, outside the bubble of the campaigns with all their promise and promises.

St Patrick's Day, 2008 had been something of a reality check for ILIR and other reform backing groups. Taoiseach Bertie Ahern had arrived in Washington for the annual shamrock summit with the American president. George W. Bush was in his final year in office – the proverbial lame duck. But the stage that he offered Ahern was as big as in any year. On that stage, Ahern caused something of an uproar when he stated that the undocumented Irish should consider celebrating St Patrick's Day 2009 in Ireland. Following the traditional Speaker's Lunch on Capitol Hill, Ahern said, 'The concept of an amnesty for people that were here for ten, twenty or thirty years, that's not in the ball park.' When asked how his pre-lunch meeting with President Bush had gone, he told reporters, 'I don't want to be gilding the lily. The concept of an amnesty is not on. People shouldn't be trying to give the impression that something that isn't on might be on. It's no good saying that. They're talking nonsense and that's not just me. That's the view of all my friends here.'

Ahern's blunt remarks, not surprisingly, didn't go down with immigration activists quite as well as the lunch. They were far and away a sharper cut than Brian Lenihan's remark, also directed at the emigrant Irish, in a *Newsweek* magazine interview back in the 1980s, 'We can't all live on a small island.' A statement, by way of reaction, from the Coalition of Irish Immigration Centers described Ahern's words as 'deeply offensive'. This was an especially interesting response given that the centers under the coalition umbrella relied, in part, on Irish government funding.

ILIR's response was equally critical and more bluntly delivered. Penning an op-ed in the *Irish Echo*, San Francisco-based immigrant activist and ILIR board member Bart Murphy wrote that Ahern had delivered his remarks with 'all the subtlety of a head-butt'. Regardless of any physical danger, real or imagined, ILIR executive director Kelly Fincham stated that the group was seeking 'urgent talks' with Ahern.

What would happen was that ILIR would hear Ahern talk. The taoiseach, as he prepared to leave office, was accorded the remarkable opportunity and privilege of speaking to the United States House of Representatives. This he did as April gave way to May. In his House address, Ahern said, 'We ask you to consider the case of our undocumented community in the United States today. We hope you will be able to find a solution to their plight that would enable them to regularize their status and open to them a patch to permanent residency.' Listening in the public gallery were ILIR's

Murphy, Fincham and Vice Chairman Ciaran Staunton, all guests of Congressman Joe Crowley. Fincham saw Ahern's words as a prelude to a closer working relationship between the Irish government and ILIR.

Things were looking up and looking better. And then they weren't. Before the end of May came the news that Senator Edward Kennedy had been diagnosed with a brain tumor. This was a shock. Kennedy had been around seemingly forever. He would have to stay around for comprehensive immigration reform to be passed. And that process seemed not unlike forever. Some who hadn't prayed for years prayed for Kennedy, who would soon undergo surgery.

Kennedy wasn't the only reform champion, of course. Campaigners had lines open to other Congress members, including Charles Schumer and Kennedy's close friend and ally Chris Dodd from Connecticut. And, of course, there was John McCain on the other side of the political aisle, now running hard for the presidency. Both Democratic presidential contenders, Hillary Clinton and Barack Obama, were reform-oriented. Still, the question persisted. How much would the legislative landscape change if Kennedy was out of the picture? More prayers went heavenward.

As the battle for the presidency intensified, and Kennedy's battle against cancer proceeded from day to day, sobering news beamed across the Atlantic. The Irish would be leaving their island again the following year, and by the thousands. The prediction was coming from Ireland's Economic and Social Research Institute, which was envisaging a recession in 2009 – the first of such since 1983.

The bad news was beginning to mount for Irish immigration campaigners. The last thing they needed was a jump in the numbers of undocumented Irish. Kennedy's illness was always part of the conversation, and while hopes were rising for a presidential forum appearance by John McCain, the man from Arizona was sounding more and more like a candidate as opposed to a senator. Candidate McCain was talking up border security where Senator McCain had once focused on immigration reform within the nation's borders.

But high summer would bring a few brighter moments. Bertie Ahern's successor as taoiseach, Brian Cowen, landed in New York in July and immediately caught the mood of the moment. At a packed reception in the lobby of the Park Avenue tower that housed the Irish Consulate, Cowen said he would make the visa and immigration issue a priority for his government. It would be, for him personally, a priority in the months and years ahead.

Cowen's words followed his meeting with representatives of ILIR, the Coalition of Irish Immigration Centers and Bruce Morrison. It had clearly been a positive gathering. ILIR's Ciaran Staunton said after the meeting that Cowen had ushered in a new era in the transatlantic Irish relationship, 'He knows his stuff. He knows this issue, and what we really like about him is that he really understands this whole idea of Irish America.'

Interestingly, the meeting had covered a matter that was beginning to come into sharper focus. All understood that it was virtually impossible for Irish nationals to secure a green card and live and work legally in America. Cowen also addressed the flip side of this – how difficult a proposition it was for Americans to secure legal residence in Ireland. The idea of *quid pro quo* was entering the arena.

And there was of course that other arena – the one in which the presidency was to be decided. Barack Obama would win the nomination for the Democrats and raise the hopes of Irish immigration campaigners by choosing an Irish American, Joe Biden (codenamed 'Celtic' by the US Secret Service), as his running mate. John McCain would be partnered with Sarah Palin. Irish campaigners, like many Americans, would shrug and ask 'who?'

There would be quite a degree of sparring between the Obama and McCain campaigns over Ireland, though mostly with regard to Northern Ireland and the matter of a US envoy to the peace process. Still, immigration would be a frontline topic when McCain turned up for his big Irish day in Scranton. He would acknowledge 50,000 undocumented Irish who, if he found himself in a position as president to throw them a lifeline, would have to do 'certain things' on the path to citizenship. John McCain was sympathetic, but he was no pushover.

And then John Sidney McCain got pushed over by Barack Hussein Obama.

CHAPTER 47

Yes We Can, Well Maybe

Barack Obama would begin his presidency with a bigger 'In Basket' on the Oval Office desk than just about anyone could remember. Saving the economy of the United States and much of the rest of the world from falling over a financial cliff was at the top of the 44th president's pile. Immigration was in the pile somewhere. But where exactly?

Obama began his first term with a Democratic majority in Congress. That was no guarantee of significant immigration reform. But it all but guaranteed at least an attempt to secure meaningful change on an issue that was always a political third rail for both parties on Capitol Hill. Reform, in character and of necessity, was an issue that demanded a bipartisan solution. And while it attracted support from members of both parties, it also made members of both extremely skittish. And as the first month of 2009 gave way to the second and subsequent months, it would be remembered that immigration reform had not been one of the main policy objectives laid out by Barack Obama during his presidential campaign.

Still, Obama could not ignore the fact that Hispanic voters broke in large numbers for him and helped him secure four battleground states – Colorado, New Mexico, Florida and Nevada – in the 2008 vote. And, of course, the fate of the reform effort now depended most heavily on growing Hispanic political power.

The Irish, too, continued to wield political power – and out of all proportion to the numbers of undocumented from Ireland. This would mean that Hispanic and other reform backers would keep a wary eye on the Irish, who were now beginning to talk of solutions that were not entirely within the generally understood boundaries of broad and comprehensive immigration reform.

Irish Lobby for Immigration Reform's (ILIR's) Bart Murphy took the Irish argument down a new path when he advocated a bilateral treaty between Dublin and Washington that would provide renewable E-3 visas along the lines of those that had been available to Australian citizens since 2005. Murphy, in a statement from his San Francisco base, said that the system of Irish immigration had been broken since 1965, 'For over forty-four years it has been nothing short of a haphazard, sporadic mess that, every now and then, has been temporarily tidied up by once-off fixes such as the Donnelly and Morrison visa programs.' Even comprehensive reform, laudable though it might be, would not suffice. It too, Murphy argued, would be just another one-time fix:

> Even if it comes to pass it is no substitute for a proper and sustainable system of Irish-US migration. Successful negotiation of an Irish E-3 visa is the way forward. Let us hope our leaders in Ireland and the US have the conviction and moral courage to push for change, to fix an old, broken system and truly embrace the history and accomplishments of our two countries.

If it sounded like ILIR was raising the stakes, it was because they were. Still, the idea of a bilateral deal was taking shape in Dublin too. Taoiseach Brian Cowen arrived in Washington to make Barack Obama's first St Patrick's Day as president a memorable one. Cowen arrived with the traditional gift, a bowl of shamrock, and a bowlful of accompanying text derived from a major review of Irish–US relations carried out by the Irish Embassy in Washington under the stewardship of Ambassador Michael Collins. Contained in the review was the proposal to develop 'Ireland-US bilateral arrangements' with a new reciprocal and renewable two-year working visa arrangement, a 'reenergized' J1 visa program and a 'long term solution' for the undocumented Irish.

ILIR wasn't overly energized by J1 visas, which were awarded to students for summer work or, down the road, a full year in America. But 'renewable' and 'reciprocal' were words to ponder seriously. And there would be plenty of time to ponder. Three months into Obama's term, his White House Press Secretary, Robert Gibbs, told reporters that reform was not imminent. 'I don't think he expects that it will be done this year', the *Irish Echo*'s Washington correspondent, Susan Falvella Garraty, reported Gibbs as stating on the eve of an Obama visit to Mexico.

Falvella Garraty further reported that a member of Congress who had long taken an interest in immigration reform, speaking under the condition of anonymity, said that any effort to secure a special bilateral dispensation for the Irish would not be achieved. The Congress member said, 'The old days of the Morrison Visa, or a special pass for the Irish, is just not going to happen. It was a one-time only opportunity.' Perhaps. But there were still a lot of members of Congress with one-time only ideas.

One of them was Senator Charles Schumer, who, by spring of 2009, had replaced the ailing Ted Kennedy as chair of the Senate Immigration Subcommittee. Schumer moved to convene new hearings on Capitol Hill. Encouraged by this new burst of energy, ILIR organized a rally where Schumer had first addressed the group in 2006: Yonkers. While Schumer would be talking up overall reform, ILIR was focusing on a twin-track approach that encompassed E-3 visas and Irish future flow – something which it felt it could have a direct role in bringing about – comprehensive reform that would cover the undocumented Irish. The latter would be under the control of Congress, where Schumer was talking about a reform bill by Labor Day – the traditional early September bookend to summer.

Just before Labor Day, On August 25, Senator Edward Kennedy lost his battle with cancer. He was 77 years of age. (John McCain would pass nine years later – on the same date – and as a result of the same kind of brain cancer.) Kennedy wasn't a president, but the funeral of the last-surviving Kennedy brother was worthy of one. Amid all the sadness and tributes, there was, of course, some criticism. Kennedy, after all, had been in politics all his life. Some Irish blamed him for the 1965 act and all that followed. Kennedy was all too aware of those unintended consequences, stating in an interview with *Irish America Magazine* in 1997:

The 1965 immigration act worked in a way we never predicted. It was a good act in the sense that it helped ethnic groups from nations that had suffered under racial bias but it put restrictions on nations like Ireland. During the 1970s there was an average of only about 1,000 visas a year from Ireland. I was strongly committed to changing that. The gates are swinging open again as they should be.

But not widely enough. *Irish America*'s founding publisher, Niall O'Dowd, would later conclude that what Kennedy 'unwittingly did' was: 'effectively end forever – or at least to this date, any legal emigration from Ireland'. He continues:

Kennedy later acknowledged that the end of legal emigration from Ireland was an unintended consequence of the bill he pushed through Congress.

Before his death on August 25, 2009, he appeared at several Irish Lobby for Immigration Reform events in Washington D.C and vowed to try and right the wrong to his ancestral countrymen.

There were warnings at the time. 'Tip' O'Neill, later Speaker of the House, asked the Irish government if they wanted an exception in their case.

The government of the day amazingly replied no, sealing the fate of hundreds of thousands of their emigrants who have lived illegally in America since then. There was opposition from Irish organizations but Kennedy brushed it off …

It was the time of huge civil rights breakthroughs and Kennedy saw immigration in the same light.

On September 22, 1965, the Senate voted 76–18 to pass the new bill that utterly excluded emigration from Europe save in a very small per centage of cases.

We Irish are suffering the consequences since.

And suffering they were. In October 2003, Kennedy had described the state of America's immigration laws as a 'national scandal' and compared the plight of millions of undocumented immigrants to that of slaves. Perhaps it was no surprise that Kennedy was once described as a real-life version of Senator Sempronius Gracchus as played by Charles Laughton in the movie *Spartacus*. He certainly played an outsize role in American politics, and he had walked the extra mile and then some in an effort to open America's doors once again to the Irish. Ultimately, though, the Senate's 'liberal lion' ran out of road.

Ready and willing to now take up the Irish cause was Senator Schumer. There was no formal passing of the torch, but there was a moment when Schumer presented himself as the one indispensable legislator – a new Irish champion. That moment came on an April 2010 evening in Queens. Bruce Morrison had just stated to an ILIR public meeting in the Sunnyside Community Center, 'I think we're in a good place right now, the best place in a few years.' Morrison was finishing up on a positive note on a night where, depending on their state of mind, listeners could pluck positive notes, negative notes, or simply vaguely reassuring notes from the Queens air. An eclectic crowd of US citizens, green card holders and undocumented had turned out in what was yet another year of the comprehensive reform campaign, and they were told that reform still had a chance in Washington.

The Sunnyside meeting was something of a test. ILIR, now five years on the road, had found itself having to organize more meetings of this kind than it had perhaps expected – or certainly wanted. But this meeting had its optimistic side, even as it was addressed by others than the main billed speaker, Morrison, and his unbilled colleague Chuck Schumer.

ILIR's Ciaran Staunton had opened the meeting with a call to legislative arms. Dan Dennehy of the Ancient Order of Hibernians set the stage with a dose of hard reality. Only 1,296 Irish people were naturalized in the US in 2009 – 298 of them in New York. At such a rate, Dennehy said, 'our heritage, our neighborhoods' would die.

Hughie Meehan of the Gaelic Athletics Association (GAA), in from Boston, spoke of efforts to prevent 'younger folks' who could not travel back to Ireland because of their status from becoming disheartened. Meehan, however, was himself dissatisfied with the attention given, by the Irish government in particular, to one aspect of the reform push: a hoped-for Irish E-3 visa scheme. The idea, he said, had been sent back to Ireland and 'put in a drawer somewhere'. What's more, the Irish government had shown disrespect towards Bruce Morrison. Comprehensive reform on its own was not good enough, Meehan said. Sticking with Morrison and securing comprehensive reform with an E-3 plan 'tagged on' was the way to go.

Joe McManus, president of the United Irish Counties, pledged his organization's members and efforts to reform. He said that he would be urging the presidents of all the county organizations to back the campaign.

The Irish Deputy Consul General in New York, Bréandán O Caollaí, vigorously defended the Irish government's role and record, stating that Taoiseach Brian Cowen and Foreign Minister Micheál Martin had only the highest of praise for Bruce Morrison. The Irish government, he said, was juggling with the practical day-to-day difficulties of the present situation and was doing so with the 'deepest concerns'.

O Caollaí said that those at the consulate 'do as much as we can'. Other consulates around the country, which had to work with limited resources, and the Irish embassy in Washington were in constant contact with Congress. The government, he said, was 'definitely determined' to find a solution which would be the E-3 plan and comprehensive reform, the latter being the 'dam buster' that would solve all the issues. 'The official stance of the Irish government is to support you, and to try to address the very real problems you face,' said O Caollaí.

Ciaran Staunton told the gathering that the Irish had a friend in Senator Schumer, who, as if on cue, appeared in the room. He had, minutes before, arrived at LaGuardia Airport from Washington.

Schumer told his listeners that he was committed, 'with every atom in my body', to getting 'a strong comprehensive immigration reform bill through this year'. He was working towards having a comprehensive immigration reform bill ready for congressional debate by May 1.

Schumer gave the room a rundown on the essential points of the reform bill that he was putting together with Republican Party co-sponsor Senator Lindsey Graham of South Carolina. He spoke of the difficulties in getting a second GOP backer but stated that beyond Capitol Hill the coalition supporting reform had broadened to include evangelicals, Southern Baptists, business and labor, which, in the case of the latter group, had 'brought the last bill [McCain–Kennedy] down'.

Schumer said that it might turn out that he would ask Lindsey Graham to 'go alone with me', but if a significant number of Republicans said they would vote for the bill, and then a second Republican co-sponsor was found, the odds were 'pretty decent' for a win. At that point, Schumer said, it would be time to 'let it rip'. 'I believe in this cause; we're going to get this immigration bill done,' Schumer said to a standing ovation before taking his leave.

Bruce Morrison, who joked that he did not mind Schumer stealing the show, told the audience, to renewed cheering, that it couldn't have had a better demonstration of what was needed to win reform and that they were lucky to have Chuck Schumer behind that effort. Schumer, Morrison said, was in the key position of being chairman of the immigration subcommittee in the Senate, and that when he (Morrison) had secured the Morrison Visas, he had been chair of the equivalent House subcommittee. There was, Morrison said, no one better than Schumer to get the reform job done. Morrison described Schumer as being a super campaign leader in the perfect place. 'But he's not God, he needs us,' he said. Morrison said, in what amounted to a rallying cry, 'We do not need to lobby Senator Schumer, but we need to be available for Senator Schumer.'

Morrison added a note of caution, however, 'I also want to level with you how hard it's going to be.' 'Maybe', he said, 'we get the job done this summer, or maybe we will be back in November after the elections, or in January to continue the fight.'

Morrison said it was 'vital', as part of any immigration reform deal, that 'we get something' with regard to 'future flow from Ireland'. This, he said, stemmed from the fact that Ireland, and he was speaking of the entire island, was a small country and could only ever hope to get a small slice of the overall immigration pie. That's why the solution to the problem was 'some other kind of visa' – an E-3 program that would provide 10,500 visas a year. So,

Morrison added, the agenda for ILIR had to be 'broad legalization and future flow'.

If there were no reform in the summer or fall of this year, Morrison said, it would be necessary to 'run it up the flagpole' again in January. 'I think we're in a good place right now, the best place in a few years', Morrison said, even while stressing that it was also necessary to be ready to be in for the long haul.

There followed an address by New York City Council member Danny Dromm, who chaired the council's immigration committee. Dromm said that the Irish had a 'special message' to deliver on the reform issue. He pledged his support, and that of the council, to getting the message out that this was an issue that profoundly affected all of America. Which, to be sure, it did.

The meeting, which lasted over two hours, concluded with questions and answers, and also cautionary words from a young woman, recently arrived from Ireland. She spoke of an economy in tatters, and a lot of anger and frustration – the very same combination that had spurred earlier generations to leave Ireland for America. This was a nuts-and-bolts meeting. All who left it knew that there was a lot of work to be done. And while there was no longer a Ted Kennedy, there was now a Chuck Schumer.

CHAPTER 48

A Last Full Measure

Washington isn't at its best in the middle of August. America's capital was laid down in grand architectural fashion – atop a swamp. High summer weather by the banks of the Potomac tended to reflect this soggy, sweaty reality. But today's Washington enjoys the merciful benefit of air conditioning. It is a luxury that has the unwelcome side effect of further warming the city – not to mention the rest of the planet. But business must proceed.

It was on an August day in 2011, under the steely gaze of Teddy Roosevelt – a man noted for action – that the near-total inertia on the immigration reform front was the subject of discussion in a White House meeting between Obama administration officials and a delegation of Irish reform campaigners.

The Obama team was led by White House Chief of Staff Bill Daley. The visiting Irish delegation was comprised of Ciaran Staunton of the Irish Lobby for Immigration Reform, Ned McGinley and Dan Dennehy of the Ancient Order of Hibernians (AOH), Stella O'Leary of the Irish American Democrats lobby group, and former congressman Bruce Morrison, by then acting as a consultant for the Irish Lobby for Immigration Reform (ILIR) in the nation's capital.

The high political ground that the Irish yet occupied was made plain by the fact that there were two White House meetings: one to air the concerns of the Irish and reform advocates speaking for a number of other European countries, the other focusing solely on Irish concerns and objectives.

Away from the presidential mansion, Senator Charles Schumer had been going about his business seeking Republicans to step aboard the reform bus with himself and Republican Lindsey

Graham. The bipartisan twosome were the newly minted Kennedy and McCain. As such, they had to temper optimism with caution. The gathering reform effort, as was to be expected, would make for national news.

Somewhat less noticed was an effort that same year to extend the E-3 visas to the Irish. This was also a Senate effort – in this instance, one that produced two bills. The initial bill was put together by Schumer. Schumer's measure, S.1983, or the Fairness for High-Skilled Immigrants Act, was, like many bills, effectively an amendment to existing law – in this case, a 1992 measure dealing with Chinese student visas. Immigration legislation, by its very nature, is a complex weave. A glance at S.1983 would not immediately give away its core purpose until such a time as it, as highlighted in the Congressional Record, 'includes nationals of Ireland coming to the United States under a treaty of commerce to perform specialty occupation services in the nonimmigrant E-3 visa category'.

As 2011 neared its end, Schumer's bill suddenly had a companion. Or, more accurately, a rival. That bill, crafted by Senator Scott Brown of Massachusetts and Mark Kirk of Illinois (both Republicans), reflected, in part, the Schumer legislation. But it differed in one key respect. While the Schumer bill, which was co-sponsored by senators Patrick Leahy of Vermont and Dick Durbin of Illinois (both Democrats), contained a provision granting waivers for undocumented Irish hoping for relief by means of an E-3 visa, the Brown–Kirk measure – a standalone as opposed to an amendment to something else – did not.

The Schumer measure proposed to allocate ten thousand E-3 visas a year for eligible Irish applicants. It had come on the heels of a House of Representatives move that upped the annual green card numbers for citizens of India, China, Mexico and the Philippines – this, while keeping the overall annual immigration limit static.

The Schumer bill emerged into sight after a series of meetings between senators and members of the Irish Lobby for Immigration Reform, the Ancient Order of Hibernians, Chicago Celts for Immigration Reform, and representatives of Irish immigration centers in various US cities. It was initially anticipated that the Schumer Senate move and the House green card measure would be somehow paired. But the arrival of the second Senate bill muddied the waters.

The Brown–Kirk bill, dubbed the Irish Immigration Recognition and Encouragement (IRE) Act of 2011, added the 'Republic of Ireland' to the ongoing E-3 visa program, providing 10,500 employment visas that, according to a statement from the two senators, would have no limit on the number of renewals allowed. Senator Brown said, 'The United States and Ireland have a close bond, and our people remain tightly knit through a long history of Irish immigration. Sadly, inefficiencies in our immigration program have resulted in increasingly poor prospects for Irish immigrants.' He continued:

> This legislation rectifies the decades-long plight by including the Irish in a special visa program that encourages their skilled workers to come to our shores. Legal immigration is the foundation of America, and we must continue to find ways to improve our visa and green card programs, especially when it comes to the treatment of our strongest allies and closest friends.

The accompanying statement additionally said that the Brown–Kirk bill 'recognizes the damage done to Irish immigration prospects in the Immigration and Nationality Act of 1965 and therefore adds the Republic of Ireland into the E-3 visa program'. It specified an annual total of 10,500 employment visas to be made available for the Irish – so, at one level, this was Schumer plus five hundred.

The measure was described as 'a standalone bill that does not include controversial immigration provisions that could weaken national security and rule of law'. It 'recognizes the history between Ireland and the United States, and the importance of increased Irish immigration'. The end-of-year holiday recess arrived before there could be any action on one or both of the Senate bills, so the two carried into 2012 – year two, as it was, of the 112th Congress.

The 112th Congress was not seen as a promising incubator by comprehensive immigration reform backers, hence the focus on, and interest in, the more limited E-3 bills. Irish doubts about the 112th were not hard to justify. In the House of Representatives, the final month of 2011 had witnessed passage of HR 3012, which would permit highly skilled applicants from several countries, though not Ireland, to gain legal entry to the US

The *New York Times* reported that the bill, penned by Representative Jason Chaffetz, a conservative freshman Republican from Utah, and Lamar Smith, a Texas Republican and chairman of the House Judiciary Committee, 'sailed through by a vote of 389 to 15'. And it sailed right by the Irish. Exclusive meetings in the White House were all well and good, but Congress was the more crucial, and certainly less predictable, forum.

Still, as 2012 arrived and advanced, there were expectations of a vote on at least one of the Senate Irish E-3 proposals by St Patrick's Day. But there would be a hitch. Both the E-3 packages were attracting bipartisan support, but even across-the-aisle agreement isn't a guarantee of ultimate success. So as St Patrick's Day 2012 drew close, there was less than total surprise that there was an objection. It was voiced by Senator Charles Grassley. The Iowa Republican had concerns that the E-3 visas would undercut American workers. This argument could have been made with regard to immigration in general, but Grassley's gimlet eye was fixed on the E-3s. There it remained, and the Irish E-3s of 2011/12 would have to wait for another day. Or another year.

But separate to all the E-3 talk, there was still the greater goal of comprehensive immigration reform, and its cause would be reflected in what would become known as the Senate 'Gang of Eight' bill. Reform certainly needed a gang behind it, but would eight senators suffice? This was a question that closely matched the one asked in the Hollywood screen classic, *The Magnificent Seven*. As it turned out, the gang of eight were pretty accomplished political gunslingers. The Democrats were Schumer of New York, Dick Durbin of Illinois, Michael Bennet of Colorado and Bob Menendez of New Jersey. The Republicans were Graham of South Carolina, Jeff Flake of Arizona, Marco Rubio of Florida and Arizona's John McCain, playing a now-familiar role as a reform champion. And so the geographically diverse eight lined up behind the Border Security, Economic Opportunity, and Immigration Modernization Act of 2013.

The bill, S.744, was introduced by Schumer and co-sponsored by the other seven senators on April 16, 2013. The Senate Judiciary Committee quickly held hearings and the bill was voted out of committee on May 21. This was fast track. It came up for a Senate vote on June 27 and passed by 68 to 32, just two votes shy of what had been dubbed in advance as 'Magnificent 70'. Because of various amendments, the bill that passed was actually named 'Leahy 1183'. But 'S.744' would survive and make it into most news reports.

It was noted by more than one Irish American observer that S.744 passed muster just as the nation was preparing to mark the 150th anniversary of the Battle of Gettysburg. During the first days of July 1863, Irish immigrants and the descendants of Irish immigrants slugged it out amid the pastoral beauty of Pennsylvania. Nobody had fussed over the precise immigration status of the combatants.

Crucially, for the Irish and a host of other nationalities, S.744 – if it now passed muster in the House of Representatives and was then, as expected, signed into law by President Obama – would clear a path for undocumented immigrants to gain legal status and, ultimately, US citizenship. But getting it through the House would be a battle – a political Gettysburg.

To help sell S.744, and as McCain–Kennedy did a few years previously, it proposed a significant strengthening of border control and security. It also contained provisions for work skills visas – a turning away, to a degree, from the emphasis on family reunification. S.744, interestingly given its lead Democratic sponsor, proposed an end to the Diversity Visa lottery – very much Schumer's legislative baby – and a turn towards immigrants already in the US and in line for full legal residence.

But there was more. As S.744 was being considered by senators, the *New York Times*, in a front-page report, informed readers that some countries were indeed looking for more. The three countries named in the headline were South Korea, Poland and Ireland. The report stated:

> The government of South Korea hired a former C.I.A. analyst, two White House veterans and a team of ex-Congressional staff members to help secure a few paragraphs in the giant immigration bill.

The government of Ireland, during St Patrick's Day festivities, appealed directly to President Obama and Congressional leaders for special treatment.

This effort from the Irish government was led by Taoiseach Enda Kenny, with Bruce Morrison working behind the scenes on ILIR's behalf. The Poles took a tried and tested path at an embassy party for lawmakers. They fed them with pirogi and three types of Polish ham. They also 'squeezed' Vice President Joe Biden and top lawmakers.

The efforts worked. Ireland and South Korea, according to the *Times* report, 'extracted measures that set aside for their citizens a fixed number of the highly sought special visas for guest workers seeking to come to the United States'.

The Poles, in return for their ham – if not the squeezing of the vice president – secured a place in the visa waiver program that allowed their citizens to travel to the US without first getting a visa. Canada won the right for Canadian citizens over the age of 55 to stay in the US without visas for up to 240 days – up from 182 days.

Chuck Schumer's fingerprints were all over these goodies, but he was quick to defend them. They made sense on their own merits, said a spokesman, 'They each solve iniquities in the existing immigration law.' Schumer, or his people, didn't have to convince the Irish campaigners. The National President of the Ancient Order of Hibernians, Brendan Moore, penned a letter to Schumer congratulating him and his 'Gang of Eight' colleagues for the overall bill and its allotment of 10,500 annual E-3 visas, which were already being labeled 'Schumer Visas'. Moore wrote:

> Senator Schumer, both you and your staff have our gratitude for decades of your dedication to ending the disparity that was created when Irish visa quotas were removed in the 1965 US Immigration and Nationality Act, and in aiding our 50,000 Irish undocumented. We feel that these contributions to the security and reform measures engendered in the current bill lead us to confidently and respectfully urge House members to pass this legislation.

ILIR's Ciaran Staunton reacted by stating that 'this is the best opportunity in fifty years for Irish America to open a door that has been closed. It is also a golden opportunity for our 50,000 undocumented to get started on their pathway to citizenship'. Staunton was aiming for a national call-your-Congress member campaign by Irish America so that the Irish would not 'get left out on the cutting room floor again'. What was needed, Staunton said, was 'for everybody, both in Ireland and the US, to use their contacts and get backing from the House for this bill'.

Ah, the House, home to 435 opinions, and many more shades of them.

CHAPTER 49

An Anniversary Falls

It is a common enough occurrence in American politics. A Senate bill goes to the House of Representatives to die. House bills can suffer a similar fate in the Senate. There is no intensive care unit between the two.

The Gang of Eight bill landed in the House and was met with a bigger rival gang. Discussion, matched by the lack of meaningful action, continued through the second half of 2013 and into the following year. On January 30, 2014, House Republicans issued a statement saying they would not go into conference with the Senate's immigration bill. Border security and 'interior enforcement' was required before all else.

Of course, 2014 was a midterm election year and bold legislative moves have a habit of hiding in corners and recesses in such years. Still, after the election, which resulted in a Republican majority on Capitol Hill, there were reports that there might be action on the Gang of Eight measure, which had been gathering dust in the Senate.

The new Senate majority leader, Mitch McConnell, indicated that he was inclined to blow the dust off the bill, or at least parts of it. He was eyeing a strategy to carve up the Gang of Eight bill into individual pieces for individual consideration. The *Hill* newspaper reported that President Obama and most Democrats opposed such a piecemeal approach.

Obama was frustrated by the failure of Congress – its entirety, or at least a majority of it – to grasp the nettle on immigration. It was such frustration that had spurred him into signing into effect DACA, or 'Deferred Action for Childhood Arrivals', a policy device designed to protect as many as 800,000 young people who had come to the US with their illegal parents.

DACA recipients could renew their status every two years. There was no path to citizenship in the program, which was first signed into law by Obama in 2012 and expanded by him in November 2014. DACA recipients are often referred to as 'Dreamers', although this term is rooted in the Dream Act of 2001, which was never actually voted through Congress. The Dream Act included a path to citizenship. Those covered by DACA vary in ages from late teens to late thirties. There are Irish citizens covered by DACA, though the number is very small. The Trump administration, spurred on by threats of lawsuits from Republican attorneys general in a number of states, moved to end DACA in 2017. The result was a Supreme Court hearing in November 2019.

The year 2014 passed without comprehensive immigration reform while the arrival of 2015 would be a reminder to Irish reform backers of why a comprehensive bill was needed in the first place. Also, 2015 marked fifty years since the signing into law of the 1965 Immigration and Nationality Act – the well source of Irish anger and frustration, which was compounded by the lingering memory that an offer to set aside visas for the Irish had been turned aside by the Irish government of the time.

Irish Lobby for Immigration Reform's (ILIR's) Ciaran Staunton began the New Year with a train journey to Washington and yet more meetings with congressional legislators to discuss the plight of the undocumented Irish. It might have been 2015, but 1965 was on mind:

> The Irish government took the decision to close the loop to stop people leaving the country and coming to America. But they could still go to England anyway. Our community has paid a high price for it. What would Irish America look like if the door had remained open in 1965? Put it this way, I probably wouldn't be making this trip to Washington.

This was an accurate, somewhat restrained, conclusion on Staunton's part.

As it turned out, 2015 would be a year for considerable criticism of the 1965 reform act by Irish American community leaders. At one point, Dan Dennehy, the National Immigration Chairman for the Ancient Order of Hibernians (AOH) who was born and based in New York, penned a report that decried the consequences for America's Irish as a result of the legislation signed into law by President Johnson on Liberty Island. Johnson, Dennehy wrote, was literally on the wrong side of the iconic statue when he signed the bill. Sure enough, a photo shows Johnson at a lectern, the Statue of Liberty in the background and with Lady Liberty's back turned to the president. There was no avoiding this, it has to be said. Space for the signing and all in attendance was behind the statue. Still, the symbolism was powerful, accidental or no.

Dennehy expounded beyond the photograph, writing, 'Not a week goes by without an appeal to this chair by AOH members seeking advice for an Irish immigrant desperately trying to stay or enter the US legally. Our Irish Immigration Centers serve as a life preserver for the neediest and a trusted advisor to all others.' Irish immigrants, Dennehy stated, wanted to enter the US legally and live in the country safely, 'Against the millions of immigrants that have arrived in the US in the past fifty years, the relatively tiny number of Irish that are living here as undocumented face the nightmare of deportation.' This nightmare included separating 'honest hard-working, community-minded people' from their 'children and spouses'. The nightmare entailed being 'ripped away from livelihoods, homes and businesses' that the undocumented Irish had developed while 'trying to live the American Dream'.

To say that the 1965 act, in an Irish context, was not being remembered fondly was an understatement. Dennehy took some solace in looking ahead to 2016, the 1916 rising centenary year, so a highly symbolic one, and a presidential election year. He wrote that 2016 would be a year for the Irish and Irish America to stand up and be counted.

As it happened, at the tail end of 2015 something to be counted was emerging into clearer view: a possible tally of visas that might end up in Irish hands – E-3 Visas. In November, a House of Representatives bill, HR 3730, proposed an allocation to Ireland of E-3 visas not taken up by Australians, who enjoyed a dedicated annual E-3 allocation. The bill was placed before the House by Congressman James Sensenbrenner, a Republican from Wisconsin. It was taken up by the Judiciary Committee but no action was taken at the time. Still, the fact that the proposal had come from a Republican with a reputation as a hardliner on border security was seen as promising.

The E-3 was a two-year renewable visa, allowing the holder not only to live and work in the US but also to bring over immediate family members, a spouse who could also legally work and children who could not. Its full formal title was the 'Australian Specialty Occupation Professional' visa. It had first emerged in 2005 as part of the Australia–United States Free Trade Agreement. There were specific requirements for applicants. They would have to secure a US job in advance. A bachelor's degree and significant work experience in the chosen work field were also necessary.

Bruce Morrison and Niall O'Dowd worked to tweak the Irish E-3 so as to accommodate possible future holders with a more varied skill set, and not necessarily a college degree. There would be considerable back and forth between the two men in America and the Irish government. There would also be back and forth travels prompted by the E-3 plan, most especially by John Deasy, a Fine Gael TD who would act as a liaison between the government in Dublin and Congress. Deasy had interned on Capitol Hill, knew his way around the place, and was familiar with its habits and working rhythms.

Regardless of its precise form, the E-3 would be no general open door to the Irish and would do nothing for the undocumented. Still, many viewed E-3s as being better than nothing. Irish Foreign Minister Charlie Flanagan, in a visit to Washington, met with Congressman Sensenbrenner and encouraged the Wisconsin man in his efforts.

The 2015 effort would falter. But the E-3 would return, Douglas MacArthur-like. In the meantime, there was a presidential election to contest.

There was no Irish American Presidential Forum in 2016. This was partly due to the expectation that a Republican winner – Jeb Bush, for example – would maintain Washington's role in the Irish peace process. If the winner was a Democrat, and that Democrat was Hillary Clinton, well there was no reason for any concern at all. The very existence of the peace process was due, in part, to Hillary's work and that of her husband.

Still, there was the immigration issue, and while any action by Congress was not expected prior to the election itself, activists and interested observers were keenly studying the emerging candidates. And some were trying to forget the words of Donald Trump when he announced his candidacy in Trump Tower, Manhattan, on June 16, 2015, 'When Mexico sends its people, they're not sending their best. They're not sending you. They're sending people that have lots of problems, and they're bringing those problems with us. They're bringing drugs. They're bringing crime. They're rapists. And some, I assume, are good.'

Trump was the longest of long shots as he shocked all and sundry with his words. By the summer of 2016, that had changed, and the tenor of his remarks had penetrated the immigration section in the Republican Party platform. It was headed 'Immigration and the Rule of Law'.

Immigration and immigrants, as far as the Republican Party would be concerned, fell within the category of legal or illegal. The platform stated that America's immigration policy:

> must serve the national interest of the United States and the interests of American workers must be protected over the claims of foreign nationals seeking the same jobs. With our fellow citizens, we have watched, in anger and disgust, the mocking of our immigration laws by a president who made himself superior to the will of the nation. We stand with the victims of his policies, especially the families of murdered innocents.

Illegal immigration, the platform continued, 'endangers everyone, exploits the taxpayers, and insults all who aspire to enter America legally. We oppose any form of amnesty for those who, by breaking the law, have disadvantaged those who have obeyed it.' The president accused of mocking immigration laws (by passing DACA legislation in 2012 and 2014) was Barack Obama, who had nevertheless earned himself the sobriquet 'deporter-in-chief'. The Republican platform was pure Trump, or, more accurately, pure Stephen Miller, who was Trump's primary advisor on immigration issues. It called for the building of a wall covering 'the entirety of the southern border'.

The undocumented Irish knew all about walls – the legal ones confining them within the boundaries of the United States. The Trump pronouncements on immigration were disconcerting – frightening, even. But there was Hillary, who was surely a wall between the illegal and undocumented and all harm. And backing Clinton was the Democratic Party platform. Its section on immigration was headed 'Fixing Our Broken Immigration System'. The platform stated that the Democratic Party supported legal immigration, 'within reasonable limits', but very quickly got to extolling the view that 'the current immigration system is broken'. There followed what looked like, and largely was, a wish list for comprehensive reform backers. The platform immigration rollout concluded with a shot across Donald Trump's bow: 'Finally,' it stated, 'Democrats will not stand for the divisive and derogatory language of Donald Trump. His offensive comments about immigrants and other communities have no place in our society. This kind of rhetoric must be rejected.'

It was rejected by the majority of voters in the November election. But the Electoral College would mean that Democrats and others who found Trump's language offensive would have to endure it. Trump's election triumph was a shock to the reform backers. And yet, as he readied himself to take over from Barack Obama, the incoming 45th president began talking of a 'great immigration bill'. Perhaps things wouldn't turn out so badly after all. Perhaps Donald Trump was really Santa Claus in a Trump designer suit.

The cold winds of January 2017 would quickly blow such thoughts away.

CHAPTER 50

A State O' Chassis

It was warm for the time of year on January 20, 2017. The new president, Donald John Trump, wouldn't have to cope with the cold so evident in the old film of President Kennedy's inauguration in 1961 – or, indeed, that of Ronald Reagan in 1985, the coldest inauguration day on record at seven degrees Fahrenheit, with added wind chill.

Trump's words, to the ears of the illegal and undocumented, would be anything but warm. The 'American Carnage' speech would send chills down the spines of millions, and by no means all of them living in the shadows. Gone was the 'great immigration bill' of just a few weeks before; instead, as Trump proclaimed, 'a new vision will govern our land'.

The new president then outlined his vision:

> From this moment on, it's going to be America First. Every decision on trade, on taxes, on immigration, on foreign affairs, will be made to benefit American workers and American families. We must protect our borders from the ravages of other countries making our products, stealing our companies, and destroying our jobs. Protection will lead to great prosperity and strength ... We will follow two simple rules: Buy American and Hire American.

Trump was telling the world that he was going to be a tough guy on immigration. But Trump in front of a crowd and Trump within the walls of the White House would not infrequently send out conflicting signals. A few weeks after his inauguration, Trump was reportedly sending signals to Congress that he would entertain a return to the debating floor of the 2013 'Gang of Eight' reform bill. At the same time, a series of high-profile raids by federal authorities were resulting in scores of undocumented immigrants being detained pending deportation, and Trump was also now talking about 'a total rewrite' of America's immigration system, with a replacing of the family reunification model by a merit-based system akin to Canada's.

On Capitol Hill, there were stirrings that reflected Trump's emerging view as the months of his first year in office rolled by. With something approaching a glaring absence of irony, on Wednesday, August 2, 2017, the White House, as part of 'American Dream Week', was the venue for the unveiling of a Senate immigration bill that would clearly put a stop to many dreams of America around the world – Ireland included.

The Reforming American Immigration for a Strong Economy Act (the 'RAISE Act') was the work of two Republican senators, Tom Cotton from Arkansas and David Perdue from Georgia. Their bill, as it stated in its opening lines, was intended to 'amend the Immigration and Nationality Act to eliminate the Diversity Visa Program, to limit the President's discretion in setting the number of refugees admitted annually to the United States, to reduce the number of family-sponsored immigrants, to create a new nonimmigrant classification for the parents of adult United States citizens, and for other purposes'.

If enacted, the bill would not only drastically reduce the number of legal immigrants entering the United States each year but also, in putting an end to the annual Diversity Visa lottery, drive a dagger into the one program that allowed Irish applicants the semblance of a non-conditional application process when applying for legal entry to the United States.

According to the White House website, President Trump introduced an act 'which will address our current outdated immigration system which fails to meet the diverse needs of our economy'. It further stated that senators Cotton and Perdue would be joining the president to introduce a measure 'aimed at creating a skills-based immigration system that will make America more competitive, raise wages for American workers, and create jobs'. The piece concluded with the line 'Americans deserve a raise'.

At first glance the bill, S.354 by its numerical designation, appeared to be an embrace of an immigration system more akin to the merit-based one that Canada used – this, as opposed to the family reunification model that the US had operated since the 1965 reform act did away with national quotas. As such, the RAISE Act could meet the definition of comprehensive immigration reform, but not of the kind that would have included provisions for the relief of the illegal and undocumented. The RAISE Act looked to the years ahead and envisaged far fewer immigrants – legal and illegal.

Cotton and Perdue, according to a *Washington Post* report, had been working with the Trump administration to refine a bill they first introduced in February 2017 – one that aimed to cut immigration by half from the prevailing level of more than one million green cards per year. The *Post* report stated:

> The legislation would mark a major shift in U.S. immigration laws, which over the past half century have permitted a growing number of immigrants to come to the country to work or join relatives.
>
> To achieve the reductions, Cotton and Perdue are taking aim at green cards for extended family members of US citizens and legal permanent residents, including grown children, grandparents and siblings. Minor children and spouses would still be allowed to apply for green cards.

Cotton and Perdue also had the diversity program in their sights; the program allocated 50,000 visas a year to specified countries. Ireland was included in the program, with separate allocations for the Republic and the North – the latter being considered distinct, under the program's rules, from Great Britain, which was not included in the lottery.

The diversity visa lottery had indeed been a solitary banker for the Irish over three decades, though a very modest one. In a typical year, Irish applicants might secure only a couple of hundred lottery green cards. By way of example, a mere sixteen applicants from

Northern Ireland would secure green cards for 2018 while the total for the Republic would be just 123.

According to the *Washington Post* report, the RAISE Act was expected to face 'fierce resistance from congressional Democrats and immigrant rights groups' and could face opposition from business leaders and some moderate Republicans in states with large immigrant populations. From an Irish point of view – the pragmatic version – the RAISE Act was a combination of the good, bad and indifferent. Given that so few Irish were entering the US on a legal basis each year, the act would have very little negative effect in cutting the legal annual immigration total. At the same time, if the Irish were to be afforded an opportunity to compete on the basis of work skills, a reduction in legal levels would mean cut-throat competition for that reduced number among an array of countries, many of them far bigger than Ireland.

Still, the introduction of the act was viewed by some as at least the opening move in a renewed reform debate on Capitol Hill. Something – anything – was better than absolutely nothing. And there were other bills floating about the place. Most bills given birth on Capitol Hill do not make headlines, or at least big ones. One headline, the 'Gang of Eight' bill, had been passed when Barack Obama was president and still existed as a possible template for change under Trump.

There were moments when Trump would seem to soften on the immigration issue. He especially seemed to harbor a soft spot for the young people covered by Deferred Action for Childhood Arrivals (DACA). In the opening days of 2018, a year into his presidency, Trump had left behind his 'great' bill and was talking up a 'bill of love'. He was also talking about 'shithole' or 'shithouse' countries (depending on Democratic or Republican assertions), Haitians as people with AIDS and Nigerians as people who lived in huts. Trump was like Irish weather: four seasons in a day.

And Irish reform advocates were perplexed by this no less so than other groups. By 2018, the concept of immigration reform had fractured and now amounted to a series of standalone issues that had the capacity to aid each other or cancel each other out, depending on the prevailing mood in Congress or the White House.

There were seeming constants. Trump had his 'big, beautiful wall', and within the White House walls there was a prevailing animus aimed at 'chain migration' – the administration's updated term for family reunification. The growing hostility towards immigrants, migrants, refugees and asylum seekers would be well explored and explained in a 2019 book, *Border Wars: Inside Trump's Assault on Immigration*, by Julie Hirschfeld Davis and Michael Shear of the *New York Times*.

The thing about Donald Trump was that, via Twitter, he had an unerring ability to put the inside story on outside display. And certain members of Congress were listening intently. House Republicans, led by Judiciary Committee chairman Bob Goodlatte from Virginia and Homeland Security Committee chairman Michael McCaul from Texas, had authored the Securing America's Future Act, a hardline measure certain to please the president. On the Senate side, the 'Gang of Eight' had reformed into the 'Gang of Six' – again, a bipartisan grouping with three Democrats (Dick Durbin from Illinois, Michael Bennet from Colorado and Robert Menendez from New Jersey) and three Republicans (Jeff Flake from Arizona, Lindsey Graham from South Carolina and Cory Gardner from Colorado).

There were no clear-cut Irish-American legislators in the various front-line pairings and gangs, but the Ancient Order of Hibernians (AOH) went ahead with plans to form the National AOH Immigration Working Committee, which was chaired by Dan Dennehy, who opened proceedings by pledging to work with other organizations 'as we fight fifty years of inequitable US immigration policy towards Ireland and for the 50,000 Irish undocumented people waiting for a visa'. The committee would include members from a number of states and Washington, DC. The Hibernians now had their own gang.

With March came St Patrick's Day and Leo Varadkar's first visit to Washington as taoiseach. St Patrick's Day, and all the ballyhoo surrounding it, offers the Irish government annual, guaranteed, highest level Washington access that is virtually *sui generis*.

Varadkar, like his predecessors, made the most of it and included an appeal on behalf of the undocumented Irish in his Oval Office talks with President Trump. Trump came across as being sympathetic. The Irish pitch was made sweeter by an offer to make anything that was done for the Irish in America reciprocal for Americans living in Ireland.

Varadkar was trying out his own version of Trump's 'art of the deal'. But any deal involving the undocumented Irish would be separate from any agreement on E-3 visas. The Irish, like Congress, were now finding themselves dealing with separate and standalone immigration proposals.

The Hibernians, meanwhile, would convene for their biennial national convention in July in Louisville, Kentucky. The AOH is not a political party but at times presents an appearance not dissimilar to one. At this gathering, those attending would be presented with a 'White Paper on US Policy on Irish Immigration'. It would be a 'where we are at and what we must do' assessment of the situation. It made for sober reading.

An especially sober moment fell on August 25 with the passing of Senator John McCain. McCain would be remembered for many things, but his partnership with Ted Kennedy on immigration would ensure his place in a very particular pantheon – that of the Irish immigration story in America.

Reform on the scale envisaged by McCain and Kennedy remained elusive, but the Irish E-3 Visa was seemingly still alive. John Deasy was still on the case. Also, and often very much behind the scenes, there was Bill Lawless, a Galway native and Chicago-based restaurateur who had formed a friendship with the Obamas. Lawless had been appointed to the Irish Senate by Taoiseach Enda Kenny in 2016. Such an appointment had been promised for many years and was widely welcomed.

Lawless was well known in the US Irish immigration reform community, and in 2014, he had introduced President Obama when the president delivered a speech in Chicago related to his executive orders on immigration – specifically, DACA and its parental extension, Deferred Action for Parents and Lawful Permanent Residents, or 'DAPA'. Lawless was co-chair of the National Democratic Immigrant Council with Bruce Morrison. He was additionally chairman of Chicago Celts for Immigration Reform and vice president of the

Illinois Coalition for Immigrant and Refugee Rights. Groups such as Chicago Irish Immigrant Support applauded the appointment, 'Since his arrival in the US, Mr Lawless has been a leading advocate for the undocumented Irish community and a proponent of comprehensive immigration reform.'

Lawless, as effectively as a de facto Irish government representative, had one interesting advantage over John Deasy. Deasy was a TD. Most Americans had no clue what a TD was, but they readily understood the title of 'Senator'. Regardless of a comparative lack of backup political power, the title could more easily open doors for Lawless than would have been the case had he merely been 'Mister Lawless'.

Still, the 'mere TD' would have his own very special moment of celebration. In November 2018, and in a rare example of bipartisanship on Capitol Hill, the House of Representatives approved legislation, that Deasy had advocated for, that would allow Irish applicants to gain access to the E-3 visa program, which, up until that point, had only been open to Australians. The bill, HR 7164, was crafted by Republican Congressman James Sensenbrenner from Wisconsin and co-sponsored by Massachusetts Democratic Congressman Richard Neal, chair of the congressional Friends of Ireland group.

The bill had been in the pipeline for several years and had been tweaked several times, partly due to Australian objections to the Irish being allowed to directly compete for the visas, 10,500 of which were awarded each fiscal year. The House-approved bill would instead allow Irish hopefuls to apply for those visas not taken up by Australians in each fiscal year. It was a second place, of sorts, but it would also be the first Irish access to large scale legal residency in the US since passage of the Morrison Visas in the early 1990s.

Sensenbrenner, whose hardline credentials on the matter of illegal immigration were long established, waxed lyrical about the Irish – to the surprise of many Irish. He said:

> The United States was built on hard work and the determination of immigrants – many of them who hail from Ireland. Through

their perseverance, they have enabled this country to grow and prosper.

I believe in the value and opportunity that comes with legal immigration. I am pleased to have authored this legislation to make the process more efficient for one of our oldest allies, and add to the great legacy of cultural diversity celebrated by our country.

This modest proposal would give Irish Nationals the opportunity to work in the US under the non-immigrant visa category of the E-3 Visa, previously reserved only for Australian nationals. Ireland in the meantime, has proposed a reciprocal work visa specific to US nationals so that those wanting to live and work in Ireland can more easily do so.

Currently, 10,500 E-3 visas are allocated each year, yet only half of these are used. This legislation would allow Irish nationals to apply for those visas unused by Australian nationals.

This significant addition to the US immigration system will not only benefit Irish nationals seeking employment in the United States, but also ease restrictions on Americans wanting to live or retire in Ireland.

Congressman Neal would invoke the mass passage of the Irish across the Atlantic during the years of the Great Hunger and its aftermath, 'America, to its everlasting credit the land of the great, home of the brave, welcomed them.' Neal described the US relationship with Ireland as 'one of the great relationships in terms of allies that we have in the history of America'.

John Deasy welcomed the vote in the House, but sounded a note of caution, stating that it needed to gain approval in the Senate. He told the *Irish Times*, 'This is an important step for it to have passed the House, but this now goes to the US Senate where it will need to be considered under unanimous consent which will require all hundred senators to agree for it to be signed into law. I am under no illusions how difficult that may be.'

The *Journal.ie*, a web-based daily, carried a reaction from Senator Lawless:

It is my ardent hope that in addition to creating future flow Irish immigration to the USA that many undocumented Irish will also qualify for this scheme … We have seen disappointment in the past on immigration legislation, particularly in 2007 and 2013 when we came close, but I am cautiously optimistic in welcoming this new deal, given that the President, the Homeland Security Chief and the Speaker's Office are pushing this bill forward during the lame duck session.

Lawless was highlighting the fact that any future E-3 availability would not, as initially constituted, bring relief to the undocumented Irish or, indeed, open the US to potential Irish immigrants with a full spread of job skills.

There was general agreement that this was a big breakthrough, though past experience had taught Irish advocates to be cautious, as John Deasy had been. The caution was well warranted. Simply put, the high hopes at Thanksgiving 2018 would be dashed at Christmas. With the 115th Congress heading for the exits, the prospects for Senate approval of the House E-3 bill headed out the door too. Seeming order would transform into confusion and chaos – a veritable State O' Chassis.

What had transpired sounded innocuous at first mention. Half a dozen Republican senators had placed 'holds' on Senate approval of the Irish E-3 bill. Holds could be softened or withdrawn if concerns were assuaged, and the six senators, one by one, followed this pattern. Then a new, final, and apparently lethal hold was placed by Senator Tom Cotton of Arkansas. The champion of the RAISE Act was about to lower the boom on Irish hopes.

Clouding the waters in the run-up to Christmas had been a report, carried by *Breitbart News*, claiming that retiring House Speaker Paul Ryan was 'quietly pushing' a bill to outsource many thousands of US college graduate jobs to Irish graduates and 'deliver amnesty to Irish illegals'. There was no evidence or indication that Speaker Ryan had been working a deal for the undocumented Irish, and amnesty for one nationality would be a virtual political impossibility outside the bounds of comprehensive immigration reform legislation covering the illegal and undocumented from all countries. But poisoning the well was an old Capitol Hill tradition, and the broad array of partisan online news sites provided abundant channels to the well.

An E-3 bill that had stalled just before Christmas 2011 did propose waivers for the undocumented Irish that would have allowed them to apply for E-3s. That Democratic proposal was countered by a GOP bill and the entire effort ultimately floundered.

At the end of 2018, the prospects for Irish E-3s – up to 5,000 annually – looked distinctly brighter. Until the Senate holds began appearing. But the six initial Senate holders – like Cotton, all Republicans – did not appear to have specific bottom-line objections to extending the E-3 program to Ireland. The specific reason, or reasons, for Senator Cotton's objection was not openly explained. He reportedly rebuffed overtures from Irish diplomats and even, according to an *Irish Central* report, a phone call from Irish Foreign Minister Simon Coveney.

Like so many years before it – all the way back to 1968, the first year of the 1965 act's full implementation – 2018 would end in frustration for Irish immigration reform advocates. But it would also end in an altogether unfamiliar manner. Since 1965, the talk had been of 'unintended consequences' for the Irish. What took form in the United States Senate in those closing days of 2018 was something new and alarming: a seemingly intended consequence.

Regardless of intent, the senatorial hold was sufficient enough to stall the Irish E-3 initiative through 2019, though the bid to extend the scheme to the Irish was renewed in the early days of 2020. As such, the effort to forge a new legal link between Ireland and the United States was now entering a new decade – its sixth.

In the decades now fading into the past, there had been Donnelly Visas, Morrison Visas, Berman Visas, Schumer and their follow-on Diversity Visas, and indeed Walsh Visas, a program under the banner of the Irish Peace Process Cultural and Training Program. The latter allowed for temporary work visas for applicants from Northern Ireland and the border counties of the Republic; it was devised by Congressman James Walsh, a Republican from upstate New York.

There had been no lack of effort on the part of individual legislators on behalf of the Irish, but the long shadow of 1965 was far harder to erase than it was to secure legislative passage of numerical and time-limited visa schemes. That shadow yet extends across the deep Atlantic waters.

'Afterwords'

As he led the 2019 New York St Patrick's Day Parade as its grand marshal, Brian O'Dwyer was not entirely focused on the cheering crowds and the seemingly endless line of marchers on Fifth Avenue behind him. With the spires of St Patrick's Cathedral now to his rear and a lengthy walk up the avenue still ahead of him, O'Dwyer stopped. As a result, the parade stopped.

Decked out in traditional formal regalia complete with sash and top hat, O'Dwyer turned and faced an office building on the west side of the famed street. Almost all of the spectators standing behind barriers were unaware of why he had stopped, or what he was actually doing.

What he was doing was paying homage to the memory of his grandmother, Mary Agnes Rohan from County Galway. As a young immigrant, and like so many young Irish women who had crossed the Atlantic alone, Mary Agnes had found work in domestic service. The office building had once been an uptown mansion in which Mary Agnes had toiled, doubtless for long hours and little pay.

Facing 680 Fifth Avenue, O'Dwyer took off his top hat, placed it over his heart and bowed. This was not an isolated, empty gesture. The grand marshal was publicly expressing an emotion that runs deep among Irish Americans. There is a reverence to be found in the hearts of millions of America's Irish for their Irish immigrant forebears. The stories of struggle in the homeland, exile and poverty in America, and ultimate triumph against the odds is a potent fuel that powers Irish America. Brian O'Dwyer, on Fifth Avenue, didn't utter words. But he said everything.

Another testimony, one of the seven provided for this final chapter that underline what is an all but unbreakable attachment, can be found in the actual words of Dan Dennehy, the Ancient Order of Hibernians' (AOH) tip of the spear on the immigration issue:

I grew up in a home that continually welcomed visitors from Ireland, whether immigrating or visiting, relative or stranger, no matter. The welcome was warm and sincere.

My Mother, Dora, was a beautiful young girl from a tin-sided house in Leitrim. She became a trusted advisor and gracious hostess for countless young visitors. My first-generation father was born in New York, but at the age of two, at the onset of the Great Depression, he was brought to Millstreet, County Cork. His father had left Millstreet hastily after waiting for Casement one fateful day on Banna Strand in 1916.

My dad was a Korean War veteran. Neither he nor his father talked much about those experiences. However, they shared with me a favorite comic strip in the Sunday Daily News. Dondi was a small Italian boy orphaned by war, adopted by an American GI, and brought to a very normal, but also calamitous, boyhood in America. To me, Dondi's integration into America made sense. It is what this country was made for. The ebb and flow of immigrants and our visits 'home' mutually shaped our family and our environment.

There were many relics and pictures of the life and times of our only Irish Catholic President, John F. Kennedy in our family homes. In my first real job, working in a Park Avenue building, I met Jacqueline Kennedy, and shared this. Because of those images, I used to think we were related. With the passing of that beautiful woman, and then her son, John Jr., the Emerald Isle Immigration Center hosted Month's Mind Masses, a most Irish Catholic family tradition.

My wife, Siobhan, was a J1 Student from Trinity College Dublin when we met in a pub in Yonkers. Siobhan made me aware that an unscrupulous lawyer was attempting to extort money in exchange for returning her travel documents. So began our shared involvement in immigration reform and advocacy. We joined the Irish Immigration Reform Movement and began the work of our lives.

As a young couple, we would soon experience congressional visits, interaction with Ireland's envoys and emigrants/

immigrants, followed shortly by legislative success and the establishment of a network of Irish immigrant centers around the United States.

Today, my wife runs a center, Emerald Isle, with an Irish name, yet it serves every accent and language in New York City. The preamble of the Ancient Order of Hibernians instructs its members 'to encourage an equitable US immigration law for Ireland and to cooperate with groups for a fair American Immigration Policy'.

We have yet to recapture the legislative victory of 1990. We have experienced hardship under the current climate of anti-immigrant sentiment and will overcome it, just like the founders of the AOH did in 1836.

We keep the line of communication open to our members, and our community. They are informed and aware of the obstacles. I am confident that we will rectify the inequities the Irish have dealt with for over fifty years and our people will continue to contribute to what is good about Ireland and America.

They will indeed continue to contribute, even in a time of an ultra-restrictionist immigration policy echoed in a statement from the White House and issued, in the waning days of November 2019, in response to a decision by a court in Oregon that did not please the Trump administration. It stated, in part:

Congress plainly provided the President with broad authority to impose additional restrictions or limitations on the entry of aliens into the United States.

The relevant portion of the Immigration and Nationality Act provides: 'Whenever the President finds that the entry of any aliens or of any class of aliens into the United States would be detrimental to the interests of the United States, he may by proclamation, and for such period as he shall deem necessary, suspend the entry of all aliens or any class of aliens as immigrants or nonimmigrants, or impose on the entry of aliens any restrictions he may deem to be appropriate.'

And in a landmark decision last year, the Supreme Court recognized the President's broad authority to so impose such restrictions. That broad authority formed the foundation of this most recent proclamation that was designed to protect the United States from the detrimental effects of uninsured immigrants. The district court's decision enjoining the proclamation disregards the statute's text, in violation of the Supreme Court's decision. We look forward to defending the President's lawful action.

The Trump years would be characterized by quite a few actions on the immigration front, most of them running contrary in spirit and effect to the more idealized version of the nation's immigrant past.

Even so, and as the *Washington Post* was to point out, though President Trump had made cracking down on immigration a centerpiece of his first term, his administration lagged far behind President Barack Obama's pace of deportations:

Obama – who immigrant advocates at one point called the 'deporter in chief,' removed 409,849 people in 2012 alone. Trump, who has vowed to deport 'millions' of immigrants, has yet to surpass 260,000 deportations in a single year.

And while Obama deported 1.18 million people during his first three years in office, Trump has deported fewer than 800,000.

It is unclear why deportations have been happening relatively slowly.

The answer to that question does not require a degree in rocket science. The rhetoric behind the Trump administration's immigration policy is inflammatory and inspires frequent court challenges. In addition, the administration's day to day functioning, at many levels, is little short of chaotic. The Obama version, quite simply, was a lot quieter and a lot more efficient in going about its business.

This is not necessarily a criticism. It was Obama who moved to protect the Dreamers and their parents, while in the absence of decisive action from Congress the system merely did what it was supposed to do: enforce existing immigration laws. Continued enforcement of these laws and a failure to pass the kind of comprehensive reform that would open America's door wider will have harsh consequences for the story of the American Irish.

Debbie McGoldrick, Senior Editor of the *Irish Voice*, takes what many would agree is a starkly realistic view:

> The death will be slow, and hopefully not too painful, but make no mistake, Irish America as we've known it for decades is in the process of dying.
>
> Is there an emergency prescription that could stop the bleeding? Immigration reform is essential for sure. The legal options for coming to America are narrow and complicated for those without an immediate family link. Long gone are the days when a relative would act as a sponsor and a visa given almost on the spot. That's how many of our Irish American bedrocks came here back in the day, populating Irish centers and clubs all over the country and ensuring that Irish America was a force to be reckoned with. Many of those organizations are now a shadow of themselves, and the outlook for future survival is bleak.
>
> Understandably, in this day and age, no Irish native wants to be undocumented in America, and with a robust Irish economy (for now) and historically low unemployment figures there's no pressing need to leave home.
>
> For those who wish to, there are many countries all over the world that offer fairly quick legal status and an opportunity for a different cultural experience. America is not the first port of call anymore and probably wouldn't be even if US immigration law was more relaxed.
>
> Comprehensive immigration reform is a term that's been tossed around the halls of Congress for years and years. Everyone agrees the current system is a mess, but the political guts to enact change has been sorely lacking among both Republicans and Democrats. In these hyper-polarized times, it doesn't appear that will change anytime soon. Irish America will be collateral damage.

But the fight for reform will continue, as Irish Lobby for Immigration Reform's (ILIR's) Ciaran Staunton points out:

> When I first came to America in June, 1982 I was told by a senior official in Tip O'Neill's office that there was no legal avenue for the Irish and there would be none in the future.
>
> But we would still manage to secure the Donnelly, Morrison and Schumer visas and maybe even the E-3 visas. Remember, things can get done when you have a group of dedicated people. That said, things are not good now. The White House is anti-immigration reform, indeed anti-immigrant. But we'll see how the pendulum swings.
>
> We need someone in the mold of Senator John McCain but critically we have to make sure we are ready for anything that happens. We have to learn from 1965 and 1986. We weren't at the table in those years and the Irish were left on the cutting room floor. We missed the boat. But now we have everyone ready and reading from one page. We also have a very pro-active Irish government. This is a legacy of the Kennedy–McCain era. We're keeping the engine oiled and ready for anything that comes up or down the road. We want to ensure future flow for the Irish.

As for the Irish living in the shadows of illegality? Siobhan Dennehy works on a daily basis to alleviate the harsher consequences of such a life. She is one of a number of advocates working under the umbrella of the coast-to-coast Coalition of Irish Immigration Centers. Dennehy is an Irish immigrant whose work heading the Emerald Isle Immigration Center (EIIC) in New York sees her advocating for immigrants from all over the world. Work, from her perspective, is no longer confined to matters purely Irish. But the Irish still matter. She states:

> Here's hoping future generations of Irish New Yorkers get to know and understand the indelible contributions the founders of the Emerald Isle Immigration Center made when they established the center in 1988. The center was established in the

aftermath of collaborative legislative efforts for immigration reform. The center's founders saw the need to provide support for then and future immigrants.

The center has risen and flourished with support from many private and governmental funding sources and the Irish government in particular should be commended for recognizing the work of the center and their financial support of the center's infrastructural capital plans when they provided capital financial support for a new Emerald Isle facility in the Bronx.

EIIC draws upon the vast ethnic diversity of the clients it serves in the city of New York and at the time of writing is planning to participate in outreach efforts to ensure that under-counted communities participate in the 2020 Census. The under-counted communities it seeks to engage with include immigrants from more than seventy countries along with Irish nationals, and particularly the undocumented Irish.

We need to ensure everyone gets counted. Ultimately at risk is the number we, as Irish America, hold dear. We once could say that more than forty million US citizens claimed Irish ancestry. That number is today declining.

Celine Kennelly, from Moyvane, County Kerry, immigrated to San Francisco in 1999. She is Executive Director of the Irish Immigration Pastoral Center, San Francisco:

As this book has told, the journey of Irish immigrants has changed since the Immigration Act of 1965 and indeed has changed considerably in the twenty years that I have been in the United States.

My arrival in 1999 was in the midst of an influx of twenty-somethings who had not been enriched by the Celtic Tiger, were full of life and ambition and determined to make their way in the world. The first decade of the new millennium saw a vibrant community supported by the immigrants of the 1980s who remembered not to pull the ladder up behind them, and marveled upon by earlier immigrants who just did not understand this new generation.

Move on twenty years and we find ourselves in a very different situation. The Irish immigrant community across the United States is fading away as is reflected by the demise of the neighborhood Irish bar and the amalgamation and sometimes disbandment of GAA [Gaelic Athletics Association] teams. Young Irish graduates come to experience US culture and work ethic only to be told that they are not wanted beyond their 365 days. Each summer, more young families pack up and move back to Ireland.

It's not that the desire to be part of the American Dream has changed. It's that things have gotten continually worse since the Immigration Act of 1965. Doors have continually closed and despite promise after promise of change, reform and immigration relief, subsequent administrations have failed to enact either comprehensive immigration reform, or any other form of relief for our community.

And this current administration continues to take it to a whole new level as it tries at every level to squeeze the life out of immigrant communities. It has not been for lack of trying. A new face when ILIR was founded, I now find myself a seasoned veteran of the Irish immigration reform campaign.

The Irish born community is now an aging one, and my work at the Irish Immigration Pastoral Center is undergoing another shift – supporting immigrants in their 40s, 50s and 60s who, after a life of working in construction, bars, as nannies, are facing an unsupported retirement, no support system, and ultimately, homelessness.

Without immigration relief, we are no longer supporting excited new faces arriving to embark on their journey on the wonderful roller coaster that is the United States; instead, we are walking with the work weary and abandoned faces of those with no status, tired bones, and no support system.

The demise of the Irish born community will translate into one thing – the demise of Irish America. As the generation gap grows, so too does the connection to the motherland. The hard fought E-3 visa campaign, if ever won, will be but a stop gap to the future of Irish America. It will allow entry to a limited number of Irish immigrants in an increasingly limited number of occupations.

The real future of Irish America lies in comprehensive immigration reform. The mantle falls to Irish America to ensure its future continues.

And still, JFK sits with the Sacred Heart on many mantelpieces.

Aileen Leonard Dibra is Executive Director of the Coalition of Irish Immigration Centers. She speaks for an umbrella organization covering eleven centers across the US that are facing not just an ever-heavier workload but also a more complex one resulting from a political landscape that is increasingly hostile to immigration from Ireland, and elsewhere around the world:

The late 1980s and early 1990s saw the birth of a new young Irish activist community in the United States. The Irish Immigration Reform Movement (IIRM) was founded in 1987 with a primary objective to legalize the status of undocumented immigrants from Ireland and 34 other countries adversely affected by America's 1965 Immigration Act. Based in New York, but with 17 branches in other Irish communities around the country, the IIRM not only led advocacy efforts, but also filled an immigration advisory role for the undocumented immigrants they lobbied to regularize. Following its success with the Donnelly and Morrison visas, the IIRM disbanded in 1992.

Subsequently, the Coalition of Irish Immigration Centers was established in 1996 to promote the welfare of Irish immigrants in the United States. In the past two decades, the Coalition has grown from an ad hoc group of likeminded individuals calling for immigration reform into the national umbrella organization for Irish immigration centers throughout the US. The Coalition continues to be a strong, cohesive and representative voice for the needs of its membership, and thus the Irish Diaspora at large, prioritizing the sharing of information and creation of best practices as a concrete way to support and assist its member centers in their direct service work.

The Coalition, in partnership with its regional member centers, provides a national perspective of the Irish immigrant community. Focused on the needs of the diaspora, this perspective informs the work and priorities of the organization, and in recent years led to an expansion of programmatic scope and a targeted strengthening of its community reach and impact. A recent and tangible example of this can be seen through the lens of the current immigration climate within the US.

Within that current immigration climate, the mood of the Irish community across the nation has been one of anxiety and confusion. The immigrant community in the US has been impacted by increases in enforcement efforts, scrutiny, backlogs and processing delays for immigration benefits, inspection efforts during entry and departure, as well as ever changing immigration policies. In response to the community need, the Coalition launched several initiatives directed at providing current, accurate and reliable information to our membership, our diaspora partners, and most importantly the Irish community.

Since 2017, the Coalition has created and distributed community information infographics to educate and provide clarity for the Irish immigrant community on pertinent topics regarding US immigration policy and enforcement.

Several areas of focus included applying for US citizenship, securing reputable immigration legal support, social media and technology inspection, the public charge rule and the Diversity Visa Lottery, among others. Further, the Coalition began providing impactful learning and professional development opportunities for its membership and diaspora partners on topics related to immigration policy changes and procedures, wellness in the Irish community, organizational best practice, capacity building and program impact with the aim of enhancing service provision and information sharing.

Finally, the Coalition prioritized the consistent crafting of national level reports to keep the Irish government up to date on the needs and challenges faced by the diaspora in the US, with particular focus on those that are undocumented and the impact of current and proposed immigration policies on the Irish community.

Though the Coalition has grown and changed since its inception, the organization has continued to stay true to mission and takes great pride in providing support to the Irish immigrant community in the United States and beyond. In the future, the Coalition will continue to engage with the community to assess and best address its needs in partnership with our member centers, external diaspora groups, and Irish diplomatic and government representatives.

In the second half of 2019, the Coalition of Irish Immigration Centers issued a release announcing the Irish share in the 2020 Diversity Visa Lottery. As was the case in every year, 50,000 visas would be on offer. Nearly 84,000 entrants were selected worldwide from over 14 million qualified entries for further processing. Ireland received the lowest number of selected entries ever with a total of 32 selected entries between Ireland and Northern Ireland. That's one visa for every county.

Bruce Morrison, now looking at Congress from the outside, but all too familiar with its ways, is not ready to fully bring down the boom:

In 1990, we passed the Immigration Act of 1990, including Morrison Visas. It was an upbeat time for the idea of increased access to green cards and openness to immigration reform. In this spirit the Jordan Commission on which I served proposed priorities of legal immigration and prevention for unauthorized entries.

But immigration activists made a fateful choice in 1996, untethering legal reforms from enforcement, hoping for better deals on both. Instead, they got a worse than expected deal on enforcement, three and ten year bars, and nothing at all on legal reform. This was the birth of the 'all or nothing' comprehensive reform demand. To make a long story short, the result has been nothing.

There are a lot of people and circumstances to blame. But the constant is the best as the enemy of the achievable. And so, we are now going on thirty years from the 1990 Act with nothing much but talk on the horizon. DREAM seemed possible as Democrats took the House majority for 2019, but it is dying in the Senate. The only bills moving are going to make things worse for everyone in the name of reform.

Employer interests are pushing the system toward 'temporary worker' programs – more people with fewer rights – to hold down wages and compete with Americans using indentured workers who do not get green cards for decades.

This is a corrupt bargain in which 'restrictionists' talk about protecting workers by opposing green cards while approving of the worst enemy of all workers: people who do not have the freedom of movement in the labor market that only a green card can provide. This was the xenophobic European model, contrasted with the permanent residence pathway to citizenship offered by the US and Canada.

Solving all the challenges of our immigration system all at once sounds good. But it is unattainable. In the simpler times of the 1980s one bill on legalization and enforcement and one on legal reform were necessary. Now it will likely take many smaller bites to get broad reform. I call it 'stepping stones,' the way you cross a stream when it is too wide to jump all at once. Just like in that analogy, you get to the other side slower, but you get there.

The key to reform in this stepping stone world is not to insist your reform go first, but to be ready for something with more support or urgency to go ahead, with a promise that you can be 'next'. Never has the public been more open to reasonable immigration rules and never since the 1920s has the Congress been so bad at delivering it. Until a spirit of compromise and slow and steady progress return, it will be a long rush to nowhere.

I hope we can learn to do it right in the 2020s.

Index